Penguin Books
Space Below My Feet

Gwen Moffat was born in Brighton in 1924 and educated at Hove County Grammar School. During the war she worked on the land, then joined the Army, spending four years as a driver and dispatch rider.

In 1953 she became the first woman mountain guide and climbed professionally for twenty years in Wales, the Lake District and Scotland. She was the first woman to make a number of ascents in the Alps and Dolomites, and in later years was on various committees of the British Mountaineering Council.

She has contributed short stories and talks to the B.B.C., and written features for the *Guardian*. Married twice, she has one daughter, and now lives in Wales writing crime novels with an upland background.

Gwen Moffat

Space Below
My Feet

Penguin Books

Penguin Books Ltd,
Harmondsworth, Middlesex, England
Penguin Books Australia Ltd,
Ringwood, Victoria, Australia
Penguin Books Canada Ltd,
41 Steelcase Road West, Markham, Ontario, Canada
Penguin Books (N.Z.) Ltd,
182–190 Wairau Road, Auckland 10, New Zealand

First published by Hodder & Stoughton 1961
Published in Penguin Books 1976
Copyright © Gwen Moffat 1961

Made and printed in Great Britain by
Hazell Watson & Viney Ltd,
Aylesbury, Bucks
Set in Linotype Juliana

To My Mother

Acknowledgements

To the Editor of *Scots Magazine* for permission to
reprint matter already published in *Scots Magazine*
for November 1954 and April 1955.

To the Editor of the *Pinnacle Club Journal* for
permission to use matter already used in the *Pinnacle
Club Journal* for 1950.

Contents

List of Plates

Acknowledgements to Plates

The author and the publishers acknowledge the following for permission to reproduce the photographs in this book: Gordon Moffat (1, 2), Planair (3), John Lees (4), *Woman* magazine (5), Popperfoto (6), The Ministry of Defence (Air Force Department), Crown Copyright (7), Sam Cochrane (9), Alan Kragh (10).

Foreword

This is the remarkable book of a remarkable woman, and I do not remember a climbing biography which has so completely absorbed me or which I have enjoyed more. Gwen Moffat is probably the best all-round woman mountaineer in this country and was the first qualified woman guide. But this – and I have read most of them – is much more than a book of climbing experiences. It records with an artist's eye and with quite startling candour the growth and maturity of an unusual and fascinating personality.

In these pages, the first thing that compels the admiration of a male reader is the quality of her courage and endurance. You find her going five months without a bed, sleeping out in all weathers, walking and hitching from North Wales to Cornwall and back again; rebuilding a derelict boat into a home until the moment when she climbs ashore, down-ladder and up-ladder, just in time to give birth to her baby; leading difficult climbs a week after her daughter is born, or, later, with foot and leg encased in plaster from a broken bone; swimming in winter pools with snow crusting the edges, or life-saving a companion caught by sudden cramp; giving herself up to bewildered military police, after deserting to share the hard existence of a wandering group of Bohemian artists, and then staying in the army until she had finished the job; going hungry, and teaching herself to live on starvation wages, surrounded by the fat plenty of the welfare state; climbing barefoot in the Dolomites, or sitting out a frozen bivouac, high in the Alps, and reminding us with a justified spurt of feminism that women usually survive nights of cold and exposure which are too much for their male companions.

Then, too, she has done so much so competently in a few short years. She has been cowherd, agricultural labourer, forester, gardener, corridor maid in a select hotel, secretary, theatre property mistress, helmsman of a schooner, and driver of a travelling grocer's van supplying scattered Highland shielings. Gwen Moffat has never escaped into security, though she could have done, has never allowed herself 'to be steam-rollered into mediocrity'. And yet she is a romantic whose romanticism is tempered with a strict sense of honesty.

She writes indeed with a compelling honesty: about her loss of nerve on a rock-face, or the stretches on a great climb which you hate at the time, numb with cold, fumbling with iced rocks, fighting the wind. She is honest about her motives, accepting lifts or food and drink when broke; about her friends and lovers, about her convictions and the reasons why she changed them; or about the unromantic nature of real poverty, alone with a baby and with a husband out of work. And so you trust her description of her emotions at those times of vision and delight when her world glows brightly round her. Here she is, scrambling down from the foot of a Dolomite tower, her companion having raced on ahead, after a climb no woman had done before, and on which she was burnt by the friction of the rope.

'He trotted off into the darkness and I followed at my own speed. I could feel my lip [hit by a falling stone] swollen like a wasp sting, and my eyes were still misty. I was stiff and aching, and the new burns were sore, but there were glow-worms about my feet and the two towers rose above the empty cirque. There was a moment of supreme awareness which I might have thought was only the satisfaction which followed achievement, or relief after tension, but I didn't think . . . I knew my moment of truth.'

With the same clarity of perception she succeeds in conveying what is almost incommunicable, the moment before a fit and expert leader tackles a really difficult piece of rock:

'I felt the familiar feeling that came when I was about to do something hard. A mental and physical relaxation, a loosening of the muscles so complete that even the face relaxes and the eyes widen; one's body becomes light and supple – a pliable and co-ordinated entity to be shown a climb as a horse is shown a jump . . . In that exquisite moment before the hard move, when one looks and understands, may lie an answer to the question why one climbs.'

You see, Gwen Moffat is neither a tough nor an Amazon. Tough people may be intrinsically interesting, but they seldom enlist your interest when they write about themselves. Part of the charm of this book is that its author is brave and enduring but vulnerable. She has not encountered enough kindness in her life, particularly from the men who have been attracted to her. She missed some of the pleasures other women take for granted, and when at rare intervals they come to her, she is the more intensely delighted. 'I went into Brighton shopping for the first dress I had bought in nine years,' and, after wandering round in a skirt made of black-out curtains, she rejoices in the attention her tan and her frock together bring her on the cross-Channel boat, and in the surprised and flattering reception she gets from her climbing companion when he meets her in Paris. Intensity of feeling brings her to tears when a climb is postponed from bad weather, or when she first sees the wild beauty of the valley that leads up to Zermatt. She is obsessed with the woes of animals, borrowing a tin mug from some sailors to milk two goats, abandoned on a station platform, adopting a dog who turns instinctively to her on one of her Welsh journeys, genuinely sorrowing over an enormous rat she killed with a kukri, or inveigling another climber into the hair-raising rescue of a sheep, stranded on the cliffs of Pavey Ark. And she blossoms in the warmth of uncomplicated delights, swimming in warm mountain pools, drinking Chianti on the hut terrace while watching her friends at grips with a climb, relaxing into the comfort of a sleeping sack after a day of wind and rain, drowsing on a sun-drenched mountain top, or absorbing the sensuous pleasure of steep summer rocks – 'The general memory is of air – very clear and blue – above, behind and below, the quiet tapping of the hammer in the great stillness, and of a red anorak against a cloudless sky.'

She has taught herself most things the hard way, her climbing included, and it is no surprise to find her practising solitary glissades round Ben Nevis, or learning how not to carry early morning tea-trays to shy couples in hotel bedrooms, or when not to accept a lift from a car containing only men. Her courage and resilience have not only brought her safely through, but have helped to make her the continuously interested and interesting person that she is. It has been my privilege to know Gwen Moffat, and contentedly to follow her neat and confident leadership up difficult rocks. This book will greatly enlarge the circle of her friends and admirers, will allow many readers to share her serenity at the end of a great and hazardous alpine climb made with her husband in a bad weather season, as she sums it all up:

'Life was the power and the glory of all the mountains I had ever climbed – as I walked along the frontier in the moonlight.'

JACK LONGLAND
Crich,
Derbyshire.

1. The Beginning – Wales

It started when, as an army driver – whose wartime dream had always been to become a guerrilla – I met a conscientious objector one sun-drenched afternoon in Merioneth.

I was driving slowly down the side of the Mawddach estuary, quite alone and idly dreaming (probably of table tennis because I was being fattened for the Command tournament in the autumn), when I saw a man ahead. He was big and hard and golden in the sunlight: a Greek god in bell-bottom trousers. I stopped and offered him a lift.

That summer afternoon under Cader I was a typical product of the war: impressionable and frustrated – for with peace declared, all the excitement was over, and now there was only the bewildering prospect of demobilization and beyond that . . . nothing.

I had left school during wartime and gone into a newspaper office, where I stayed for a short period, and then joined the Land Army. But I wanted a fighting service, not animals, and after eighteen months of the land, I lied about my age and joined the Auxiliary Territorial Service.

Now, after four years, I felt I was too old to go back to journalism as a cub reporter. I had made no permanent attachments in the services (although I had been engaged twice, once to a master from Christ's Hospital and the other time to an engine driver from Kansas City).

The brown man, who hadn't wanted a lift, sat in the car and talked. He found in the cubby hole a book about Saint George: an intriguing and rather heavy story concerned with the conflict of Good and Evil. It must have seemed an odd choice for an ATS driver (I was no glamour queen but I got my share of wolf whistles); in fact, I suspect I had been attracted to it by the spirited dust jacket which depicted the saint, on a superb horse, slaying a very scaly dragon.

Having leafed through the book and stared at me rather disturbingly, he launched straight into a description of an astonishing world completely outside my experience, a free and splendid world of mountains and mountain climbing, and hidden lonely cottages which he shared with friends (who appeared, from the telling, far larger than life). My imagination pictured supermen and lovely, casual girls subject to no ordinary rules or conventions, wandering gaily about the country, laughing, working and making love – and having a multitude of shocking adventures.

I don't know how long I listened; I had started by being my normal, gay, superficial self, but I was enormously attracted by this picture. I lost some of my self-consciousness but I remained wary. I wasn't uneasy about the man and the more obvious designs he might have on me; it was the life itself that was frightening. The very fact that it seemed to be the quintessence of everything I had ever wanted – adventure, freedom, rejection of authority – carried the knowledge that, once committed, I should find it terribly difficult to go back. Not that I seriously considered committing myself; I pretended to ponder the, to my mind inevitable, invitation to the cottage, but, of course, I rejected it – and drove away.

He wrote several times and I replied, once. Suddenly I was detesting life on the camp. This enchanting glimpse of a new world had come at the psychological moment when I was halfway to complete frustration. I replied saying that, as far as I could see, life – not only the Bohemian one – held nothing for me. I threw myself into table tennis practice because it was the only thing that could hold my attention.

Then I fell in love with a Marine and for one glorious week I was completely happy. It was autumn now, a very wet autumn, and we cycled along dark lanes at night, over yellow leaves, to little lost pubs where he played the piano. I wrote a great deal of poetry afterwards, all very sad and suicidal, and four or five years passed before I stopped going cold and looking for the pianist when I heard Chopin played in a pub. He was married. He didn't tell me then (I don't blame him; in his shoes I would have done the same), but he wrote after he was posted at the end of a week. The letter broke me for a while, and since I had formally applied for marriage leave, my commanding officer was sympathetic and posted me immediately at my request. I didn't care where I went: anywhere to get away from Wales.

I was sent to Stoke on Trent.

*

I left Merioneth in a trance – indeed, I hadn't felt anything since the initial shock when I had the letter – but I began to come round when I reached Stoke. The awakening was ghastly. In my memories of Stoke it is always raining; wet grey streets gleaming in a dim grey daylight, or drizzle drifting across acres of sodden waste-land, where dirty canals wound about the five towns.

At night it was more dramatic as the fog lifted and the bellies of the clouds flashed dusky red from the pottery furnaces, or perhaps they were just ordinary factory furnaces – it was immaterial. We were stationed on a hill above the town. Coming back to camp at night, I would stand in the rain, staring at the reflection of those fires, feeling utterly impotent, my moods alternating between a savage hatred of life and depression so overwhelming that I felt physically sick. People are quite wrong when they say being young is fun. When you were miserable you were almost mad with despair to think that there was no way out – that you would never find a way out, and yet, in a day or a week, it was all over. Conversely, the only time you were certain that a situation wouldn't last was when you were happy.

In the New Year of 1946 I was in hospital with influenza, bad enough to be granted ten days' sick leave. I was due for privilege leave too; in all I had three weeks. I lay in bed and knew that nothing mattered now. I couldn't be hurt any more and there was nothing to be afraid of. I had my railway warrant made out to Bangor and I wired Tom, the brown man of Cader Idris, to meet me there the following evening.

*

He called the valley the Nant Ffrancon. We drove up it one frosty morning, sitting on the back of a lorry and eating custard tarts.

There had been a light snowfall the night before and the tops of the mountains were sprinkled with white. Everything was too new and strange for me to appreciate it properly, but I found the very strangeness delightful. Although I had spent several months in Central Wales, the mountains here were bigger, more wild and rugged than the hills of Merioneth.

Before we reached the top of the pass, Tom banged on the roof of the cab and we stopped. He handed down the rucksacks and we crossed the road and leant on the stone wall, looking down the hillside to the river flats where a barn stood close to the water and some distance from a farmhouse. That barn was to be my home for the next ten days.

When we reached it we found it full of hay, fortunately, for the nights were bitterly cold. We had sleeping bags, but even then we had to burrow deep into the hay to keep warm. We lived quite a spartan existence. Tom was a food reformer and vegetarian and we ate no cooked food. We had nothing to cook on, anyway. We lived mainly on bread and cheese, chocolate and apples. We drank water from the stream.

In the evenings we went up to the farm and sat round the fire while Tom talked to the old farmer. The rest of us, the house-keeper and her son, myself and the dogs, sat on the fringe of the circle in the shadows thrown by the lamp, nodding as the evening wore on. After the first hour or so, heavy with the milk that was pressed upon us whenever we showed our faces at the house, I would be dozing unashamedly, half-hearing the conversation: talk of the mountains, of quarrying, of the sheep and the salmon . . .

Then down through the bogs, dry now and frozen hard, to the barn, with the big black mountains (which always seemed to come closer at night) looming against the stars.

My first climb was, said Tom, very easy – a novice's route. It was the Ordinary on the Idwal Slabs. I wasn't very impressed. The holds were iced in places, but the slabs themselves were set at such an easy angle that it seemed more like walking uphill than climbing as I had imagined it would be. The terrace at the top was icy; I found this and the descent more interesting. Fortunately we had brought ice axes; we had to cut steps along the ledge and up the side of the broken cliff above. Then Tom put the rope round a knob of rock and slid down it for about forty feet to the ground. I wasn't new to abseiling; among other things I had been a physical training instructor in the ATS, and one of my first moves, on being posted to a new unit, was to go out and inspect the men's obstacle course. My pet problems were the abseil ropes and the scrambling nets. I could abseil as efficiently as most male instructors, and now I felt very smug as Tom turned to shout directions and found me halfway down. For several years I went on being smug until I came up against a hundred-foot abseil in the Dolomites, ten feet out from the rock all the way down and about a thousand feet of air below. It shook my complacency.

The day after we did the Ordinary we went to Tryfan. I liked the look of the big grey buttress running down towards the lake – it was more mountain-like than the Slabs – and as soon as I was off the ground and starting up the Direct, I knew that this was what I had been waiting for. It was different from yesterday's uneventful progress; this was a series of strange and delightful movements – coming round corners on to unexpected slabs, long sideways strides up little walls, pleasing pulls on the arms using the strength in one's shoulders – and all the time the ground dropping away, a hundred feet, two hundred, and then – nothing, and we were climbing in the cloud. I couldn't see Tom, the rope ran up the rocks and disappeared into the mist.

I loved everything about the Milestone Direct. I don't think I realized that it was wet and cold (for the thaw had set in and the climb streamed with water); I loved the feel of the rock under my hands, rough and satisfying; I loved using the strength of my body to haul myself out of the cracks and chimneys (I had yet to learn that climbing is mostly balance); above all, I loved the intimate feeling of shared adventure between the two of us, alone on a big mountain.

We reached the top of the buttress some time after eleven o'clock, in plenty of time, Tom said, for us to scramble up the north ridge to the summit. When we had left the barn that morning and called at the farm for our jug of milk, the woman had been washing the dishes, so, since my watch had stopped in the night, I set it for nine o'clock.

Now I untied the rope reluctantly at the top of the buttress and we started scrambling up through the sodden heather. The mist grew thicker and the day darker and it began to rain. Once some goats appeared in the gloom, yellow and smelly: the wild goats of Snowdonia, according to Tom.

We reached the summit some time in the afternoon. It was very dim on top, but being totally unversed in mountaincraft this didn't worry me, although I did remark on it to Tom, who said it was only very thick cloud and that as we descended we could come out into daylight again.

We started down and it grew darker and darker, until we realized, rather belatedly, that we had been out of the mist for some time, and it was night. I looked at my watch. It said three o'clock.

'She was washing up the *lunch* things !' I said.

We had no torch. We were coming down the west face of Tryfan – a mixed mountainside of grass, cliffs and scree, easy enough in the daytime if you keep to the grass. Tom tried to do this, but he warned me that there were drops, that we must take no risks. So we descended about fifteen hundred feet of Tryfan on all-fours, but upside-down as it were, and feet first. I was in front, in retrospect I cannot think why, edging downwards very gently with my feet and taking most of my weight on my hands. When my foot slid forward over air, I would shout a warning and lower myself with infinite caution, on to my bottom, and start to fish warily for the next point of contact for my feet. If I decided I was sitting on the edge of a drop (and there was no way of telling whether it was five feet or fifty), we would resume our crab-like motion sideways, until we hoped we had come to the end of the obstacle.

The wind was rising, and the rain that we'd had for most of the day was now interspersed with sleet and hail which came driving across the mountain, slashing viciously at the rocks and stinging our faces. The wind was very cold and combined with the sleet and rain to remind us that we had been soaked to the skin by earlier showers. While we were climbing, we had moved quickly enough to keep warm, but now the wind cut like a knife and, hearing the gusts sweeping towards us, I tried to shrink inside my clothes and offer less resistance.

Once a car passed along the road below. It lit up the mountainside like a searchlight for a few seconds and I got up and ran like a rabbit. Then the light passed and I sat down again, but we'd saved about fifteen minutes in those few seconds. In my imagination I saw the interior of that car, rushing through the black, stormswept night, a soft, warm, dry interior, perhaps two people going to a dance (Chanel No. 5 and Turkish cigarettes), or a com-

mercial traveller hurrying towards his dinner with the radio playing and the heater full on. Did it cross their minds, as the wipers
clacked across the windscreen, to pity any poor devil out on a
night like this?

Again my foot touched nothing. My arms were so tired, my
hands so numb, that it was a great relief to sink on to my back
and lie there awhile, idly swinging my feet over the edge and
speculating on the height of the drop. We were tired of feeling
along the tops of precipices – even the smallest boulder was a
precipice that night – so I tied the rope round me and lowered
myself over the drop.

We couldn't hear each other for the noise of the storm, but if
I wanted slack I was to jerk the rope. I was very tired by now and
Tom, for reasons of his own, lowered me partway and then stopped, so that I dangled, spinning slowly, and stared downwards,
trying to pierce the darkness. I thought I could sense the ground
not far below and I jerked the rope. Nothing happened. I kept
jerking. Suddenly the slack came and I fell about eight feet on to
turf. I picked myself up and started to swear, but I hadn't time to
be really bad tempered, because in another moment I was knocked
flat again by Tom who fell on top of me. He was six feet tall and
well proportioned.

Then another car came and we grabbed armfuls of rope and did
another sprint.

Eventually we reached the road. There was a stone wall topped
by wire, then the grass verge, and then the flat, solid, friendly
tarmac.

*

The thaw had come in earnest now. The river rose and we waited
in the barn for days, watching the water creeping nearer until it
almost lapped the walls. Then we retreated – making an attempt
on Snowdon as we went. We reached a height of about two
thousand five hundred feet on Crib Goch, walking into the teeth
of a south-westerly gale. My hair froze and rattled in icy strands
on my cheeks; I was crying with the pain of the sleet on my face
and at last I made some tentative little remark like, 'Will they
keep dinner for us?' – a remark fraught with meaning despite its
apparent irrelevance – and we looked at each other – and turned

back. With the wind behind me I was ashamed. I asked if they would have persisted on Everest in such weather. Tom, laughing, assured me that they would never have set out.

2. Desertion

The cottage stood at the top of a ravine, among the wooded uplands that lie between Cader Idris and the Mawddach estuary.

We came to it one dark night when the stream in the ravine was in full spate. We had no torches. At first the path seemed to be a few hundred feet above the water and Tom warned me to keep away from the edge (with the loads we were carrying, we wouldn't have stopped had we started to roll), then we dropped down the side of the ravine and stumbled along a path only a few feet from the river. The noise was shattering. Speech, of course, was impossible. Once I walked into Tom. He pushed me against the bank and I realized that I was meant to stay on that side; I edged forward unhappily, splashing through water, knowing that there would be no warning if the path collapsed and Tom went with it.

The track swung back on itself, climbing through thick trees just sensed in the darkness, and the noise of the river faded gradually, then dropped to a low murmur as we came out into high open country.

I felt rather apprehensive as we crossed the fields. I had come to know Tom slowly : the long talk in the car back in the summer, the letters, the last ten days' climbing. The man himself tended to overshadow the life he led. When one is in love, the lover is, in one sense, taken for granted; there is no criticism : eccentricities are accepted, perhaps with mild surprise, often with amusement, always with approval. Now, suddenly, I realized that the people only a few hundred yards away in this fascinating cottage were strangers in every sense of the word and there would be no buffer between us. I would see them and their life more objectively than I saw Tom, and I wasn't sure that I was going to like it – and them. Least of all, that they would like me.

Tom had told me a little about them : they were all artists of one kind or another; there were several men and one girl. I had built up a picture of a tall, elegant woman in smart country clothes, beautiful and sophisticated. Her beauty would be of the flawless, mass-produced Hollywood type.

A light showed, a soft yellow square in the darkness, and I smelt wood smoke. Our boots rang on slate, there was an open door, a flagged passage and then a room, seemingly full of men. They were huge, all six footers and over, and they wore enormous fishermen's jerseys, exaggerating their size. They wore beards too, and long hair. They looked like benignant vikings. And when their welcome was over and they had subsided on to mattresses (on the floor) to sit and beam silently at me, I became aware of Barbara, sitting on a low stool by the fire, very soft and womanly in shabby brown velvet, with red-brown hair hanging long and straight to her shoulders. No make-up, of course, but violet eyes. I think she was Irish. Anyone less like the sophisticated picture I'd had in mind would have been difficult to find. She had been an art mistress in an exclusive girls' school, had met one of the men and given up everything to join him in this strange wandering life between the mountains and the sea (they spent a lot of their time in Cornwall).

They earned their living by felling trees. They lived very cheaply, travelling by road, hitching or walking, carrying only rucksacks and their axes and saws. They rented various cottages in Wales and Cornwall: bases where they kept a few books, blankets and odd tools.

I liked the cottage on Cader best; it was the most comfortable, and it possessed atmosphere: the happy feeling of an old house, much lived in. Tom maintained that when he first came into the kitchen, when they had just rented the place, he saw an old man sitting by the fireplace. After a while he wasn't there. Tom felt no apprehension at all; on the contrary, he said he had the unmistakable feeling that he was being welcomed.

Life at the cottage was very simple. Invariably we talked until late at night or the early hours of the morning, so we never woke up before ten or eleven. There were no beds; we slept on mattresses on the floor, and when we got up we didn't eat but went swimming. On the first morning, with a heavy frost on the ground and

January snow lying a few hundred feet above the house, I was too shocked to accompany them. They grinned tolerantly and scampered off like great shaggy dogs – except Barbara, who was like a red setter. When they came back, red-faced and rowdy, their hair was wet, so they *had* swum.

Next morning I went.

There was a small brick reservoir built in a high gorse-filled valley – a kind of hanging combe above the estuary. It was about ten feet deep, deep enough to dive – and I have to dive in winter. If I had to wade, I should never get there. I watched them dive, swim, and emerge gasping and shouting with laughter. Slowly, reluctantly, I took off my clothes, and climbed on the brick parapet. Mad, I thought, utterly mad, as my poor white body, rough with gooseflesh, swayed and shivered in an icy blast. Tom roared at me and splashed. Thinking that the shock might kill me, I dived.

It was cold, but not too bad if you kept your head. I surfaced. There was an aching pain across my forehead.

I thought, you're in water, cold certainly, but still water; swim! I swam to the side of the reservoir and hauled myself out, gasping. Then I joined the others, running frantically up and down the frosty grass between the gorse. When we were breathless, we did exercises and slapped ourselves, until we were dry and shining like a lot of boiled lobsters. We never used towels.

Sometimes we swam in the ravine where a dam had been built across the river and a deep pool formed behind. When the river was in spate, the water poured over the top of the dam and it was hard work to reach the other side without being swept over. Even when the snow was thick on the ground and glassy icicles hung from the banks, the dam pool seemed warmer than the reservoir, possibly because there was more life and excitement here; you thought more about the danger and less of the cold.

After swimming and eating we spent the rest of the day walking, shopping or getting in fuel. We burnt wood, and there was an old forest of oaks at the back of the cottage which supplied us with logs. Shopping meant walking to Dolgellau and back – about ten miles. 'Walking' was less strenuous: a scramble up Cader and along the four tops, or a ramble over the foothills, watching birds or talking. Sometimes people went alone, sometimes they all stayed together. There was no consistency in the arrangements; there were no arrangements.

To me the life was completely absorbing in its simplicity, but as my leave drew to an end I began to feel uneasy. In the evenings the others criticized me gently for my way of life. They had been conscientious objectors during the war. I listened to them and – when I became too bewildered – turned to Tom and he smiled and changed the subject. One night we brought a young naval officer home with us from Dolgellau. They were less tolerant with him and, for the first time, I heard the word 'deserter'.

One morning they decided to go down to Cornwall, and the next day they were gone. Tom and I walked with them to the foot of Cader, and stood there, watching silently as they scrambled steadily upwards to the skyline. After a while Tom said,

'Go on, go back and get your pack and go with them.'

I turned away, remembering the grey fogs and the dirty canals of Stoke. I couldn't speak.

I overstayed my leave by three days, but I went back eventually. I arrived in Stoke early one evening.

When I came into the Nissen hut that was my billet it was empty, except for one girl. She told me I was to report to the sergeant-major. I did this and was asked why I was late back. I said carelessly that the floods were over the railway line. Had I a signed statement from the police to that effect? I hadn't, but I had one from a Welsh Nationalist stationmaster. Inexplicably, even to me, I didn't trouble to produce it. I walked back to the billet and started to pack a few personal belongings. I realized that I was shaking as if I were cold, but I felt nothing: no elation, no fear; my mind was completely blank.

I tied up my parcel, addressed it to my mother and went next door to the pub. There I gave it with ten shillings to a disreputable-looking customer to post. Surprisingly, it reached its destination. I went back to the billet, washed my hair and bathed. I wasn't sure when I would do either again – in hot water. While the other girl was out of the room for a moment I hid my rucksack in the bushes outside the hut.

An hour after I had come back, I nodded casually to the girl, murmured something about a drink, and slipped out of the hut. I scooped up my pack, slunk through the shrubbery to the main road, and started walking.

It was not until then, trudging along the wet pavements, that I started to think again. I was committed now – in my own mind. Of course, I could have turned round and gone back, but I never contemplated it. In my mind I was already a deserter and, now that I'd done it, reaction set in. My mind had been dead for an hour; I don't remember making any decision to go. I don't remember thinking at all since I walked into the Nissen hut and hated it on sight. Now all the emotions which had been held back during that blank hour came flooding in. Fear: of police first, and, secondly, of the extraordinary life that lay ahead: on the run, homeless, with no money (I had about ten shillings). But the same things which frightened me roused a wild elation. I may have been a little hysterical at first, but after a while the necessity of thinking calmed me down.

I didn't dare go back to the cottage; I thought that anywhere in Wales would be unsafe, since the ATS knew that I had spent my leave there. I don't know if I was traced to the cottage or the barn in the Nant Ffrancon, but I like to imagine large military policewoman (and the local constable) conscientiously prodding in the hay for me, or peering through the cobwebbed windows of the cottage, trying to discover my crouching figure in the shadows under the table.

I went to Yorkshire. At first I had had the intention of leaving the country altogether, not realizing at the time how easy it was for a deserter to lie low in Britain. I was in a lorry travelling north when I made this decision and I started questioning the driver about the chances of getting on a boat for nothing. He said my best chance was the crew. I thought about this for a while, and then changed the subject. That night I slept, bolt upright, in the passenger seat, outside some public conveniences at Knutsford, a position which had its advantages at dawn, when I needed a wash.

That day another driver enlarged on the theme of persuading a sailor to stow me on board a boat. I became uneasy; Greenock seemed to be on the first lap to South America, but even this destination didn't worry me so much as the thought of conditions on the ship on the way out. In the end I decided that Greenock must wait until I was better able to take care of myself, and I settled for the West Riding.

I came back to Settle in the early dusk of a winter afternoon. In the crowd in the market place I caught a glimpse of the hostess with whom I had been billeted five years ago. I was seventeen then, sitting for Higher Schools, already what *they* called irresponsible. We were only allowed out in threes, but I explored most of the surrounding district alone, or with an Irish terrier called Paddy. So I knew exactly where to go this winter afternoon to find a bed.

I walked upriver towards Stainforth (past the copse where the goldcrests used to be; they weren't there now), and I found the pool where we used to swim in summer, and, above it, the barn.

I moved in, to share my new home with eight cows. I saw the farmer and struck a bargain: I was to be given my meals (by his cowman) and my lodging (in the barn) in return for milking once a day, watering the cows in my barn, and helping in the fields.

The first few nights in the barn were intensely cold; I had no bedding except hay. I burrowed as deep as possible but there was little difference between the temperature of the hay and that of the air – and the frosts were heavy. I was frozen. I would have gone and slept against my cattle but their bedding was too dirty. I sent an urgent SOS to Tom for the sleeping bag which had been lent me in Snowdonia, and when I judged it had arrived, I took the afternoon off and went into town. I loitered on the other side of the road until I saw that there was a crowd in the post office, then I went in and asked quietly for my parcel, half-expecting a policeman to spring across the counter; but the clerk wasn't interested in me, and I got my parcel.

Tom had done me proud. He'd not only sent the sleeping bag, but a pile of warm clothing as well. He sent, too, his congratulations and three pounds and said that they would welcome me in Cornwall. I swaggered out of the post office as if I owned the world.

After the sleeping bag arrived, it was a terrible trial getting up for the early milking. I had to resort to the river to wake myself, although the deep black water under the dripping trees (it was always foggy in Yorkshire) was not only cold, but terrifying. But it woke me up.

After I'd milked at the farm and had breakfast with the cowman's family, I went back to the barn to attend to the dry cattle. The first day I unchained them and they lurched into the yard to drink, but one of their number sat down in the gutter by the door and stayed there. I had been warned that one was 'a little unsteady on her legs'. I brought her water in a bucket and swept round her as best I could. I cleaned out the byre, put down fresh bedding, forked hay into the mangers and still the old cow sat in the gutter. I decided to let the others in, hoping that the sound of their munching would get her on her feet again.

I had forgotten the extraordinary meanness of some animals when one of their kind is at a disadvantage. I stood at the closed end of the byre while they entered, and as the leader came in the door she gave a vicious lunge at the beast in the gutter. She responded with a bellowing groan. I leapt forward, to be met by the incoming tide as they plunged towards their hay. I broke through, dodging horns, and leant across the cripple's back, flapping at their noses when I saw the mean glint in their eyes. But instead of going quietly into their stalls, they started fighting. I had no idea how they stood in the byre and I weaved frantically in and out of the slipping, lurching bodies, trying to mark down – in all that welter of tossing horns and bellowing groans – at least one cow who knew her place. Fortunately I had mostly blunt ends towards me until I waded in to start chaining them, and then I talked loudly to let them know it was me coming, and not some upstart young heifer. I was kicked a few times, but that was to be expected in the circumstances. In the end I had them all chained and munching steadily. I don't know if they were in the right stalls. During the fracas the cow in the gutter had managed to stagger to her feet and find a stall, where she had collapsed again. Next day I let them in one at a time.

I worked at the farm for a fortnight. The work was monotonous but easy – the field work, that is; I was never tired of the cows. The weather was very grim. Since I had come to Ribblesdale the fog had thickened and it never lifted. Bare trees stood sodden in the fields, and it was raw cold day and night. The only time I was warm was in my sleeping bag, and milking – when I pressed so hard against the cow that we became a sort of mutual support society and if one moved the other fell over.

At the beginning of March I had the sudden incongruous feeling – in all that mud and fog and bitter cold – that it should be spring; so far as Nature was concerned, it *was* spring. The sun would be shining somewhere; there would be catkins and primroses and lambs in a more hospitable country.

The farmer showed no surprise when I said I was going. Heaven knows what they thought of me. I told them I was a writer without money.

*

I travelled back to Wales almost without incident. One night I was picked up by a member of the Women's Institute, who took me to her house, where I slept in green silk sheets (after a bath) and in the morning my tea was made by one of those electric kettles beside the bed. It was fantastic and, once on the road again, unbelievable. It was the first time I had slept in a bed for five weeks, and it was to be five months before I slept in one again.

3. On the Road

It was night when I reached the cottage. This time there was no square of yellow light, no smell of wood smoke to welcome me. But I hadn't expected to find the house occupied, although I'd wondered if Tom might come on the chance of meeting me. When I realized the place was empty I assured myself I was using it merely as a stage on my route to Cornwall, not as a rendezvous. But I didn't continue south; I hung about the cottage hoping he might come.

I was profoundly bored. The memory of those crowded days a few weeks ago, our rollicking puppy-dog rambles, and the intense and gentle evenings, was painfully vivid. I had no idea of how to live with myself. The daytime was worse because then I felt I had to go out (a relic from childhood: 'You can't stay indoors when the sun's shining') and I never liked walking for its own sake. As yet I had little interest in plants or birds. In the evenings, and in desperation, I turned to the books. I found Rilke and Lorca, William Morris and Pater. Until now my idols had been Kipling and Somerset Maugham. All I remember of the new ones is a laburnum tree in one of Rilke's letters and the description of the Gioconda in Pater's essays '. . . and the eyelids are a little weary'. How I would have loved to be a *femme fatale*!

In the middle of this orgy of culture I met Thomas.

I was walking out of Dolgellau one afternoon and he was sitting on the kerb, watching some children at play, I had the impression that he had stopped for a moment for a rest before going on his way.

He was a dog-tramp. Not a bedraggled waif, but a kind of affable super-tramp who had taken to the life through choice, not necessity. He was a black and white collie with a fine head and a long plume of a tail. I flicked his ears as I passed.

A few minutes later, when I was clear of the town, I realized that he was trotting a short distance behind. I stopped and spoke to him, and he came up, wagging his tail. When I started again, he ran ahead, sniffing cheerfully at the banks, checking and waiting, ears cocked, to see if I still wanted him.

We arrived at the cottage after dark. Thomas – already I'd given him a name – after a preliminary sniff about the lower rooms, and a heavy lolloping up and down the wooden stairs, flopped loosely in front of the fire and went to sleep. When I'd made my supper I shared it with him and afterwards he sat beside me staring at the flaming logs, and nudging me now and again with his paw.

When I went to bed I left the front door open in case he should want to go back to his old home during the night. I told him to sleep in the living-room, but after I'd gone to bed I heard him pattering over the house in the darkness, to pause in the doorway of my room, and then turn and go heavily downstairs again.

Next morning I was wakened by a large and indelicate paw dabbing persistently at my face. With the sharing of breakfast I knew that he was here to stay.

That morning was the first of many glorious days that spring: bright and warm with a thousand scents about the cottage that sent Thomas into wild rushes of ecstasy, scampering across the primroses and splashing through the marsh, snapping at the orchids and covering himself with mud.

We took long walks over Cader, where sometimes we were caught in mist or snow showers on the ridges, and Thomas came leaping round corners having great fun pretending to be the Hound of the Baskervilles. Either he had an extraordinary sixth sense, or a highly developed imagination. There were times during the night when he rushed out of the cottage after one half-stifled bark, and I'm certain there was nothing outside. He would return slowly, grumbling to himself, and I'd hear the heavy flop of his body as he settled to sleep again.

He ignored mice rustling in the log box as we sat in front of the fire; he ignored even the mouse who ran solo obstacle races along the chimney piece, and he was quite deaf to the owl in the sycamore outside the window. But if all the night creatures were silent, we could imagine anything outside. I would look up from my book and catch him watching me. We stared at each other, and as I tensed and stiffened, he would copy me. 'What is it?' I'd whisper – and his mane bristled and the deep snarl would start in his throat. He rolled his eyes at the window, then he whirled and flung himself at the door. The game had to be played out to the end, so I got up and opened it and ordered him to go and get them. After a while he came back and went to sleep without a word. I'd be deep in Rilke again.

One day we were walking round the little lake below the north face of Cader: Llyn y Cader. Up the slope from us and about two hundred feet away was a big boulder resting on the scree. Thomas stopped suddenly and stared at the rock. His hair began to rise. I walked all round him but his eyes didn't shift. He started to growl. 'Go on,' I said, 'go and get them!'

He wouldn't go alone. I walked towards the rock and he followed, stiff-legged, the growls and snarls coming faster until he was barking quite hysterically. I couldn't see anything except scree. I walked right round the boulder and there was nothing, not even a dead sheep. Thomas approached, relaxed completely, lifted a leg and trotted away.

Did he really see something invisible to me or was he, like some children, pretending, to gain attention? Or was it, more likely, an extension of our nocturnal game?

With other dogs he was very aloof, an attitude which was a great success with strange animals. He was large and possessed an air of ponderous middle-class superiority, which intimidated farm curs, but which failed with the unpleasant bitch who lived at the farm where I bought my milk. One day she flew at him, and every dog on the farm joined in with enormous gusto. Thomas sat down on my feet. It was like being attacked by a wolf pack. Flying bodies were coming at me from all directions and, since my feet were firmly anchored, my back felt very vulnerable. I was fighting with the milk cans. It was pandemonium. I must have put up a fairly good show because neither of us was bitten, and I can still hear the satisfying clonk of aluminium on furry skulls above the bedlam of snarls. We were rescued by the farmer. After that Thomas came with me to the penultimate field where he sat down (out of sight of the buildings) and waited.

I stayed at the cottage for a few weeks. Tom came, bringing

friends. He laughed a lot at my escape, was amused by Thomas – and then he left again. When he had gone the loneliness was more pronounced, in spite of the dog, and – on a more practical level – I was broke. In Cornwall they were cutting down trees. I would be one more mouth to feed, but another pair of hands to help the timber gang.

*

As soon as I had cleared the food left by Tom and his friends, I started the long walk south, coming up the slope of Cader early one morning when heat haze shivered above the rocks and all the little lakes came into view as we climbed, shining like jewels.

The afternoon found us in the hills north of the Dovey estuary, where we were picked up by a doctor and his wife travelling in a very small car. The doctor's wife, Thomas, myself, and all our gear were squeezed together on the floor and the door fastened with rope to keep us in.

We slept in a barn that night and crossed Plynlimon the next day – Sunday. It was a bright cold morning with the wind sweeping across the moors and numbing my bare legs. There was no sign of a house anywhere, only the sheep moved in the windswept heather. Far away to the right glittered a cold white lake. Everywhere was high and flat – a lonely wilderness of moorland and lake, heather and bog, crossed by one dry, dusty road. And then I came on Dylife: shells of cottages with crumbling walls and fallen roofs. Stunted thorns grew out of the stones. The village must have been deserted for years. But it wasn't completely deserted; standing back from the ruins was a pub – but even that was closed and shuttered.

Where the road ran through the ghost village it widened to four or five times its normal width and it was surfaced with ashes. like a dirt track. To complete the illusion, three powerful motor cycles came sweeping round the bend ahead and roared past me in a cloud of dust. There were few things I regretted leaving behind with the Army, but my motor cycle was one of them. I walked on, feeling cold and a little depressed.

However, I was as resilient as a rubber ball – usually; it was seldom that there wasn't something strange or beautiful round the next bend to excite my interest. This time it was a stream which disappeared over a cliff. One moment I was walking along the road above the stream, and then I realized that the mountain ended suddenly and the valley was several hundred feet below. I looked back to see how the stream had managed, and I saw the cliff, and a waterfall shining in the sun.

By degrees we came to the Wye valley and were picked up by a man delivering a new car. All the windows were closed and there was a strong smell of upholstery, petrol and tobacco. An old raincoat had been spread on the back seat ('the dog's paws might be dirty') and I glanced back after a while to see if he were still on it. He stared at me reproachfully. I was feeling queer too. Surreptitiously I opened a window. I began to feel that something was wrong. I turned and stared at Thomas again. This time I realized that the look in his eyes wasn't reproach but apology.

I sat in the car staring at the road beyond the bonnet, frantically thinking of a way to break it to the driver. At last I said in a small voice,

'I'm afraid I've got bad news for you.'

Fortunately we seldom ate until the evening, so Thomas couldn't be very sick. I expected to be kicked out of the car, but after I'd cleaned up with grass, on the principle, I suppose, that it was spilt milk, we were allowed to re-enter. The spilt milk theory wasn't foolproof; where he got it from, I don't know, but Thomas repeated his performance twice. On the third occasion, with the dog's head hanging from remorse, and mine from embarrassment, we cleaned the car and let it go.

*

As we came south the weather grew milder. At first we had spent the nights in barns but now we slept out, under hedges, in haystacks: anywhere that we happened to be when we felt tired, so long as it was not too public. I have been wakened by cows and an embarrassed cowman trying delicately to creep past because I was stretched across the path, and once, somewhere on the Shrewsbury by-pass, I think, I had to lie idle for hours in my bag, because, in the dark, I'd picked a spot close to a railway embankment, and before I could dress (I used my clothes as a pillow) I had to wait for a pause in the shunting.

With the milder weather I was in a hurry to reach Land's End;
I saw myself picking daffodils in my long skirt, talking through
the soft spring evenings, swimming . . . I was impatient to get off
the road and settle down again. Thomas was the snag. The affair
in the new car was the point of no return; afterwards he was unhappy and ill in all cars. However, I had friends in Gloucester-
shire who were farmers, relics of my driving days in Western
Command, and they, having accepted the lie that I was on demobilization leave, were quite willing to look after him for a few
weeks. I chained him to a kennel and then, with his frenzied
barks in my ears, hurried blindly through the lanes to the main
road. I had betrayed him. There was no way of telling him I
would come back. I hated myself.

*

I found the others in a wooded cove several miles from Land's
End. It was a Sunday evening when I arrived. I had been walking
along the cliffs in a thin drizzle and I came to a bend with a gate
on the angle, and beyond it the land dropped away to the combe.
I looked down on the tops of trees where smoke rose straight from
invisible chimneys. Seawards a gaunt old derrick stood on a
crumbling pier. The water was smooth and quiet.

I heard them coming before I saw them: familiar accents and
laughs; and then they came into view, straggling up the road –
Barbara in the old brown velvet and the others in their fishermen's jerseys. They put my rucksack under a hedge and bore me
off to Penzance and a chamber concert. Their numbers had been
swollen – by a boxer from Wolverhampton. Although rather
surprised at his profession, I reflected that he had two things in
common with the others: a powerful body and the delightful
philosophy that obeying one's instincts was not only rewarding,
but right. He was a disturbing influence, towering beside me in
that hall with its palms and string orchestra. His shaggy clothes
smelt of dew and earth and green things.

It was late when we returned to the cove and I could see nothing of the village. I remember a long steep garden through which
we climbed towards a window with lighted candles standing on
the sill. There was a bare kitchen with a few crates ('Furnished,'
they said, 'so we can't be turned out') and there was supper of

grey mullet and watercress. Their vegetarian principles were elastic.

*

My life as a deserter was completely strange and rather wild. I took to it like a duck to water. I was twenty-one and it was my first taste of freedom. At eighteen I had joined the ATS, where any spark of initiative and individualism had been ruthlessly suppressed. For four years I had been ruled by convention and employers who, on the whole, exercised more authority than sense. It is rather surprising that the sudden lifting of restrictions didn't go to my head. Had it done so, I'm not sure what would have happened. Perhaps some people, in similar circumstances, would become criminals to fulfil a need: power, wealth, social position? But I didn't want anything. I wasn't even a rebel; I had got my freedom (Tom would tell me I wasn't free, but I forgot when he wasn't there).

People told me during the next five months: 'You know, you're not cut out for this sort of thing,' but since they were conventional people, I wouldn't listen, taking any such remark as criticism of my friends – the best of whom were, in my opinion, the prophets of a new religion.

Despite the fact that, to a casual observer, I might seem more cut out for the life than, say, Barbara, this wasn't so. She travelled with the others, was attached to one man and, at a guess, I would say she was placid and contented. I travelled alone – between Wales and Cornwall – unable to settle for long; always torn by my emotions: ecstatic in the realization of a love affair, or depressed, remorseful and insecure, trying to find peace in work or long lonely walks from which I'd return clean and empty and eager for the next impression.

We lived simply: the men felling trees, Barbara and I lending a hand occasionally. Or we would cut up wood on our own: old trees which were taking up space in the corners of farm yards (and would continue to do so after we'd gone, for we merely cut them into lengths – we had no circular saw – and left them just as unwieldy as when we'd started). But the farmers invariably succumbed to our pleas for work, although, at the end of the day, instead of one enormous log, they had four or five. Sometimes we earned money, sometimes cauliflowers, eggs or milk – sometimes both. Always we were given large meals.

We were artists at begging. We stood on the quays, barefooted and with skirts halfway down our calves (long before Dior brought out his New Look), and waited for the fishing crews to throw us fish. The tourists loved it.

We picked watercress from the beds on the cliff top: that was free. On dark evenings we picked cauliflowers: that wasn't, but the farmers wouldn't miss one or two, we said.

At first I revelled in the softness, the lush, indolent atmosphere of the cove. Sometimes wild gales came raging in from the Atlantic, but the prevailing mood was of lethargy, of fecund earth breathing slowly and heavily in the green twilight of the woods. They said the trees took all the oxygen out of the cove. I began to feel stifled. I thought of high uplands with the wind whipping through last year's grasses, and lonely, desolate cwms above the tree line. I wanted to go, but had become too lazy to leave of my own accord. Then we lost the cottage.

Originally the others had arrived one night, liked the look of the place, and squatted there. The owner politely, but rather casually, tried to remove them, with no success. Then one afternoon, as I was returning from cutting down a tree for the Bird Hospital at Mousehole, axe on shoulder and feeling very professional (with my fee in my pocket), I came up the garden and stopped – to stare in astonishment at the cottage.

Workmen were removing the roof. It was raining slightly and people were rushing in and out of the front door: going in empty, coming out with armfuls of books, sleeping bags and best clothes. (They had 'best' tweed jackets and trousers, and good shirts, very colourful and expensive.) Slates were flying all over the place. Really it was very dangerous. People ran crouching as if they offered a smaller target. The men on the roof worked phlegmatically, puffing at their pipes.

Fortunately, after the last big timber job, the boxer had bought an old horse caravan and had it transported to the cliff above the cove. Now it had to house all our possessions, but since there were only two bunks, Barbara and Jim had these and the rest of us slept out on the cliffs – or between the wheels when it rained. I had a waterproof cover for my bag, and as it was rather congested under the caravan, I continued to occupy my favourite ledge on wet nights – just below the lip of the cliff. I could see the Lizard light when it was fine, but when the fog banks came rolling in, I seemed to be suspended in space, for the fog horns filled the air and, by some acoustic trick, seemed to emanate from a point vertically below my ledge. Whenever a horn sounded I waited, terrified, for the inevitable crash as the ship piled up on the rocks below.

Although I didn't mind sleeping out, it was rather a bore cooking and eating in the confined space of the caravan. I began to think – on wet days – it would be nice to spread myself in an empty cottage, instead of living cheek by jowl with so many other people. So one morning I packed my rucksack and started walking.

4. Deckhand

Some hours later I was heading up the north coast when I saw, above the roofs of warehouses, the masts of a ship. Idly curious, already bored with walking, I strolled on to the quay and discovered a real sailing boat – a schooner. She was being loaded, but I found her skipper sitting on a pile of sacks, looking very green and nursing a bloody hand. He had just caught it in some machinery and was waiting for the doctor. I sat and sympathized with him for a while and worried over the doctor. The skipper was touched by my concern and said he could find me a passage to Cardiff if I would wait until his relief arrived. He came then – with the doctor; my friend was bandaged and sent home, I was signed on as a deckhand, told the ship sailed at six and sent away to find eggs. These were very scarce at that time.

It was a grand evening; very still and calm when we chugged out of harbour on our auxiliary engine, and once on the open sea I was given the wheel and a bearing, and the skipper disappeared below. There were two others in the crew: a boy who seemed to attend to the cooking, and a man, about thirty-five, who wore a greasy cap (first mate?) and seemed to do everything else.

I had never steered a ship before; I had never been in a wheelhouse, but the sea was completely empty and there was nothing to worry about except my bearing. Below, they drank.

I was happy. To have the responsibility of an eighty-foot boat in my hands (she may have been more) was awe-inspiring; I felt I would like to take her round in a circle to see what it felt like, and admire the wake.

The captain came into the wheelhouse as it grew dark, told me about lighthouses and asked if I were all right. He brought me a bottle of beer.

I must have been in the wheelhouse about five hours, at the end of which I was gently shifting my weight from one foot to the other, when the captain came back and started to talk. After a while he moved in on me but I couldn't retreat, for I felt that the boat was my responsibility, the more so because I knew myself sober but felt none too sure about the others. I started to talk sensibly about the ship and her cargo. I doubt if he heard a word. An enormous arm, like the tentacle of an octopus, came round my waist. He was a very big man. The annoying thing was that it was such a crazy situation; I was finding it hilariously funny, yet knew that the only thing to stop him was to lose my temper or have hysterics (or both) and scream at him like a fishwife. Then suddenly, and without any warning, flames belched from the smoke stack. The engine faltered and stopped, and we were left floating in a great silence, broken only by feet thudding along the deck.

The flames died, and everyone except me went below to play with the engine. I carried my bag up into the bows.

I woke about eight o'clock. It was a glorious summer morning. At first the stillness and the gulls' cries were very familiar and I thought I was on the cliffs above the cove. Then I remembered, and knew something was wrong. The boat had stopped again. (We had been under way when I dropped off to sleep last night.)

Although no one was about, there was a smell of bacon frying. I crawled out of the bag and stood up. The schooner was anchored off a small fishing village. It was all very romantic and remotely South Sea Islandish. My skipper reminded me of Somerset Maugham's Red. I went aft to the galley and took over the cooking from the boy. I wanted my eggs done my way.

The captain, he told me, had gone ashore. I wasn't told why. The morning wore on. The mate came up from the engine-room and we all lay on the deck and smoked and read Westerns. About midday we saw a boat approaching with three men in it.

The captain was accompanied by a very large sack, which chinked, and a little old man, not too clean and with a face like a ferret, who grinned a lot and agreed with everything that was said. I never found out who he was nor what he was doing on the boat. Perhaps, like me, he was hitching to Cardiff. Maybe he was just coming for the ride.

I cooked a meal for them (I was getting nervous about the boat again, and I suspected the captain hadn't eaten breakfast) and afterwards the boy was left in the wheelhouse and the four of us went below with the sack.

We had quite a party; it seemed only a short while before the boy was shouting that we were coming in to Cardiff. Three of us scrambled on deck (the old man had gone to sleep) and, sure enough, we were close up to Cardiff docks.

Now, there is a signal at the end of a pier flanking the entrance to one dock, a signal which may be three balls arranged in a triangle like a pawnbroker's sign. If the signal is the right way up, the way is clear, but if it is reversed, something is coming out and you have to wait. I can't remember the details, but I know that the two signals were very similar.

The captain, the mate and I stood in the bows and stared at the signal. The captain said he thought it was All Clear. He turned to us for confirmation. We strained our eyes and agreed. What none of us knew at the time was that we were all short-sighted and no one would admit it. Each of us thought the others had really seen the All Clear signal.

So we went ahead.

We were passing an enormous American tanker when the wind lifted my very full skirt. As I struggled to get it off my head, I was appalled to hear the siren shrieking loudly from the tanker. Just as it stopped, and the wolf whistles died, there were wild shouts from all directions; another siren sounded with great urgency and, holding my skirt firmly with both hands, I turned and saw a huge ship bearing down on us as she came out of harbour. Our little boat acted like a toy dog which has decided, after all, not to attack a bull. She veered in a wide circle right under the black bows (which towered above us like monstrous overhanging cliffs) and came round towards the entrance again. We were right under the signal now. It was *not* All Clear. We saw a harbour official, too, waiting for us to pass. I started below, but the captain yanked me back.

'You go and stand forrard,' he said. 'He'll think you're my wife, and then he won't say what he wants to.'

So I stood in the bows and smiled weakly at the official as we passed. He stared back grimly.

We tied up at a wharf and the old man, who had woken up, the captain and I went very fast out of the dock gates and into

the first pub across the road. We had been badly frightened –
even the old man, who had been below, but knew something un-
toward was happening from our sudden change of course in the
harbour entrance, and must have been rather bewildered at the
speed the scenery changed outside the portholes. Very close
scenery, too, as we went under the bows of the other ship.

When we had settled down a little, we emerged and started to
pub crawl up Bute Street, a proceeding which, interesting at first,
became monotonous as the evening wore on.

*

It took me two days to reach the cottage again. I walked up the
ravine at noon on the second day, steaming in the hot sun. The
previous night I had been soaked as I slept on a hillside in the
Wye valley. The bag grew wetter and I became colder until, just
before dawn, I could bear it no longer, and, grabbing a torch,
toiled up the hill naked in an effort to get warm. Then I dressed in
my wet clothes and went down to the road to start hitching in
the dark.

As I approached the cottage Tom came walking out of the open
door and I ran into his arms.

'I came up on a boat,' I said after a while.

He looked down at me, smiling.

'The *Teresa*'s my boat,' he said.

Teresa was the name of *my* boat. Now, we had no mutual
friends who knew I had come up by sea. I begged him to tell me
how he knew, but he insisted he *knew* and that was that. It is a
measure of my regard for him that I should accept such an example of psychic powers; it wasn't for many years that I remembered that the original skipper of the *Teresa* – the one who'd hurt
his hand – had asked me for my address and I'd given it to him as
the cottage on Cader.

Tom, the boat and the return to Wales had driven all thoughts
of Thomas out of my head, but after a few days I remembered
him and rushed down to Gloucester. He was overjoyed to see me
again, and since Tom had parted with the fare with great good
humour, we returned to Wales by train – to a district just south
of Snowdon. Here the hills were craggy but small, and the valleys
were soft and well-wooded, full of rhododendrons. We settled in

a lost valley between the Aberglaslyn Pass and Cnicht and close to a youth hostel where the wardens were friends of Tom's. They were Penny and Bill Condry. Bill was an enthusiastic ornithologist; walks with him were sheer delight. He seemed to know where nests were by instinct. Birds had been just birds before, although I knew a curlew now and coloured ones like woodpeckers, but most of the others were little brown birds, or big brown ones, just flashes across the landscape. Now I started to distinguish between them, to see shades of colour and observe behaviour. A whole new world was opening before me.

There were other friends of Tom's about; usually they came singly, drifting through the valley, descending on the hostel in the evening. Sometimes they stayed only the night, sometimes a few days, then they wandered off again – to destinations unknown even to themselves. Joe Gianelli (who afterwards became the warden of Snowdon Ranger hostel) was often in Nantmor, his small stocky figure appearing in the evening. He was older than the rest of us and under the woollen cap, which was seldom removed, his disconcerting eyes missed nothing. Tom talked and Joe listened. I was a little afraid of him. He seemed to regard me with a detached fatherly air, as if I were a precocious child amusing its elders.

That was a perfect spring. I needed no money. I wore old clothes donated by my relatives or Tom's or even earned by odd jobs (I had come by a pair of shoes by digging for an hour in the garden of a Cornish guest house). I helped in the hostel and was repaid with meals. Bill lent me his tent and I slept on the hillside above the valley. Nights were starlit and silent – except for curlews and owls and foxes.

By day we walked the lovely upland area east of the valley – an undulating plateau between Nantmor and the Moelwyns, where we swam in tiny lakes set in the heather, or wandered through abandoned quarries dropping stones down bottomless shafts, exploring the silent alleys where the only sound was slate shifting on the tips under the fleeing hares.

Bill found nests and Joe photographed them – and Tom came and went, so that I ran the whole gamut of emotions: ecstasy and despair and terrible, racking jealousy.

It seems strange, looking back on that time, that I should have stayed so long in Nantmor before moving on to the climbing area. But I had not yet caught the bug, nor did I have anyone to climb with. The dog and I explored the Moelwyns and Cnicht, but there was no one for the other end of a rope; even Tom – when 'he was there – was too lazy to stir far from the valley. He did take me once to Lliwedd but the climb left little impression on me. It was misty and I saw nothing of the cliff. Probably we followed the general line of Rocker on the west buttress, avoiding the difficulties; hardly an inspiring route, but, considering Tom didn't know the cliff, it showed something of the old pioneer spirit to go without a guide book, to the foot of a cliff in mist (a cliff which is intimidating at the best of times) – with a novice – and climb straight to the summit.

Although the climb itself left little impression on me, the feel of the rock and the sense of exposure awakened memories of the Milestone Direct. I wanted to go back to Idwal.

Then Mother sent a pre-birthday present – money – enough to last me quite a few weeks at the rate I lived. Feeling it was a great adventure, I set out with Thomas one fine May morning to do the Snowdon Horseshoe en route for Idwal.

*

It was very hot. For some forgotten reason I carried my boots and walked in plimsolls. The long grind to the top of Lliwedd was agony. I had a full rucksack (including the tent) and there was no track. We went straight for the Far East peak.

The ridge was very dry that day, as dry as a ridge on the moon. Tom was a great believer in fasting. Not necessarily to cure illness, but general fasting : a periodical 'clean out'. To lighten my load and save money, I had started a fast the previous night, but how I longed for a cup of tea on the top of Snowdon ! The staff gave Thomas water, but I didn't like to ask for some myself if I were buying nothing, so I sat in agony and listened to his lapping, wishing the café would empty suddenly so that I could get down and join him.

After Snowdon itself the rest of the horseshoe was perfect. We had found our second wind at last and the slight pull up to Crib y Ddysgl went unnoticed. Then we were on the knife-edge of Crib Goch, myself balancing airily and happily along the top in my plimsolls until – to my incredulous horror – something pushed heavily against the back of my knees. Thomas slipped past scrabbling, then waited on the next move, motionless and grinning nervously.

I sat down to recover.

We managed to complete the ridge without falling off or my losing my temper, both remarkable achievements, as Thomas refused to go ahead and would stand stupidly, rooted to his holds with horror, right on the place where I wanted to step (so that I would have to traverse underneath, when he would move convulsively to the next hold – the point where I wanted to regain the ridge). On the other hand, if he were second, he thought he was being left behind and pushed past with that breath-taking shove against the knees to leave me sprawling white-faced on the crest of the ridge. And so we dodged and pushed and cursed our way in short rushes along the razor-edge of Crib Goch. Then he jibbed at the descent to Bwlch Moch and I was forced to climb down outside those silly little corners with half a hundredweight of dog hanging over one arm.

We reached the grass and the place where Tom and I had turned back last winter, when the blizzard swept across the cwm from Lliwedd, and Llydaw was a black and awful pit seen through the shifting mist below our feet.

It was evening now : a still May evening, very quiet except for the streams. Two or three miles away was the Pen y Gwryd hotel and a meal for Thomas. I wondered if I were justified in breaking my fast to the extent of having a drink. We hurried down.

The Riddetts were very good to Thomas. They brought me his dinner plate to inspect. It was heaped with chicken, gravy, stuffing, roast potatoes . . . (our vegetarianism had never excluded white meat). I left him in the kitchen and went to sit in the smoke-room trying to lose my hunger in mild beer and Riddett's praise of the new BP boot nails. I knew that, eventually, I would derive immense spiritual uplift from my fast, but just at the moment I felt plain earthy.

That night we slept in the lee of a boulder below the summit of Glyder Fach. The last of the afterglow faded as I crawled into my bag, and the next thing I knew was waking in the cold grey dawn with the sunlight on the tip of Snowdon – although somewhere in that night is a dim memory of a world of moon-silvered peaks and long white wraiths of cloud lying up the valleys like sleeping fish.

I kicked Thomas to wake up and talk to me, but he opened a bloodshot eye, grumbled about no breakfast and the cold, turned round and went to sleep again. When the sun reached us we thawed and crept out into the open. We were too high for streams so there was no wash. I put the bag in the rucksack, combed my hair and pushed on.

The heat wave was holding. We reached the top of Glyder Fach and looked down through the dancing haze to Idwal. Suddenly I was excited. I could see no cliffs; they were all below me or hidden on the far side of Tryfan; but I knew what the excitement was. I don't think I tried to analyse my mood (judging from my contacts at the time, this is surprising). Perhaps I'd thought of all the climbs there must be in the area I was looking at, bigger and better than the Milestone, or perhaps I had a premonition of the life ahead of me. Probably I just knew I was in love, completely and overwhelmingly, and this was the last time. I had always fallen in love at second sight, which is puzzling, because you can never understand what went wrong the first time. Now, walking along the plateau between the Glyders, I knew that I had come home.

*

We met Paul Russell on the slopes of Glyder Fawr; he was the first of the older climbers that I was to meet that summer. People like George Dwyer, Dicky Morsley, Appy Hughes, Taff Williams . . . perhaps it is because we had people like these around when we started climbing that there seemed to be far fewer accidents than there are nowadays.

Paul showed me four things that day : a big red fox on the slope below the Fawr, how to run the screes down to Llyn y Cwm, the Devil's Kitchen and the route down beside it. I had been up to the foot of the Kitchen in the winter, but it was sensible of Paul to show me the top of the track. Accidents have happened here because people thought the track went literally down the great cleft instead of down a natural rake on the cliffs at the side.

We trotted cheerfully down to Idwal, where we arrived at the hostel at opening time. I had eaten nothing for forty-eight hours but it had had no effect on my mountaineering.

*

The assistant warden at Idwal was Frances Payne – a small, slight girl who had reached the same standard in climbing as I, starting in similar fashion by (almost) being benighted in Y Gully the night after we had performed that harrowing descent of the west face of Tryfan. During the week there were no climbers at Idwal so, feeling rather devils, we started climbing on our own. Between us we had about half a dozen climbs to our credit, and neither of us had ever led. We kept to what we knew – at first. I climbed bare-footed in imitation of Tom (I only wore shoes in towns and when hitch-hiking anyway). Frances and I travelled light, carrying only the rope and gym shoes slung at our waists.

On our first climb we were solemnly leading through on the Milestone Direct when Dicky Morsley and Paul Russell came solo-ing gaily up the Ordinary parallel to us. Dicky's bright moon-face appeared round a corner and he stared in astonishment at our feet. (Actually we were equally amazed at their being without a rope but we didn't say so.) They trotted upwards, their incredulous remarks floating back until they died away in the direction of the east face.

The great cliffs were not for us. We moved among the lesser climbs – starting up the Ordinary on the Slabs, and after long and serious discussion, deciding it was too easy, doing Hope instead and coming *down* the Ordinary – a strange experience this: to see the drop all the time below your feet. We worked through the easier climbs on the Slabs but left Tennis Shoe well alone. We graduated to Very Difficults by way of Monolith Crack – a safe but strenuous introduction and hardly typical of the rest of the standard. Then the more experienced people showed us the real V. Diffs. Tom came and took us up Zig Zag (Frances' husband, too, all four on the rope) and Frances fainted at the top of the last chimney, and when she came to, announced that she was having a baby ... And one Sunday afternoon I persuaded Appy Hughes to go to the Slabs and do Tennis Shoe. But when we reached the climb he wouldn't lead, so I led it and found out what exposure was and the meaning of the word 'delicate'.

The following day we all climbed solo up different routes to the Luncheon Stone at the foot of Holly Tree Wall – until then only a name, or, perhaps, steep rock to be studied idly after Hope or Faith or Charity, a wall where one knew there were routes; but these were Severes and Severes were, quite literally, unthought-of in connection with oneself. So I lay there idly, wondering in a disinterested sort of way why people struggled so hard in the scoop on the first pitch of the Direct Route. It looked so easy (but I didn't say so). Two men stood above the scoop, but for all their efforts they could bring no more of their party up. In the end the two men went on, up the wall, alone.

The spectators on the Luncheon Stone stirred.

'Right,' said Tom. 'Want a go?'

'Oh yes!' I breathed. To be taken up a Severe – my first – and that, Holly Tree Wall!

But Tom stood back and I realized that I was meant to lead. I didn't think twice about it. The scoop had looked easy and it *was*. I went up like a bird and I've spent the last fourteen years trying to discover why, because it's never gone so well since. All the climb was delightful: the lovely undercut hold on the Crescent Slab which could be used as a layback, the funny little chimney behind the tree, and the last steep crack. Tom was delighted with me, and I had a sneaking feeling of smugness because George Dwyer was on the terrace below with clients. George was the local guide.

Holly Tree marked the end of a phase for me: the initiation phase. Tom had to return to his work, but he was reluctant to leave me at Idwal. Perhaps he felt I might climb beyond my limit now. He persuaded me to return to Nantmor and there we had a sudden and very shattering quarrel.

Our relationship had always been uneasy. We had fought on and off since we met, usually because I couldn't take criticism on small points of behaviour and sometimes because I was furiously jealous of other women. The last quarrel started from some trivial cause and developed into a full-scale attack by me on the Bohemian way of life – particularly its futility – and then came my passionate and hysterical announcement that I was going back to the Army. This appalled both of us and I fled to the woods to exhaust myself in wild weeping.

The following day I left for Cornwall. Thomas stayed behind in Penny's care. I felt very much alone as I walked south. I brooded darkly on my life. I could see no future for me while I led this aimless existence. During the last few weeks I had met a different type from Tom and the Cornish crowd : people who had struck a compromise with life. They worked at normal but interesting jobs, and they climbed every weekend. I was completely converted to climbing myself and wanted no more beards and sandals and James Joyce. To me everything was in watertight compartments; it never occurred to me that a climber might read Joyce. What more did one want to read than *Mountaincraft* and the guide books? But, possibly because the Idwal climbers were younger and less sensational than the Cornish people, the latter still exerted a strong influence over me. I had quarrelled with Tom but I hadn't the courage to sever the ties completely. The Cornish community was generous and casual, they would always welcome another one; but if I turned away from them I'd be on my own. The Idwal people didn't live in expanding communities – they were at university or in town flats. I'd have to find work and a home on my own – and I was still wanted by the police.

I went back to Cornwall in a desperate and final attempt to make up my mind. I had told Tom I would give myself up, but the step needed more thought than had desertion. In the normal way I would have been demobilized by now, but I would have to wait another six months for release if I went back, to serve out the time I'd been absent. I didn't know how I could face six months in the Army after the freedom of that spring and summer.

I wandered slowly down through Devon, bored and unsettled. I felt now that I would be battening on the hospitality of my friends, taking advantage of them while I worked out my decision. I made up my mind to support myself, and be independent financially.

They were still living in the caravan when I arrived. Their attitude towards me was cooler now. Hardly surprising; I was a cat among pigeons. I stayed only a few weeks. In the mornings I picked potatoes on surrounding farms and in the afternoons I ran down to Mousehole to model for the artists – posing in sun-lit studios that were old sail lofts, with the windows open wide above the cobbled alleys, and the gulls crooning softly on the chimney pots. Sometimes I stayed the night at Mousehole to go out before sunrise on a cold grey sea and help lift the lobster pots. The painters and fishermen mingled freely; some of the painters seemed to be fishermen and vice versa, and since they all dressed the same it was difficult to tell the difference, and the village was an intriguing mixture of sophistication and simplicity, of realism and romance.

Then someone else took a proprietary – and firm – interest in my career. My mother came down for a holiday. She saw me for the first time in six months, she met the others, and she stayed at a respectable guest house in the cove and collected information. I felt something was brewing and my hackles rose. The fact that someone was about to try to persuade me to go her way was enough in itself to make me go to the other extreme, but my last stand collapsed almost without a shot being fired. Suddenly I knew that I didn't want to fight. I had lost all faith in my cause and the only thing that kept me from collapsing openly was pride and the feeling that I ought to give the Enemy a run for his money. My mother and her landlady, with the amazing cunning occasionally manifest when strangers conspire against a com-mon danger, recruited several of the more intelligent visitors (I remember that one was a lady novelist, another a playwright) and they waylaid me. They trapped me on the outskirts of the village as I came home from work, delighting me with compliments on my looks, my tan, my superb health . . . the while leading me gently back to their hotels, to dinner and wine and persuasive conversation. Mother was not present at these soirées; indeed, they never made the mistake of sending two people at a time. It was probably arranged during the afternoon. I gave them their money's worth, talking with cool detachment of the life I was leading and its attractions (but using their arguments privately, only to bolster my secret decision – to go back). Coupled with the dawning awareness of the futility of that life was the urge to tidy up a loose end. The present inconveniences attached to being on the run: being unable to obtain a passport or driving licence, having to be careful of the police – were only minor; the major consideration that sent me back was this knowledge of a job to be finished.

5. I Give Myself Up

In a heavy skirt made from a black-out curtain, sandals and one of Tom's old shirts, I felt very vulnerable as I walked along the platforms at Chester Station looking for the military police. But as soon as I saw the large woman with the flat red cap like cardboard and the bosom-bursting tunic I knew that I had the advantage.

'Good afternoon,' I said. 'I'm a deserter. What do I do?'

She stared and her eyes flickered apprehensively. She couldn't decide whether to ignore me as a civilian taking the mickey or to accept me. Training came to her help.

'Where's your pay book?' she asked.

I was genuinely amazed. I hadn't the least idea, and said so. Impasse. We waited, both thinking hard.

'Look,' I said kindly, 'how about taking me to the Transport Office and the sergeant will tell you what to do with deserters?'

Perhaps if I'd been dressed in conventional clothes and carried a suit-case they would have been more sure of themselves, but right up until the time that I reached my final destination, a transit camp outside Liverpool, I was handled with kid gloves, as if they suspected my present tractability were transient and that if they made a false move I would show my claws. I suppose they were worried because they couldn't understand me. I knew only too well how the Army hated precedents and I conformed to no set standard for deserters.

I followed the policewoman along the platform and people turned to stare at us, but furtively – afraid that, like a mental case, I might poke my tongue out at them or scream an obscenity. It was difficult to keep a straight face and when we reached the Transport Office and I dumped my rucksack on the counter, and the men looked up and grinned, I grinned back. The girl was telephoning her superiors: 'I've got a deserter here . . .'

Eyes wavered, eyebrows lifted, grins broadened. I went behind the counter and drank tea, chatting with the men while the women, with elaborate unconcern, sat at their desks and worked on papers. I felt like the returned prodigal. When the truck came for me, I was escorted to the station entrance by several Redcaps, one carrying my rucksack. They didn't think I was going to make a bolt for it; we were swopping addresses.

I sat in their mess and ate a large tea with a host of police-women. They couldn't hear enough of how I had lived in the last few months. They treated me with a kind of astonished amuse-ment, gaping at the tales of sleeping out, of rats in barns, of the *Teresa* on fire at sea. They couldn't undertand how I'd managed to eat with rationing in force . . .

A sergeant came and told me I was to go to Liverpool. I hadn't enough money and said I might take a little time, hitching. Im-mediately there were offers of loans. A warrant was made out for me, but since warrants were not provided for trams, five shillings appeared from some official source. (I imagined the commanding officer watching my exit from behind a curtain.) As I was driven away to the station they handed me a full packet of cigarettes.

*

In those days – perhaps it is still the same – it was difficult to punish an ATS girl for major breaches of discipline, and I sup-pose my breach was the worst outside a criminal court. I had known I would be confined to barracks for a period, that I would have my demobilization number put back (we were numbered according to our length of service), that probably I would have to do extra duties, like floor scrubbing.

At my court martial – in my horribly new, badly fitting uni-form – I was asked if I had anything to say. I pondered. Should I tell the truth to my commanding officer – an unsympathetic woman with hard eyes? Say I deserted because I wasn't fitted for the Army, that – with the war over and no chance of being posted abroad – I felt that there was no purpose in remaining in the Services, that there was no goal ahead? I was being steam-rollered into mediocrity. During the last six months I had become an in-dividual again, even if it was rather an unsettled one. But I saw their point of view. They were thinking how irresponsible I was to leave the Army when I was no longer getting anything out of it, to leave the other life when I had sucked it dry. There was too much doubt of my own actions and their motives to allow me to reason with the court. Reason was out, anyway. I hadn't reasoned when I'd deserted but I'd known I was right, in the same way that I knew, instinctively, that I was doing the right thing in coming back. I had done what I'd wanted to do and now I had to take the rap. Or perhaps I was merely too lazy to state my case – if I had a case.

'No,' I said, 'I've nothing to say.'

*

My sentence was so trivial I've forgotten what it was. But they had a more subtle way of bringing me in line, although the effect it had on me was to send me really wild for a time.

They put me on the switchboard.

It was the beginning of August – not a very good August, certainly, but I worked myself up into a fine state of martyrdom, staring out of the window (which wouldn't open) on to a green field where a bronzed physical training instructor showed off her body – less supple, less hard, less brown than mine. I wrote long, morbid poems, and volunteered for extra duty so that I could write more. One night I wallowed in emotion listening to someone playing Chopin in the NAAFI, only to find – when I left the telephone-room – it was a pint-sized sergeant-major.

After a week or so the poetry palled and I began to grow savage instead of morbid and resentful. I stopped writing about suicide and deep black water, and wrote about caged beasts and hate. Then I stopped writing and looked round for something else to do.

At that moment I met Georg. The camp was a transit camp for Poles returning from fighting on the Continent. Georg was a brain surgeon who was waiting to be demobilized when there was a post for him in the States. He was a quaint little man : middle-aged, balding, very clever. We must have looked an odd couple walking through Liverpool : a roly-poly little colonel, and an ATS driver half his age, deep in a discussion on life. Georg taught me that you didn't need to be a tramp to be unconventional. He also taught me that you don't have to be a long-haired artist to appreciate Art.

He took me to my first opera (a dramatic choice: *The Rape of Lucretia*), and although the music meant very little, I was terrifically impressed by the visual beauty. We went to lots of plays together, and he took me to supper afterwards, seeing me to my train at the end of the evening (we came from different camps), and kissing my hand at the barrier.

Georg didn't stop the break-out, he checked it. True, I was already rebelling in a minor degree, but only to the extent of asking the other operators to stand in for me on the board at night, so that I could stay out late. I, who had used the nights as casually as if they were the days for six months, wasn't going to come hurrying home at ten thirty pm (one pass until eleven fifty-nine pm). I didn't resent the restriction. I ignored it and came and went the back way, over a high wall, to avoid the guard-room.

When Georg went to the States I was at a loose end again. I knew a lot of people now, civilian and military, because I was sent along to the American Embassy with parties of Poles who were emigrating; since they and I spoke a kind of German, I was the interpreter.

I was invited to parties which lasted into the small hours, when I would come over the brick wall just before dawn and creep into the NAAFI to snatch a few hours' sleep before I went on duty at eight o'clock. On one occasion I had worked out our unofficial roster so that I could take three days off and go yachting with a Marine in Devon. He wasn't much of a sailor and the engine failed and we were becalmed in the middle of Tor Bay. I got into Brixham at the moment when I had promised I would relieve my long-suffering colleagues on the switchboard. I telephoned and told them they would have to sit it out until I arrived.

I got away with it that time, but, unknown to me, I was under suspicion. Only proof was needed. Now, there were two sergeant-majors on camp, male and female. The male was the little man – Herbert – who played Chopin. They were both very neat and very strict from a military point of view, but Herbert was attractive and his opposite number was no glamour puss, and, when she began to suspect us she must have been most indignant, particularly when she uncovered the switchboard angle. I expect she discovered that by making repeated calls at night and finding the voice didn't correspond with the name on the duty roster. And when I wasn't there, Herbert would have disappeared too. It must have been lonely in the sergeants' mess. They were the only members.

I was unmasked at about four o'clock one morning. I had come in from a party by way of the brick wall (I knew every hand- and foot-hold, and it had given Herbert such an inferiority complex to be pulled up each time that now he came in legitimately – by the guardroom). I walked calmly along the corridor to my room, pushed open the door and stared, fascinated, at the little red glow on the bed. I smelt cigarette smoke.

'You've been a long time,' said the sergeant-major. The other one.

I switched on the light. I had been drinking for so long that I was quite sober, but very tired.

'I'm going to bed,' I said. 'Do you mind?'

I resented her making herself at home on my bed, and I was too exhausted to be amused at her long vigil. The ash-tray was overflowing.

'Where have you been?'

'For a walk,' I said, slowly crawling out of my uniform.

'How did you get back?'

'Over the bloody wall; now let me get to my bed.'

'Nine o'clock in the morning,' she said ghoulishly, knowing that would hurt as I wouldn't get a lie-in.

*

'Anything to say?'

My crime had been read out. The new junior commander – a kind, sensible woman with spectacles, grey hair and puzzled eyes – waited. The silent escort behind me waited – and the sergeant-major. Somewhere on the camp Herbert waited, shaking in his shoes, wondering what revelations I was going to make.

'Can I speak to you alone, ma'am?'

It was more of a studied insult to the RSM than because there was any necessity for privacy.

They tramped out and shut the door of the office.

'Well,' she said, 'why did you do it? I know you've been doing it for a long time.'

That took me by surprise, but then I recovered myself and saw

my opportunity. I could explain to this woman. By this time my
exploits in Cornwall and North Wales were generally known.
There was no need to tell her about those. But I told her about my
feelings on the switchboard, despair at first, then savage resentment at being caged like an animal. The incredible boredom of
staring, for hours at a time, through a window that wouldn't
open, at a green field.

'What do you want?' she asked.

'I'm a driver,' I said. 'I want something to drive.'

'And you'll stop going absent; coming in late and climbing over
the wall?'

I would have agreed to anything if I could have a waggon again.

She was a wonderful woman. There was a man on camp who
was driving her car. He went the next day and I replaced him.
Not content with that, she had a three-ton Bedford allocated to
the camp, then a fifteen-hundredweight. I was in charge of
all of them. I was in my element. All my energy and love were
lavished on my trucks and my commanding officer. I couldn't get
enough driving. Because I was the only driver on the camp I was
in constant demand to take the other girls to dances in the evenings. If there were any questions of a relief driver, I would be
furiously angry and bully my CO into letting me work twice as
hard, twice as fast. It was hopeless trying to maintain all these
vehicles, so, trading on a friendship with the transport officer, I
used to smuggle them into the workshops of the local RAF camp
for a periodical inspection. And after I had a blow-out and, being
in the inevitable hurry, ruined the tyre by driving home on it,
an inquiry was skilfully avoided by changing the whole wheel
with the RAF. It was months after I was demobilized that the
War Office stopped sending me letters asking why that wheel had
an Air Ministry number instead of War Department.

There was no more climbing over the brick wall. For four months
I took no leave. I can't remember that I had a day off. I flung myself into the business of driving, of helping to organize dances, of
moving camp (we moved twice in those four months).

One of my pleasantest jobs – and the most dramatic since I had
been a despatch rider in Essex when the doodle bugs were coming
over – was going down to Prince's Dock to meet the troopships
coming home from the Far East.

It was autumn now, and we would go down early, lorries and ambulances and cars, all converging on the dock from the different transit camps on the outskirts of the city. We would wait for hours in our trucks (the transports were always late) until at last there would be a stir among the dockers and we'd leave our cards and gossip, and get down from the vehicles to watch the big grey shapes looming through the fog, with all the troops singing – and the girls would creep back into their cabs to get their tears over before the boat came near enough so that they had to get out and wave. Every time you said you would control yourself in future, and every time your heart turned over at the first sight of them coming up the Mersey through the fog.

The rain and grime of industrial Lancashire didn't worry me in the least. It was always raining, but I have the happiest memories of Liverpool: centred on the docks, the Royal Court Theatre and my CO's house in the suburbs where we called sometimes to have tea with her old father. The physical aspect of Lancashire became merely a background to my life, not a foreground as Stoke had been. I was trusted and treated decently and I responded like an animal. When I had given myself up, my self-confidence didn't go very deep; I was contemptuous of authority, but with a sympathetic commanding officer, who seemed a little lonely herself, the contempt faded. Because she relied on me, I began to acquire respect for authority. She brought me back to the conventional fold but I was very changed. Before I deserted I never thought of myself as being connected with authority, and, completely unaware of any social pattern, felt a natural rebelliousness, but I accepted it too, knowing it was little use kicking; the other man was much stronger than I was. It was fear that kept me under. Then, in Cornwall and Wales, I learnt that there was nothing to be afraid of, that there was nothing behind the façade; it was merely a shell of silly conventions, and rules laid down by unenlightened people inferior to ourselves. In Liverpool I unlearnt that philosophy and started again under the tuition of Georg and the less conscious one of my CO. I certainly got around, going from fear to contempt to respect in a year and, had I stayed in the Army, probably I would have developed a power complex, wallowing in frustration until I acquired my first stripe. But I didn't stay on, and my demobilization orders came to me one Sunday afternoon as I sat in Ogwen Cottage and the gales came lashing through the pass.

*

I had volunteered to work over Christmas partly because festivities were more fun in the Army, partly to help my CO, but mainly so that I could race around Lancashire in my fleet of vehicles (I had a feeling my time was running short).

I took my leave at New Year and went back to Idwal. I had kept away deliberately during the last five months because I felt the mountains would unsettle me if I returned for a weekend. But now that I knew my demobilization was very close I could risk my peace of mind.

I went back by way of Nantmor. Penny and Bill were still there. They weren't surprised to see me in battle-dress; the grapevine had been at work – now everyone knew I had been a deserter from the ATS when I was here before.

Tom was in Nantmor.

It was a strange, uneasy reunion; we were like two dogs walking round each other, stiff-legged, uncertain whether to play or fly at each other's throats. In the morning he came with me as far as the foot of the Watkin path below Snowdon. We sat on the bridge above the deep pool where we used to swim and he talked – sadly and censoriously. I listened politely (after all, I owed him a considerable debt) but I was bored, staring at the cloud low on Lliwedd, and wondering who would be at Idwal. Cars were passing empty, and after a while I said goodbye and started walking up the long hill out of Nant Gwynant.

At Idwal I met Johnnie Brownsort: a bespectacled, gangling, intense young man, just released from the RAF; correct, but not so correct that he could not consider plans for the formation of a new group: the Bar Room Mountaineering Club. With a geologist, we walked and climbed on Tryfan and the Glyders in temperatures well below freezing. An iron-hard Idwal was waiting for the big snow of 1947. I had no boots but borrowed a pair, nailed with hobs, from the warden. In these I was crucified on the Yellow Slab of First Pinnacle Rib, almost in tears that I, who had floated

up a Severe (leading) a few months ago, should now be so extended (second) on a Difficult. It is not until one starts growing old
that the excuses come fluently: the wrong footwear, numb hands,
lack of practice, one pitch of a climb which is of a far higher
standard than the general grading . . . Then I found no excuses,
but I persevered and was dragged up more of the easier routes,
gradually working up to leading them. It was bitterly cold and
usually damp; anything harder than a Difficult was out of the
question.

We had come down from Y Garn that Sunday afternoon and
were drinking tea in Ogwen Cottage when Johnnie Brownsort
appeared outside the window waving a telegram. It recalled me to
camp. No reason was given, but I knew.

'I'll be back in a week!' I promised.

I was back in three days.

*

I arrived in Warrington that evening, to be told to entrain for
Aldershot the following night. We had a hectic celebration on
the Monday, returning to the CO's office at about eleven o'clock,
where everyone crowded round to witness my signature on various documents. There were girls from the barracks with their boy
friends, the new driver who was taking over from me, and an
RAF officer whose name I have forgotten, whom I can remember
only as being large and soft. Some time before this, when our
relationship had threatened to become serious, he had told me –
while parked outside the barracks one night – that he couldn't
allow me to climb any more. I was so astonished that he talked
on for about half a minute before I could collect myself and leave
the car. I contacted him again on the last night because he was
the only person I knew with enough money to give us all a
proper party.

For some time the CO had been pressing me to sign on in the
ATS. She assured me that if I went back to my old trade of
physical training I would become a corporal automatically after
my refresher course. The prospect was alluring but it was quite
impossible for me to stay in the Services now that I had discovered
climbing. As I signed my papers she made one last effort to persuade me to change my mind (did she doubt her influence at the

last minute and have inner visions of my Going To The Dogs?),
but, even had I been doubtful a few weeks before, that last leave
at Idwal would have tipped the scales.

It was a sad parting and I cried all the way to the station, where
sadness gave way to righteous indignation when I discovered two
goats in need of milking tethered on the cold platform. Untying
them, I led them to the waiting-room, handed them over to a
party of sailors, and then stamped off to find the stationmaster to
demand that they be milked. I suspect he disappeared automatically with the arrival of demob parties; anyway, his office was
locked, so I milked the goats myself – into a tin mug belonging to
one of the sailors.

*

Aldershot, Sussex and back to Idwal – to a Snowdonia lying grim
and grey under a lowering sky. You could smell the snow.

It came the following Saturday afternoon. I had a novice on the
Ordinary on the Slabs – a foreign doctor, almost speechless with
admiration at my agility, particularly on the level, coming down
through the dusk to Idwal.

'Like a wild goat,' he kept repeating to the third man. 'A
chamois!'

The chamois, running ahead to prepare dinner, slipped on a
frosted rock and sprained her ankle. They were going down
another way. As I started the long and lonely crawl to the youth
hostel, the first snowflakes began to fall and I wept in anger and
frustration. I spend the next six weeks in Sussex, writing. The
only time I left the house was to limp painfully over the crusted
ice to the bus stop for the cinema. At Idwal they were cut off by
the great falls of 1947, countless sheep died in the drifts – even
two of the wild goats died. I would have hated to see the animals
in trouble (although I could have helped dig them out of the snow
as the weekend climbers were doing), but the mountains must
have looked glorious.

The ankle took a long time to heal – for me sprains have always
been worse than fractures – and the snow was gone and spring
was in the air when I was finally able to return.

6. The Splendid Season

I came back, still a little shaky on that leg, at the end of March. Out of my gratuity I had left a little over fifty pounds. My intention was to live at Idwal, climbing, until the money gave out. I met a snag immediately, finding that, when the weather was poor, I was eating my head off and getting no return for my money. Since it rained a lot that March, I took a job as assistant warden over the Easter period at Capel Curig youth hostel.

On Good Friday strong gales swept Snowdonia. The river in front of the hostel rose until it lapped the wall beside the road. Farmers were rescuing sheep from the flooded fields. That morning a small group of walkers had taken the bus round the Glyders to Nant Peris, planning to walk back over the tops to their guest house in Bethesda. This route took them past the Devil's Kitchen.

The weather must have been terrible on top, with mist and rain; they had the wind behind them, but they were poorly clad. That evening one of them staggered into Idwal youth hostel, exhausted. He said the rest of the party was still out. A rescue party was organized, but although they found a second and, I think, a third person in Cwm Idwal, there was no trace of the remaining girl and boy. They went up to the plateau above the Kitchen, still searching, but in the end they returned to the hostel planning to go out again at first light.

At Capel Curig we didn't know about the affair until the Saturday morning, when the warden of Idwal came down to collect climbers for the search party.

There were about ninety people assembled at Idwal that morning, and they searched the area from Cwm Cneifion to the eastern spur of Y Garn: a district difficult to measure in mileage, but comprising three great cliffs – Glyder Fawr from the summit to the foot of the Slabs, and the Kitchen cliffs, and all the broken slopes of Y Garn. The cliffs were easier to search than the broken mountainsides: from a good vantage point and with powerful binoculars it is comparatively simple to pick out a person stranded on a bare face, but on broken ground you could hide a regiment.

I was in the middle party, on the Kitchen cliffs. It was my first experience of a search party. It was, that first time, alternately monotonous and exciting. There was a slight element of hysteria, a tendency to show off. We were, in the main, unaware of tragedy although, looking down the cwm, seeing the mountain alive with slowly moving figures, one felt it too big to grasp, and in a spirit of self-defence I resorted to that pseudo-callousness that made death a subject for facetiousness or ghoulish humour.

There was one brief interlude of normality. Since we must search everywhere, we often found ourselves in places where no one would go normally, because of unclimbable or dangerous rock. In one of these places, peering over the edge of the cliff near the top of the Kitchen, Johnnie Brownsort and I found a raven's nest with eggs. Then the old birds, which had been croaking above the cwm, lost their frightening aura and became harmless, but genuinely interesting, flesh and blood.

Then there were shouts from the top of the Kitchen and we looked up to see people converging on one point: the top of the grassy rake leading up from the Devil's Cellar. When we arrived, George Dwyer was coming up to the top of the cliff with a girl draped over his shoulder. Her trousers were in shreds and her legs blue with bruises and cold. She appeared to be barefooted in ridiculous little shoes. The sight of a blue leg through a long rent in the trousers, emphasizing the utter helplessness of the child, filled me with compassion. Later, when I saw a body, I thought I must have grown hard, to find death so unmoving, but even now the sight of a helpless person still alive, is, to me, so overwhelmingly pitiful that, for a time, all the responsibility of the world is on my shoulders.

Once there was the report of an aeroplane crash in the papers – an aircraft carrying a load of children. One small boy was the sole survivor, and when the rescuers arrived, he was still sitting there, waiting for them to come and tell him what to do. Had he been killed as well it would not have seemed so pathetic; the ultimate pathos lay in the fact that he was left alone to be frightened while he waited. So while the girl was made comfortable on the stretcher, and someone came up to say that the boy had been found dead, I was only concerned that she shouldn't know.

At the time those of us who were starting to climb (and most of us had little or no experience of mountaineering – the wider aspect of climbing that is knowing the mountains as a whole and in all weathers) were puzzled when we learnt the full story of the accident.

Apparently the girl and boy, lost on the top and with darkness coming, knowing that they were in the vicinity of the Kitchen, decided to wait until dawn to continue. Perhaps they were too exhausted to go farther, in any case. They crept under a boulder, where the boy died from exposure during the night. The girl was fit enough to start out in the morning, to survive a fall over a cliff (she stopped on a ledge) and to wave when she saw the rescuers in the cwm.

To us, in our ignorance, that a woman should come unscathed through conditions that killed a man was merely coincidence. We had no idea that, given the same circumstances, a woman is more likely to survive, owing to her lower rate of metabolism. One experienced mountaineer, who is also a medical man, inclines to the belief that women have a greater will to live in order that they may perpetuate the race. One may speculate indefinitely, but whether one settles for the theory of immortality, of a more strongly developed sense of responsibility, imperviousness to panic (the cold, insidious panic of despair that is more deadly than hysteria) or merely a lower metabolic rate, the fact remains that in the majority of cases and given the same conditions, women will survive exposure where men succumb.

*

I returned to the hostel subdued, like most novices after their first rescue. Often a novice can be put off his climbing by an accident, particularly if it happens at a time when he is climbing badly. But the following day the weather cleared, the rock dried, and I was barefooted again on the Milestone – and then on the east face of

Tryfan, to lead gaily up Pinnacle Rib, where I'd slipped and slithered in hobs a few weeks ago.

The weather improved further. I gave up my job at Capel and returned to Idwal. I had bought a cheap, but excellent, American tent which I pitched in the shadow of the larch wood above the Falls.

The glorious season began.

*

I climbed nearly every day – with anyone and everyone. At weekends the same people congregated at the hostel or in tents, or slept in the doorway of the disused chapel, but in the middle of the week I climbed with strangers. I had my own rope now – three-quarter-weight hemp; nylon was starting to make its appearance at Ogwen, but it was too expensive for me (I was living on a pound a week). During the week I would walk to the foot of the Slabs or the Milestone, and, if there were no one about, I would climb solo to a higher cliff : up the Slabs to Holly Tree Wall or to the east face by way of the Milestone Buttress, and there, or on the way, I would be sure to find someone for harder climbs.

During one of these free weeks I met a man who was so desperate to climb that he was willing to pay for my food (my only expense) if I would lead him up moderate routes. It was my first experience of professional mountaineering. My main reaction was surprise that I should not be bored by such routes as Gully and Slab and Two Tree Route. Moderates. On the contrary, I was delighted that my second should derive such enjoyment from his days with me.

Then I met Dave Nott, at that time a precocious schoolboy with not enough money to buy himself a pair of boots, and now on the editorial staff of a large paper. He told me of a cottage on the moor above Bethesda, which I could have free until July. It was owned by some friends of his who would like me to keep it aired. About this time Frances and Geoff Payne – who had left Idwal when I returned to the Army – came back to Wales with their baby. They were living on a farm in Capel, but Geoff didn't like farming and Frances didn't like the accommodation, and now they were thinking of moving down the Nant Ffrancon so that Geoff could work at the quarry. If I moved to Dave's cottage we could all live together: in fact, we might become the nucleus of a new community having the best of both worlds: climbing and the *vie de bohème*.

Dave and I walked down to see the cottage one Sunday afternoon. We took a short cut through the quarry. I was fascinated as we walked round that great tiered bowl and looked down all the levels to the tiny green pool in the bottom. In one place there had been a rock-fall; you could see how the terraces had melted away before it. Later that landslide provided a magnificent climax to a short story which I sold to the BBC.

The cottage stood on the edge of the moor – a gaunt, grey house, semi-detached, but its twin was dangerously in need of repair and uninhabited. I was to be offered both houses for eighty pounds later in the year. The building was at the end of a long rural street of quarrymen's houses, but whereas the others stood on a road, mine was reached by way of an iron gate leading on to the open moor. It was only in the mornings, when the quarrymen passed, and on the occasions when the neighbours came with complaints, that we were aware that we lived in a community larger than our own. We could dodge the street when we went down to the valley by taking a short cut across the moor.

I moved in the following weekend: a weekend made eventful, first, by the weather breaking so that I was devoutly thankful that I had a roof over my head, and, secondly, by the fact that I starved for two or three days. I had run out of money and my savings book was in Sussex. I had sent an urgent telegram to my mother, but meanwhile I was penniless. There was, I remember, a large packet of cornflakes in the cupboard, and nothing else. No coal. Dave and I sat in the dim parlour (no oil for the lamps) and, wrapped in blankets, played pontoon for matches. The whole house was ransacked for cigarette stubs which we smoked in a pipe. On the third day the weather cleared and we went to the nearest plantation to collect firewood. The larches were thirty to forty feet high.

'Look,' said Dave, 'this is how Tarzan does it!'

But I could have told him they were the wrong kind of tree. I knew my Burroughs too. He climbed to the top of a larch and set it swaying furiously. As it reached the limit of its widest arc, he leapt into the next and set that moving. Suddenly there was a loud crack and the whole top of the tree, and Dave, fell to the ground. There can be no sound more horrible than the soft thud of a human body falling from a height. I waited, speechless, uncertain whether to mourn him or to scream with laughter.

He sat up, white and trembling, and looking rather surprised. I collapsed.

*

When Dave returned to school I decided to go to Capel and find out when Geoff and Frances intended to move into the cottage. It was a lovely spring afternoon when I came out on the main road above Bethesda and started walking up the valley. After a while I heard the weak but noisy sound of a motor bicycle behind me. It took so long arriving that I decided it wasn't worth hitching, but it stopped all the same. The driver was attracted by the rope which I carried, partly to facilitate hitching, but mainly because I never knew whom I was going to meet and whether I would have an hour or so to kill while in the vicinity of climbable rock.

In those days no one interested me unless, or until, they climbed, but I admitted to myself that the driver of the motor cycle might have possibilities. He was a slim, dark youth, in appearance in his early twenties, but actually about seventeen or eighteen. He was full of charm and enthusiasm. I showed him the Milestone Buttress as we passed, and, later, the spot from where we could see the Snowdon Horseshoe. This wasn't enough for him. We had to drive along to Pen y Gwryd (with the back mudguard jumping on the tyre so that we were accompanied by a strong smell of burning rubber) and down Nant Gwynant so that he could have a closer view of the peaks. Then we returned to Capel and I took him to the farm where the Paynes lived. I felt rather apologetic breaking in on their delightful domestic squalor with this gilded youth. Geoff Payne masked his disapproval for a time but couldn't resist a pointed remark on the stranger's elegant cuff links, a remark which was accepted pleasantly and with no embarrassment. When he'd gone, we found it difficult to believe that he had just been expelled from school. Already he had the poise of a man. We shook our heads, heavy with foreboding, and forgot him.

A few days later he came to the cottage with a bottle of gin. In some matters he was still somewhat ingenuous. Apparently he thought I was sophisticated and he had been told that sophisticated women drank gin. We went down to Bethesda and changed the bottle for Tio Pepe.

I took him climbing on the Milestone. He was very bad: clumsy while trying to be quick, and resentful because he was not so good as me. He says I told him he would never make a climber, an erroneous prophecy which I don't remember making, although, on that first day's showing, there was every justification for it. This was Geoffrey Sutton, who, a few years later, became a guide, then helped to form the Alpine Climbing Group and, more recently, was part-author – with Geoffrey Winthrop Young and Wilfred Noyce – of *Snowdon Biography*.

He didn't do a lot of climbing for a year or so after he first came to Wales. He was busy working his way round the world. (I had a letter from Singapore or Hong Kong where he was a radio announcer for a time, and another from North America when a millionaire was employing him to look after his motor launch. I think, too, at some period he worked in a lumber camp.) Except when his letters arrived, we forgot about him, and next time he appeared he was stationed at Chester, commuting between Eaton Hall and Llanberis Pass in a very ancient racing car shaped like a cigar. Then he passed beyond our range again and rumours filtered back that he was in the Somaliland Scouts. And while he roamed the world, we stayed at Ogwen and climbed, so that it was the more disconcerting to discover, when we met again, that, in technique, he had caught us up and passed.

*

Whitsun came, bringing the Paynes to the cottage on the moor, bringing also Johnnie Brownsort from London, Dave from Liverpool; and, with Dave, a tall, thin, outrageously funny young man, Peter Hodgkinson. He was so outrageous that, on one occasion, he was 'reported' to George Dwyer for his indelicate language on Balcony Cracks.

The main business of Whitsun was the house-warming and climbing, in that order. I wanted a large supply of beer in the house but empty bottles were unobtainable. We were too young and impecunious to think in terms of firkins. Accordingly,

Johnnie B., Dave and I left the house at about two o'clock one dark night and, carrying sacks, made our way down the mountain to Bethesda.

By some fortunate coincidence all the pubs in the village are on one side of the street, backing on the river, their yards surrounded by high walls. All the gates were locked, of course, but the walls presented no obstacle. I have vivid memories of dark figures silhouetted for an instant against the night sky, of bottles chinking but drowned by the rush of the river, of slipping stealthily along the alleys to peer up and down the empty, lamplit street, looking for the police.

We returned to the cottage just before dawn, our sacks loaded with bottles, and the same day took them all back to Bethesda in the pram to be filled.

It was a grand house-warming. Geoff baby-sat and the rest of us spent the early part of the evening in sunlit back bars where the quarrymen sang *Calan Lan* and *Sospan Fach*, and, outside, the spring-green trees swayed above the river in the golden light. Frances and I wore flowers in our hair, and the whole party glowed with beer and happiness. When the pubs closed we straggled homeward up the mountain, the gay mood leaving us (owlishly reminding each other of the stages of drunkenness in *Tortilla Flat*) until we were serious again, discussing, with nostalgia – and some exaggeration – those climbs we had done, and – with alcoholic fervour – those we were going to do. There are no climbs one cannot do when young, even discounting the influence of beer.

There wasn't room in the cottage for everyone to sleep. Hodge was in my tent on the moor and I could hear him singing dolefully to himself as I went to bed. Looking out of the window – it was light now – I saw that empty bottles were emerging in lazy parabolas from the interior of the tent. A few hours later we were wakened by the next-door neighbour, with the polite request that we should collect the bottles before the cows cut their feet.

That weekend I did my first Very Severe. I had been leading Severes for some time – my favourite being Javelin Buttress on Holly Tree Wall. From some angles the Wall seems to overhang the Slabs, and when you are on it, you find that first impressions were not deceptive: people coming up the Slabs look a very long way below. Of course, the Slabs themselves are at a fairly easy angle, but most people who have fallen from the terrace at the top haven't stopped until they reached the bottom nearly five hundred feet below. But exposure didn't worry me then, although the first time I saw people on Javelin Buttress it was its steepness more than the clean, delicate nature of the crux that appealed to me.

It is an attractive crucial move. You are about sixty feet above your second and standing on the last foothold before the hard move. Above and on the right is what the guide book terms 'a series of good holds far apart'. They are very far apart – particularly for a short person. A normal-sized climber, standing on that last foothold, can reach the next with his fingers at full stretch: the first of the guide's 'good holds'. The hard part is supposed to be getting your feet on it (it is a mantelshelf move). The hard part for me is reaching the mantelshelf in the first place, but in those days, when strength had never failed, a slip had never been known, ropes didn't break, in short – one could not fall; then the hard move was a delicate and delightful piece of footwork.

For a year Javelin Buttress was my favourite climb. I did it so often that I became used to a gallery watching me on the hard move; it was my exhibition climb. But at Whitsun, with Balcony Cracks, I had my first taste of Very Severes – and was disappointed. I thought Javelin Buttress far superior. However, the climbs that followed were in a different category althogether and, fortunately, I had met the people who could lead them competently. It was no longer a question of waiting at the foot of the Slabs with a rope. Now people picked me up at the cottage on their motor cycles, and, after a while, even Bethesda was too far away and I moved back to the larch wood above the Ogwen Falls.

I followed Hodge up Belle Vue Bastion on Terrace Wall on a golden afternoon in late June, when he chain-smoked on the 'slab on the edge of all things' plucking up courage for the hard move, and, afterwards, perched on that airy terrace above the east face and below the walkers gaping from the summit, played a flute.

While I was at the cottage I had met David Thomas – a Welshman from Wrexham, ex-navigator (RAF), who was waiting to go up to Aberdeen University. At that time he was one of the best, if not the best, climber in the Ogwen valley. At a loose end during the week, he started climbing with me.

It was a delightful and fruitful partnership. We were both supremely confident in ourselves and in each other. Literally, we never thought of falling, despite the fact that we had both seen the results of accidents. My attitude was that of the very young in wartime: other people might be killed, but not oneself. We were completely inviolate. We were to have, both of us, a very rude awakening which finished – for good – the idea that we were gods.

Through July we polished off the Very Severes at Idwal. We didn't do them from any desire to tick them off in the guide book, but there wasn't a lot of fun in doing the same climb twice. Once a problem had been solved, it was a problem no longer. If you couldn't get up a climb twice, then it meant merely that you were tired or off-form; it wasn't the technical difficulty that defeated you.

Young people are often accused of being rock gymnasts, but surely you may be excused in your first great season of being so passionately in love with the rock that you can't have enough of it? No one grudges the newly-weds their honeymoon. After all, we shall never have that first season again. And, of course, there are times when you are not concerned with the rock. In fact, in the long hot days of a good summer, a climber who spends all his time in the mountains has a chance to dawdle.

We did a lot of swimming – but very little sunbathing. That was a waste of time. And swimming was indulged in as a re-fresher, not for its own sake. Since I have vivid scenic memories of that July, I must have been aware of other things than climb-ing. I remember how the whole of the west face of Tryfan – that rather mediocre pile of broken rock – would flush copper in the sunset, and how vividly green the flats looked down the valley in the evening light. And it was Geoff Payne who remarked, one evening as we came down the Gribin, and a shaft of sunlight slanted through the Kitchen so that the moraine glowed like emerald fire, that the Emperor Concerto always sounded like com-ing down after a good day.

We went to Clogwyn du'r Arddu, that stupendous cliff under

Snowdon, and spent several cold hours in the shadow struggling up Chimney Route, while wiser people swam in the sunlit waters of the lake. (We had swum there on the way up. I had nearly collapsed when I dived off a rock and realized, too late, that this lake was situated a thousand feet higher than those in which we usually bathed.)

Although we were doing so many Very Severes, I had not, as yet, led one. David was too good to want to second me (he was, indeed, leading all these routes in nailed boots), and, in any footwear, I wasn't up to the standard of leading the hard climbs which he wanted to do.

I had my chance at the end of July, when he went north for an interview, and Ian took his place. I had met Ian at the start of the summer when I had made a great impression – according to him – by saying we would introduce him to 'one of the easier climbs': Hawks Nest Buttress, then graded Severe. (If I did say this I was showing off.) He had been passing through North Wales at the time and he didn't stay long enough for us to climb together, but now there was no one else so, rather diffidently, I agreed to go out with him.

He was of medium height, with chunky, good-natured features, and a broad Scottish accent. He was one of the most honest, forthright men I had met; simple and unselfish, and possessed of boundless energy. He was as hard as nails and his ingenuity in a comfortless bivouac – as I found later – was astounding. He had been a sergeant in one of the famous Highland regiments. I felt I could trust him implictly. He made a great impression on me, and although I disagreed with some of his principles (to Ian black was black and white was white, and there were no shades between), he had a stabilizing influence on me. I found myself thinking of a house and babies and himself coming home from a regular, respectable job, and I with the evening meal ready and his slippers by the fire. I hadn't found a man who could dominate me since Tom, and even for him I had no respect. I had a great deal of respect for Ian.

Our first day's climbing was typical of the man. We had gone to Glyder Fach to do the Direct: that old-fashioned mountaineering route of splendid and varied situations; never really hard, never easy – and when we came to the point where the route goes left by way of the Toe and Finger traverse, I looked up, at the shallow trough of Gibson's Chimney, rising smooth and vertical above us.

'That's a V S,' I observed.

He studied it solemnly.

'Do you want to do it?' he asked.

'Yes.'

He looked at it more closely, then looked at the belay, at me.

'But I want to lead it,' I said.

'Have you done it before?'

'No.'

'Have you led a V S before?'

'No.'

'Then I'll do it first.'

Secretly I was amused at this attitude of masculine superiority, although I would have taken it seriously had he been a tiger.

He had some shrapnel in one leg – a war wound – and I was a little anxious when he reached the crux and had to straddle the chimney, which is too shallow for comfort. But he heaved himself upwards, grunting, and discovered a large finishing hold on top. I followed without any difficulty, and we descended the amusing little hand traverse at the side, then the Toe and Finger traverse, to return to our original position below the chimney.

I looked up. It hadn't changed. It was as if I'd never climbed it. I put the rope round to my back, still staring. And before I started to move I felt the familiar feeling that came when I was about to do something hard. A mental and physical relaxation, a loosening of the muscles so complete that even the face relaxes and the eyes widen; one's body becomes light and supple – a pliable and co-ordinated entity to be shown a climb as a horse is shown a jump.

In that exquisite moment before the hard move, when one looks and understands, may lie an answer to the question why one climbs. You are doing something hard, so hard that failure could mean death, but because of knowledge and experience you are doing it safely. This safety depends on yourself; there is no other factor: no horse or piece of machinery to let you down. What you accomplish is by your own efforts, and the measure of your success is the width of your margin of safety.

After the climb we were delightfully tired. Already that day we had done several routes, and when we reached the top of Glyder Fach, where the big flat boulders were hot under the afternoon sun, we stretched out like animals and went to sleep. After a while we woke and felt hungry, and we came down Bristly Ridge with our last spurt of energy. By the time we reached the tents we were staggering, and we sank on the grass and slept again – until midnight, when we cooked a meal by the light of our torches, while the owls called and stars glittered above the larch wood.

The rest of the holiday was a dream; we climbed and swam, and hitch-hiked down to Capel in the evenings, where we were warmly welcomed and I basked in the approbation of the Great Ones: George Dwyer, Dicky Morsley, Appy Hughes. On another wonderful afternoon I took Ian up Bellevue Bastion, but I didn't chain-smoke on the ledge on the edge of all things as Hodge had done, because I wasn't afraid of the steep slab above. The tiny holds on that slab, although far apart, were perfectly fitted for my big toes.

We had one bad moment, but it was not on rock. We used to swim across Llyn Idwal and back when we were returning from the Slabs or the Kitchen on a warm day. It was less than half a mile but the water was cold. Ian and I were nearly back to the shore one day when he announced, quite calmly, that he had cramp and couldn't swim any farther. Life-saving him to the shore was a simple matter, but it would have been more worrying had we been farther out, and hopeless if he'd been alone. The cramp had started in his game leg. It troubled him considerably at times but he never complained. When we went down to Capel on the Paynes' motor cycle, the four of us – Geoff on the saddle, Frances on the tank, Ian on the pillion, and myself between the two men – I had to hold the stiff leg in one hand because he couldn't bend it to reach the foot rest.

He talked to me a lot about Scotland, a place which rapidly acquired the aura of a strange and desirable fairy land, the country beyond the ranges . . . There were, he said, hundreds of mountains of over three thousand feet (there were fourteen in Wales). There were several over *four* thousand. There were great cliffs in the North West where no one ever climbed. There was the Cuillin Ridge of Skye – and there was the north face of Ben

Nevis: two miles long and two thousand feet high. Ian was better at statistics than atmosphere. I promised him I would go north as soon as possible. 'Possible' meant when I felt the urge. Although the thought of this great new country intrigued me, I was sure nothing could compare with Welsh rock. (I had never climbed anywhere else.)

Ian went, and David came back – looking for a partner for a fortnight in the Lake District. The transport was there: David's Triumph; there would be no inconvenient hitch-hiking. I agreed to go with great enthusiasm.

*

We met our Waterloo in Wasdale.

It was raining when we reached Wasdalehead, but David had thoughtfully bought a dozen Penguins on the way, examples of which were A Child of the Jago and Hiroshima, typical Thomas choices. It poured for three days. We ate until we were bloated, and we read until the print danced. Then we bickered. We had never been in an enclosed space together before, and we were both mad to climb. Then, fortunately, it cleared a little and, in oilskins and nails, we tramped up to Great Gable, to stop below the vertical sixty-foot wall of Kern Knotts Buttress. Of course, David picked one of the hardest routes on the wall. I wasn't worried. I never read the guide book until after the climb, and often when we were at the top I would ask him, genuinely curious, where the hard move had been. True, I was usually second on the rope, but nowadays I have not the slightest difficulty in recognizing the crux – all the subsidiary ones, and the main one – whether leading or second.

Halfway up Sepulchre I found myself in a cave in the corner of the wall. Before me was a great block of rock like a pulpit; away to the right David was making for a tiny ledge about forty feet above the ground. This so-called ledge, an inch or two wide, led across the smooth and vertical wall to the Innominate Crack, which provided the exit for Sepulchre. David reached the ledge and seemed to be swinging along it on his hands. Actually he was trying to mantelshelf. Then, suddenly, he wasn't there!

I was so astonished that, when the jar came on the rope, I

clutched it instinctively and held on, my mind trying to take in what had happened. Then I shouted.

'Are you all right?'

No answer. I waited, beginning to be alarmed, and then shouted again . . . and again. At the third attempt I was answered.

'Hold on,' he called, 'I'm coming up.'

I held on; I had no choice, my hands were jammed between the rock and my body. The rope ran up and over the pulpit in front of me and down to David.

He climbed the rope and appeared in the mouth of the cave. His hands were a mess; there was a sharp crack at the back of the ledge and when he came off he left the tips of his fingers behind. He was adamant that he had not been knocked out, but he must have been because my third shout was the first he heard.

After a rest he removed his nails and tried it in socks. This time he managed to get his feet on the ledge and did it as a foot traverse, which is the customary method. I followed, rather gingerly, and on top we were subdued, avoiding each other's eyes.

The incident had no effect on our technique, but it was no coincidence that from this time we started meeting difficulties, and, recognizing them, even turning back.

A few days later we still had the confidence to go to Scafell to 'look at' Central Buttress: for many years the hardest climb in the Lake District and still, according to its admirers, one of the greatest classics in the country. It is four hundred and seventy feet long, most of it Very Severe, and the crux comes two hundred feet up where, near the top of a crack, is a wedged stone. The crack itself is formed by a gigantic flake, hence its name on the climb: Flake Crack, Central Buttress. The crux of the climb is the chockstone and the few feet above. The usual method is for the second man to climb to the stone and suspend himself from it by slings, and then the leader comes up and, standing on his shoulders, is able (in the case of a tall man) to reach the good holds on top of the flake. The route is seldom climbed direct, that is, without the rope engineering.

We had almost forgotten Sepulchre. As we stared upwards we thought it looked worth a try.

David went up first. He made two attempts on the crux, said

he was tired, and climbed down. I went up. By the time I reached
the chockstone I was tired too. I'll try it once, I thought, and if I
can't do it, I'll climb down, too.

I had my hands on top of the block, and I tried to heave myself
on to it, to mantelshelf. Nothing happened. I was cross and
puzzled: my power-to-weight ratio was high, I had strong shoulders and I weighed eight stone – just the physique for a mantelshelf, I thought – but that one was too much for me. I retreated
dismally, comforting myself with the thought that no woman
had led it direct before.

Our attempts had been watched by a little gallery of climbers
on the screes below, and, while we'd been studying the crux, we'd
been amazed to see a man appear round the rocks on our right,
unroped and perfectly at home on the face. He introduced himself
as Arthur Dolphin and he applauded our intentions. He had
fallen off Central Buttress a few days before – also in nails.

Arthur Dolphin became a legend in the Lake District where, in
Langdale mainly, but also on Gable and Scafell, he put up a
galaxy of new routes, most of them hard Very Severes: climbs
very near, or at the top of their standard. One can judge their
severity only by second-hand reports (they are too hard for me)
and the often wildly inaccurate graded lists of climbs at the back
of the guide books. He girdled Gimmer and Pavey and Tophet
Wall (the last is the only Dolphin route I may judge and it is very
pleasant). The year after we met him he put up his finest route:
Kipling Groove on Gimmer. I met him several times in the next
few years. He was always quiet and unassuming; his physical
appearance would have led one to think he was delicate. Tragic-
ally he was killed on the Dent du Géant in 1952.

*

We retreated from Central Buttress and did a pleasant Severe to
the right: Moss Ghyll Grooves. Even that had a surprise in store.

For some time I had been aware that funds were dwindling.
Two nights ago, on our way back to the tent from the hotel, I had
suggested that expenses could be cut drastically if we started living off the land. I cited puff-balls as edible fungi and ate one on
the spot as a demonstration. But it must have been past its prime.
I thought I had a digestive system like an ostrich, but for the next

few days I was as weak as a kitten. Stomach cramps would seize me in the most inconvenient places (once in an exposed position on Long John, where only light mist hid me from the curious eyes of the spectators below). On Moss Ghyll Grooves I felt the pain coming and had just time to shout to David before the rock shifted and faded and I felt the rope tight on my middle, I didn't leave go, and after a while the mist cleared and I was able to climb again.

We moved around the Lakes during the last week. We visited Pillar and Dow Crag and the weather cleared and we climbed nicely again, on rock that was dry and warm in the sun. We returned to Wales a little subdued but contented – and then David asked me to go to Scotland.

7. The Coming to Scotland

David had decided that, for a long run – from Wales to Skye – he
would prefer to travel alone. I was glad, for although I was so
used to discomfort now that I hardly recognized it as such, there
was a limit, and that was riding pillion several hundred miles
with a sixty-pound rucksack on my back. So we agreed to meet on
Skye, in Glen Brittle, and I was to hitch-hike.

I started from Ogwen on a Thursday morning and I didn't stop
until I was on the shores of Loch Lomond. I had travelled through
the Thursday night on a long-distance lorry : London to Glasgow,
so I had seen very little of Scotland so far; only sleeping towns
black and shuttered, with walls suddenly floodlit as we rumbled
past.

Glasgow was merely an obstacle to the Highlands, a city completely unfamiliar, where people stared curiously at my patched
trousers. Despairing of finding a way out of the centre on foot, I
boarded a Loch Lomond bus and was set down at Balloch, with
not another town (except Fort William) between me and Inverness over a hundred and fifty miles away. Already I was beginning to have some idea of the scale of this country. I looked at my
small-scale map and calculated distances. I was now, perhaps, two
hundred miles from the north coast, and on the map I traced a
line from Loch Lomond to Stirling. North of that line it was all
mountains. If you said it was a hundred and eighty miles to the
north coast and roughly an average of a hundred miles for the
breadth of Scotland north of my line, then there were eighteen
thousand square miles of mountain country ahead of me. No, it
was impossible. And yet Ian had said over three hundred Munros
. . . Dreamily I started shopping for my supper. Then I went
on slowly, up the west shore to Tarbet, beginning to feel very
tired. I had been hitching for over thirty hours.

Beyond Tarbet there were woods above the road and here I

turned aside and climbed slowly through the undergrowth until I was a hundred feet or so above the shore. Here the trees thinned out and left a glade chest-high with bracken. I swung my pack to the ground and lay down.

Hours later the midges wakened me. The sun was setting and the evening was very still. Through the green and silver birches I could see the water calm as glass, and beyond, a big mountain, blue in the haze.

I crept inside my sleeping bag and slept again until this time I was wakened by the sunlight. The midges had gone and it was a glorious morning.

I made a fire and boiled a can of water. I was so impatient to be off that I upset the first can and had to start again. Below I could hear cars swishing by on their way north. I ate quickly, pushed bag and cans into the rucksack, then plunged down the hill to crash out of the undergrowth on to two startled American tourists. Apologies served for introductions and we walked slowly up the road together. They were a middle-aged couple from Chicago. I was full of gaiety and I loved everyone that morning. I told them all about myself and, perhaps because they were complete strangers, they were delightfully unreserved and sympathetic. After a while they suggested that they were hindering my chances of a lift and they walked ahead.

Almost immediately a large car stopped and the driver, a dark, handsome young man with a well-trimmed beard, asked me where I was going.

'Skye!' I said.

'So are we. Get in!'

Off we went, speeding round the bends beside the shining water, flashing through the sunlight, and the bearded man talked to his other passenger in an accent which reminded me vaguely of Spain, and then of Ireland.

Ardlui came at the head of the loch.

'Would you have lunch with us?' he asked in that lovely accent. I accepted with alacrity. Sometimes I turned down shelter on my travels, but never food and drink. Over lunch I gathered that my companions were natives of Skye, that my host had just come out of the RAF and was now helping the family run a transport business, that the other man was a mechanic.

Then we were speeding northward again up to the head of Glen Falloch, where we left the woods behind and came out into a bare and golden country where steep grassy hills held promise of things to come and twisted ancient firs stood, solid and uncompromising, brooding on the past glory of the Caledonian Forest.

The stretch between Crianlarich and Tyndrum was uneventful: there were two railways, a river and a road sharing the valley, there were scattered farms and pastures with fat cattle. But the eye and the heart strained ahead, aware of the great shapes to the north, but unaware of names, of history, of reputation; knowing only that the *real* mountains were coming up; the ones with cliffs; the only ones that counted.

We took the right fork at Tyndrum and pushed up a long gradient to the pass on the boundary between Perth and Argyll, and all the way from Tyndrum onwards great unfamiliar mountains rose against the western sky. They told me we were crossing the Moor of Rannoch. I stared like a child, fascinated. It was a wide empty country of peat and lochan and endless heather. It was all too much, too big. I remember little in detail; the drive was a series of impressions: the flat and lonely moor and a mountain on the other side: a lump fining to a slender cone, then, as we passed down Glencoe, ridges running towards the road from somewhere in a vast hinterland, and ending in sudden walls, the last one of which was stupendous. It must have been nearly three thousand feet high, with a long slit of a cave hundreds of feet above the scree. They knew nothing of names, so it was some time before I learnt that the lovely cone was Buachaille Etive Mor, that the ends of the ridges were the Three Sisters of Glencoe, and that the last great wall was the Aonach Dubh with Ossian's Cave the black gash high above the screes.

My fleeting impression of Fort William as we sped through its one main street was that it was ugly and characterless. I was surprised to see a shop with the sign: 'Fleshing'. There was nothing to tell me that in a few years' time I would be passionately fond of its ugliness, and its inhabitants would have all the character in the world. Nothing to warn me, not even a first glimpse of what was to become my favourite mountain – for I hadn't the least idea where it was in relation to the town.

We stopped in Glen Nevis for tea, then dashed on. We were in a hurry as there was a dance being held on Skye that evening.

We drove up the Great Glen and turned west at Invergarry, where clusters of scarlet berries dripped from the rowans above the blue water of the loch, and so, in the failing light, we came to Glenelg, where a cobbled ramp led to the ferry and the swift black waters of the Sound of Sleat slid between the mainland and the Isle of Skye.

Here, they said, was an old inn where the drovers, coming home to the island after selling their cattle, were murdered for their money and their bodies tossed out of the window. I looked at the deep fast water and reflected that it was probably true.

It was quite dark when we drove off the ferry and for the rest of the journey I saw nothing but the single track road winding ahead, and rabbits' eyes glowing in the headlights. But Broadford was lit up. We stopped outside a sizeable modern house and, un-protesting, I was ushered into an enormous kitchen which seemed to be bulging at the seams with people. There were brothers and sisters of Ronnie – my driver – and, because the place turned out to be a guest house, various members of the staff. Then there were all the attendant girl friends and escorts. They seemed to be using the kitchen as a rendezvous before the dance. Ronnie's mother appeared and automatically started to feed us. It was as if they took strange hitch-hikers into their kitchen every night.

They wanted me to go to the dance but I couldn't – not in my old climbing clothes – so midnight found Ronnie and me sitting on the end of the old pier listening to the music across the water, while the northern lights wheeled across the sky and the salmon leapt beneath our feet.

The family owned a garage and many vehicles: buses, taxis, lorries. That night I slept on a stretcher in the back of an ambu-lance. Next morning one of their buses took me to Sligachan – a delightful Chestertonian road winding inland for miles round the heads of sea lochs where gaunt grey herons stood among the sea-weed and cormorants skimmed across the shallows.

At Sligachan I started walking on the last lap: a rough moor-land track, and as soon as I was on it and had got my bearings, I knew that the big pinnacled peak on my left was Sgurr nan Gil-lean, the start of the Black Cuillin.

With every mile they unfolded before me: a fantastic fretted ridge of black peaks, with cliffs and gullies and high corries. I think it was from that moment (or perhaps coming over Rannoch Moor) that I realized for the first time that there was more to this business of climbing than leading Very Severes. I wanted to become a mountaineer. I would have been incredulous had anyone suggested that in a few years' time I would be working as a guide in the Cuillin.

After walking for a long time – with many stops to stare, although my eyes hardly left the Ridge even while I walked – I came to the dusty road that leads down Glen Brittle. After another two miles I saw the youth hostel, a tall timber building beside the road.

David had not yet arrived and no climbers were staying at the hostel so I spent my first day exploring. Too cautious to go alone, I took a Frenchman with me: a well-built, flirtatious Parisian for whom I lost all respect when I left him behind on the Alasdair Stone Shoot.

I had progressed since the day Paul Russell showed me how to run the scree above the Devil's Kitchen. Scree running had become a delightful pastime, and in 1947 the thousand-foot shoot below Sgurr Alasdair was still small and free running. As you stood at the top, in the cleft like a great gateway between Alasdair and Sgurr Thearlaich, when you were thirsty and hot, it was good to contemplate the lochan nearly fifteen hundred feet below, which you would reach in a few minutes instead of the usual long jolting descent down steep grass or jumbled boulders. You plunged over the edge, and the small scree, a foot or two thick, started to move, and you ran on top of it, like going down a down-escalator, but instead of the advertisements for films and ladies' lingerie, you had the great gully walls streaming past on either side and the water gleaming below among the boulders.

*

When David came we started climbing in earnest, but the weather didn't stay fine for long. We had two or three days in which we romped on the great cliff of Sron na Ciche, where the slabs sweep away below your feet, and walls rise, vertical or overhanging above your head, and there's not a blade of grass in sight. We led alternately on the classic Severes. People had shaken their heads and said the rough rock of Skye would stop my barefoot antics, but my feet had grown as hard as nails. A few weeks before, I had run the scree barefooted down a gully on Pillar, and some time previous to that I had cut my foot on glass and the skin was as thick as leather. Bare feet stuck on Skye gabbro as if they were furnished with suckers.

Perhaps the most enjoyable day was spent in Waterpipe Gully, and we came down the corrie to bathe in the chain of pools and then walked home with the shadows deepening up the glen, and the peaks smouldering in the sunset.

We weren't ambitious in our climbing. There wasn't much harder than Hard Severe on Skye at that time. There was a great deal waiting to be done, but either because First Ascents were an unknown quantity or because we remembered Sepulchre, or both, we kept – with one exception – to the known routes.

We made the exception when we put a route up the Lagan Buttress of Sgurr Dearg. It was a pleasant climb but with nothing in particular to distinguish it. However, it was our first First Ascent; we were quite proud of it, christening it – with an astonishing lack of imagination – Lagan Route, and grading it Very Severe in boots. We weren't happy about the grading and I wasn't surprised when the 1958 guide book lowered it to Severe.

Rather foolishly we had off-days; foolishly because the summer couldn't last for ever. It was September now and the weather showing signs of breaking. But before it broke there were some hot, heavy days when we swam and sunbathed and excused our lethargy by saying that too much rock could make us stale.

One day we were beside the high lochan on the way to Coire Lagan when two sweet old ladies came up the path and approached us. 'Do you mind,' they asked David politely, 'if we swim in the nude?'

I was face-down in the heather and stayed that way.

'Oh no,' said David in his best sidesman's voice, 'we'd be delighted.'

And they did.

We spun for mackerel on the loch – myself spinning, a young medical student rowing – following the flocks of gulls which concentrated always about half a mile away, so by the time you'd rowed there, they were gone to another place. We followed them because I said they were after the mackerel. We caught three.

On the last good afternoon we found ourselves near the top of Sron na Ciche and David said,

'Let's go and look at the Crack of Doom.'

We went and looked. The crack reared above our heads, narrow and steep, with a vertical retaining wall on the left. Gallantly David offered me the lead.

It was a little like Central Buttress in the sense that there was a chockstone and exhausting work climbing the crack above it. I climbed to the stone and studied it – and remembered the Flake Crack. Then I looked at the wall on the left. Running up it was a line of tiny holds and then another line – at right angles – across the wall and back into the top of the crack: a neat and delicate detour just made for bare feet!

I relaxed and, grinning happily, went up the wall.

David had a hard time in the crack. A year later, in nails but as a second, I came to the same place in the rain, looked at the wall, shook my head gloomily and, discounting the nails, said I was old, and had to struggle up the crack.

Then the weather broke and we sat in the hostel watching the rain driving up the glen, wondering if the summer had gone. It had; the wonderful season was over – and all the days of bare-footed dancing on sun-warmed rock. We were not to know fine weather again until the frost of November.

We had one last day on the Cuillin; a day of mist and rain and great gusts of wind when we went out to search for two lost climbers. I was with two other people going up Coire na Banach-dich, staring hopelessly at the mist and what we could see of the corrie floor, and getting into stupid difficulties in steep little gullies where it seemed silly to put on the rope. After a morning of this, and staggering along the knife-edge ridge where the gullies dropped, bottomless, into swirling mist, wind tearing at our anoraks, and hands growing numb on the streaming rocks, we returned to find the 'lost' couple safe in the hostel.

We left Glen Brittle and David drove me to Fort William where I was to meet Ian and climb on Ben Nevis.

*

We met during one of the brief spells when it wasn't raining; met

in a bar and then went to eat fish and chips and discuss plans for
the Ben. There was a hut belonging to the Scottish Mountaineering Club below the north-east face but neither of us considered
using it. We had no tent but we were quite happy to bivouac
below the cliff. I had not been shown this face on the two occasions that I had passed it on the road; it lies back at the head of
a long glen and looks out at right angles to the road, so that it is
inconspicuous to the traveller if he doesn't know it's there. Yet
although I spent several days on the Ben that September, still I
didn't see the northern face.

We had planned to bivouac in the glen for a week, and accordingly we carried terrific packs that first evening as we left Fort
William. It was raining again, and we went only a mile up the
glen before we decided that we had gone far enough. We draped
oilskins over our heads and nearly suffocating, fried sausages on
the Primus stove and ate them with the rain drumming on our
heads. Then we crawled into our sleeping bags, rolled ourselves
in the oilskins, and went to sleep.

It was raining when we woke up, but we ate some breakfast,
packed all the gear in our rucksacks and left them, carrying only
the rope as we headed up the glen towards the North-East
Buttress.

The mist was down and all we could see were the lowest pitches
of the buttresses like the feet of gigantic elephants picketed in a
line up the corrie.

Ian ran out a rope's length on what he thought was the correct
route up the North-East Buttress, but rain and cold defeated him
and we retreated.

On our way back, we discovered, some distance above last
night's bivouac, a tiny hut beside a dam across the burn. It had
no door, but a tin roof and an earth floor. It was luxury compared
with another night in the rain.

An hour later we were installed.

All night the rain drummed on the tin roof, but we got some
sleep, and in the morning the rain had stopped. As we lay in our
bags blinking idly at the daylight, there was suddenly a terrific
whoosh ! ! ! outside, followed by a heavy, metallic clanking like a
great iron hoop on boulders. I stared, panic-stricken, at Ian, and
then we both rolled to the doorway and peered round the corner.

An enormous geyser of water was rising majestically from the top of the dam, curving as the wind caught it. The crest bowed and wavered. We watched, fascinated. What looked like hundreds of gallons missed the bothy and descended into the dry bed of the burn below the dam, which was transformed immediately into a foaming torrent.

The pressure of flood water had lifted the manhole cover from its concrete bed and it was this that we'd heard clanking merrily down the gully.

We recovered and laughed, a little weakly, and after a while I clambered down into the gully where the torrent had subsided to a trickle. I was brushing my teeth and idly debating baked beans or sausages for breakfast, when suddenly I heard that awful *whoosh*! again. I had just enough time to grab my sponge bag and I was up that bank like a scalded cat while Ian roared with laughter from the bothy doorway.

After breakfast it rained again. Under the persistent gaze of the bothy mouse – who sat in dark corners with his eyes on stalks – we read a book about Borneo and sympathized with the writer in the monsoon. At tea time we were tired of the bothy and trotted down to Fort William, to a bar, where Ian, fiercely protective, knocked down a large Pole who asked me the time. No one was to blame. The Pole knew very little English and, in trying to explain his request, lifted my sleeve to see my watch. Ian jumped up and hit the Pole, who collapsed on the floor. Rather naturally, two of his friends started for Ian, but suddenly the whole of the bar seemed to converge on them and the Poles were being hustled outside, and people were asking me if I was all right. I felt it had all been a little unfair.

Back we went to the bothy in the rain, and the next morning, with a wet gale blowing, we decided to move to the youth hostel.

Walking down the narrow gauge railway track of the Aluminium Company I suddenly had a most peculiar feeling. We were staggering into the south-west gale and wind always makes me uneasy, but this time, when I glanced behind, there was a very logical explanation. A train was bearing down on us.

I shouted and we leapt for the bank together. The engine passed and the driver stared stonily. Perhaps it was fortunate it was going too fast for Ian to overtake it.

We climbed the North-East Buttress the following day, climbed through shifting mist and a howling gale. Although we never saw the face in its entirety, for the first thousand feet we had occasional glimpses of another party on Observatory Ridge away to our right. We found the rock easy and, for the greater part, we moved together, carrying coils. It was a new experience for me: to be on a big, strange cliff in bad weather, where the difficulty lay, not in the rock, but in the weather itself, the length of the climb (two thousand feet), above all, in the route finding.

I was lucky in that, just at the time when I wanted to explore new country, I should have been introduced to it by Ian, who was a really tough and accomplished mountaineer. Unfortunately it was nothing more than an introduction, for I climbed with him only twice again.

My gratuity had dwindled now until there was nothing left. I had to start looking for work and in Fort William I heard that the Forestry Commission wanted girls in the Great Glen. I had visions of myself cutting down trees (I was handy with an axe), of leading teams of horses, which strained at great logs just like the Christmas cards, of working on mountainsides high above Loch Ness.

*

The only part that was correct was Loch Ness.

I was sent to a bothy a few miles north of Fort Augustus. There were five other girls – and I was wrong from the start. They were all Scottish. We were as different as chalk from cheese and neither side made any concessions. Since I had deserted from the ATS I had been more or less vegetarian and the big meaty meals at the bothy filled me with revulsion. Then I spent my evenings in a corner of the big kitchen, writing: letters, stories, articles – and that wasn't very popular. At the weekends I went camping and walking with Ian. The girls were not only astonished at my sleeping on the ground in the open, but deeply shocked, as by some form of perversion. As the last straw, I was caught swimming in Loch Ness with nothing on – in December.

It was a glorious Sunday morning with snow thick on the ground and the loch sparkling through the trees. The water didn't seem particularly cold, but when I came out the sub-zero temperature hit me like a blow. I couldn't run about on the shore for the brambles, so I padded through the trees to the road, decided the snow was too thick for traffic and started trotting up and down the A82. There were no houses in the vicinity and I had prudently chosen a place some distance from the bothy. Everything should have been perfect but for a car which appeared suddenly and without a sound. I swerved into the undergrowth, uncomfortably aware that the Forestry Commission wouldn't approve and bare branches hid very little. The car didn't stop.

I thought it was extremely funny but the girls listened in stony silence when I told them and relations deteriorated.

I made a few friends outside my work. One Sunday, hitching home from a weekend walking, I was given a lift by a girl who had been in the FANY[1] during the war. Now married to a Canadian working on the forests farther south, she was shortly going to Canada. I started to visit them on the weekends when Ian wasn't free. They were an intelligent, well-read couple; it was a relaxation and a real pleasure to spend the long winter evenings talking by their fire. In the bothy the girls read *True Romances* and knitted.

I used to catch the last bus back on a Sunday night – a fifteen-mile journey. Often I was the only passenger. It was astonishing to think that this little vehicle was overlooked by great mountains brooding through the night while snow plumes streamed from their empty summits – and here, thousands of feet below, the tiny, dim-lit world of a bus went on its way with its three silent occupants: the driver, the conductor and the passenger. But if you became a little frightened by the immensity of that which lay beyond the metal walls – toying for a moment with the idea that you were the last people left in the world (but the driver and conductor didn't know yet) – you could rub the window and, if you waited long enough, see one lamplit square, or even a cluster of them. But it was still strange and oddly pathetic to think of each little world behind its window, quietly going about its business with the occupants sitting by the hearth, or being born or making love, all unaware of the other world – the antithesis

1. First Aid Nursing Yeomanry.

of the hearth and the womb and the bed – the cold, empty, in-human world of snow and rock and space outside. It seemed that the lights and the bus, even ourselves, were on sufferance.

The other girls had thoughts too – on narrower lines. They wouldn't walk home from the village at night along the shore of Loch Ness. I did it often but, mainly because I was conditioned, the first few occasions were no ordinary walks, in fact, the very first time was terrifying.

Sometimes I went to the village to spend the evening with the minister, who was something of a writer himself. He told me stories about the loch and the monster. He, like many other people on the banks, had had his own personal experience.

He had been driving home from Inverness on a windless after-noon when he saw something moving in the water. The road there was a hundred feet or so above the shore and he stopped the car and got out. He had a perfectly clear view of the object below him, moving very fast towards the centre of the loch. He said it was a *wake*, but whatever was making it was so nearly submerged that it was invisible at a distance. It resembled the wake left by the periscope of a submarine.

The villagers were reluctant to talk about the subject, perhaps from fear of ridicule, but they seemed to think that there *was* something there.

On the first night that I walked home from the manse it was misty – a strange light mist with a moon above it. In places the road ran very close to the loch, so close you could hear the soft whisper of water. There was no wind. Suddenly a sound came through the fog which was so strange, so ominous in its intensity, that I stopped dead, keyed to breaking pitch. It wasn't repeated, and I waited, frantically trying to place the direction from which it came, to guess its origin. A description formed in my mind. It was something of a cross between a roar and a howl.

It was the first time that I had heard stags belling.

Once it was explained to me the sound lost all horror and I was entranced. I would go outside the bothy on frosty nights to listen. There are few sounds which can thrill me as much as this. Another is a curlew's call, but that is sad and lonely, making one think of lost souls searching; the belling of a stag is fierce, exult-

ant, challenging – that animal wants to fight and he doesn't care
who knows it.

*

I was in a strange, unsettled state while I was in the Great Glen.
I had loved the free life when I had money and could climb every
day, but now I felt shackled. I was leading a normal, respectable
life with a pay packet on Fridays, but I hadn't the one consolation
of respectability – I had no home life. Ian and I talked about marriage and I tried to picture a little whitewashed cottage with a few
hens and a cow but I couldn't get any feeling into it. I was unhappy at the bothy, a little irritable, and our weekends were not
exciting enough to compensate. The weather was too cold for
rock climbing and the snow too soft for snow and ice work. On
Saturday evenings we met in some remote village to sit in a bar
until it closed, and on Sunday we wandered listlessly about the
glens until it was time for us to go 'home'. We were both wary of
each other now that we were thinking seriously of the future;
perhaps I was more wary than Ian, knowing that, on marriage,
a woman gives up so much more than a man.

We agreed to meet for Christmas in Glencoe, but there was a
terrible muddle with telegrams, the outcome being that I arrived
in Glencoe, having given up my job because I thought we were
to have three weeks' climbing, and, not finding Ian at the youth
hostel, jumped to the conclusion that he had changed his mind
and gone elsewhere.

David was at the hostel – an exultant David saying he had
known it would never work out. He made me very cross and
aggressive. Also at the hostel was a funny, wiry little man with
sparkling eyes and the agility of a monkey. His name was Gordon
Moffat. It needed only a day spent with him on the hill for me
to know that I had met a fellow tramp. At that time he had a very
good job with a boatyard on the Gareloch, but he implied that he
would leave it at a moment's notice and go anywhere in search of
adventure. What would have happened if I hadn't sprained my
ankle again is anyone's guess. But going out on another rescue
one dark night, I vaulted the hostel gate and landed badly.
Foolishly I hobbled up the road for two or three miles clenching
my teeth in pain, and collapsed in the police car while the rescue

party went up and lowered some silly people off a ledge on the side of the Aonach Eagach.

I knew I would be immobilized for a week or two and a comfortable base was imperative for that period, so when Gordon suggested installing me in a stable belonging to his aunt on the Gareloch, I was devoutly grateful.

I came to the stable by devious and painful hitches. Gordon had made a sort of retreat out of it. There was a camp bed and a Primus stove, and a tap outside the door. He spent every evening with me, talking, fascinated by my way of life. Even if I exaggerated he believed everything. I found his attention and admiration flattering after the incredulity of the Forestry girls.

When my leg healed we had a good climb on the Cobbler. Gordon had done no climbing as such until he met me, but he was a prodigious reader and had an excellent memory. He listened, too, when people talked climbing and the result was that he was seldom at a loss on a strange hill. The Cobbler day was remarkable only in that, on the descent – having climbed Great Gully – I had my first fall. I was traversing horizontally from Gordon and away from the line of a buttress. I was on a rock ledge and came to a place where I had to jump down on to snow. I jumped, slipped, and was out of control, swinging under Gordon in a pendulum at the end of a hundred feet of rope. The buttress rushed to meet me with the speed of an express train. I screwed up my eyes tightly and waited for the impact. Nothing happened and I came to a halt directly beneath Gordon, unhurt except for bruises, but rather shaken. I was learning fast.

March came and the old foot-loose feeling. Gordon and the security of his aunt's stable couldn't hold me. One night I told him I was going to Skye.

8. Skye Cottage

My idea was to make my way through the western Highlands to Skye, vaguely looking for a cottage on the way. Then I would find work and write in the evenings, thus saving enough money to have a good holiday in six months' time.

It took me a week to find the cottage and, when I did, it took my breath away.

It was a calm evening in early spring and I stood on a cart track on the west coast of Skye looking at the square, whitewashed house below the road. It was a very ordinary building: two up, two down, with an iron roof of faded yellow. A hundred yards away was the sea, with islands dotted about, and – far to the west – the Outer Hebrides floated like a dream on the horizon. Behind the house, across a flat, marshy basin, were the cliffs of Loch Harport, and beyond those again – the ridge of the Black Cuillin from Sgurr nan Gillean to Sgurr Dearg. Everything was very green and peaceful; the house seemed to be settling itself like a cat, drawing its paws under itself, as it basked in the last of the golden light.

I was determined to live there. I saw myself cutting my own peat, baking my own bread, fishing, writing, climbing. It was a lovely dream and it all came true.

I found the owner of the cottage and rented it for four months at five pounds a year. That made it thirty-three shillings and fourpence. I didn't get a receipt and the owner looked so hurt when I asked for one I didn't press the point. In fact, I had the impression that he would have preferred not to take my money.

I spent that first night at a neighbouring farm and the next morning I moved in. I had no belongings, only my rucksack and rope. Immediately I sent a letter to my mother asking for books, putting at the top the proud, lovely address, Isle of Skye.

Inside the house there was a kitchen with a pot-bellied stove on stubby legs and an old car seat. Upstairs in the wood-lined bedrooms were two bedsteads with straw palliasses.

I had a Primus stove and a sleeping bag. The house was furnised for my needs. But there was something which I didn't know about . . .

I spent the day buying provisions, soap, brushes and a bucket in the store two miles away. Then I came back and started scrubbing.

The floors were extremely dirty and there was evidence of rats. I was exhausted that evening and went to bed as soon as it was dark. It seemed a little itchy in my sleeping bag but I was too tired to worry unduly.

The next day I continued scrubbing but I was not quite so tired that night. I went to bed and almost immediately was aware of something crawling. I grabbed my torch and investigated. Nothing. Straw, I thought, and lay down again. But there *were* things crawling. I lay very still, staring at the window, tense with horror. I reached stealthily for the torch, switched on and dived inside the bag. It was a flea. Half triumphant, half disgusted, I disposed of it and lay down again. There was *still* something crawling – *and something else*! I found two more and killed them, but before I went to sleep I knew there was another . . .

Next morning the travelling shop called. I explained my problem to the driver and he produced a box of DDT powder. I dusted both sides of the palliasses and all my clothes. I had a very thick, white seaman's jersey. After I'd dusted it, I put it on the grass outside the house and, a little later when I went to examine it, found fourteen dead fleas. And they littered the floor beneath the palliasses like autumn leaves. The DDT was quite successful; I was never troubled with fleas again, although the rats remained.

They were clean rats. There was no sewerage system in my cottage nor in any of those in the immediate vicinity. My next-door neighbours lived in one of the few remaining black houses. It was a little, low, thatched building and they kept cows which drank in my burn, so that one had to be careful about water. There were other crofts beyond the marsh at the back. It was amusing when you got up in the morning and went outside to see distant figures all on the same errand. So the rats were clean. They were also extremely well-behaved. It was quite usual to go upstairs and glimpse a large brown form waiting politely in the shadows on the landing to go downstairs in his turn.

They sat on fence posts and cleaned their whiskers in full view. This was when we were all used to each other. On the first day I had not been so well disposed towards them (being a town girl bred on tales of sewer rats) and when I found one in the kitchen I shut the doors and looked round for a weapon. There was, of all things, a Gurkha kukri hanging on the wall. I took it down and, with one well-aimed blow, killed the rat cold. I was astonished and very upset. I hadn't meant to do it.

After that my feelings changed towards them and I came to look upon them as company. Then a large cat called Tiger came to live with us. This was later, when there were four of us living in the cottage and the root vegetables were stored in sacks on the parlour floor. They were disappearing with startling rapidity. I accused all the other residents in turn, but they denied categorically all knowledge of raw carrots, turnips and potatoes. The root store continued to dwindle and I pleaded with them at least to replace the stock even if they didn't pay for it (it wasn't fun cycling ten miles to Portree on a cart track and ten miles back again with food for four people on your back). Furiously they reiterated their innocence. I couldn't understand why anyone should be so ashamed of eating raw vegetables, except that the quantity consumed implied criticism of my hospitality.

The situation declined until one day – after Tiger had stolen something from the larder – I chased him into the parlour, where he disappeared up the chimney. I could hear him scrabbling as I knelt on the hearth trying to reach his tail, and the next thing I knew I was almost buried under an avalanche of half-eaten vegetables which came pouring down the chimney. Tiger had stumbled on the rats' Famine Supplies.

*

I wasn't alone for long at the cottage, but long enough. I must have furnished a topic for considerable speculation among my neighbours. I was young, tolerably attractive, but quite alone. One night, very late, a man came along to find out more about me. It was *very* late and I was asleep. I woke to heavy stumbling footsteps on the stairs. I called out but there was no answer. I waited, stiff with apprehension. He came across the room, reeking of whisky, and collapsed on the bed, mumbling. Although deeply shocked I wasn't frightened, but a little worried about the problem of decency since I didn't wear pyjamas. I knew who it was as I'd recognized the voice. This was why I was shocked, for I'd met him several times and naïvely regarded him as a pillar of the community. Putting the best face possible on the situation, I slipped out of bed and threw on shirt and trousers. Then I took the torch and went downstairs. He was forced to follow me. In the kitchen I lit candles with trembling hands, and then I turned on him. My anger is terrible. It shakes me – quite literally. And, although I didn't touch him, the man was left in no doubt concerning my attitude. Finally I flung open the door shouting hoarsely, 'Get out! Get out! Don't you ever, *ever* come here again, d'you hear?'

He clutched at me frantically, begging me to be quiet. The black house wasn't far away and already their dog was barking.

When he'd gone I sat down to recover. I decided I couldn't face life alone, it was too complicated for a defenceless girl. I'd told my visitor I would send for my husband, had thrown it at him without thinking. All right, I thought defiantly, why not? It would get rather boring after a while, on my own. And I didn't want a repetition of the incident.

The following day I sent a wire to Gordon.

*

He guessed something was wrong. He came immediately, like a little cock bird rushing to defend his mate. I was touched and amused but I felt secure again. Had I been older and more mature, I could have coped with life on my own, but living as I did I laid myself open to all kinds of advances and speculations. Ordinary, conventional men thought this way of life an open invitation, and I couldn't face the resentment which I knew they felt when they were rebuffed.

When Gordon came I relaxed. We were well aware that people watched us curiously and speculated on our relationship (they didn't have to speculate long; our mail came under different names). But we had little contact with the locals. There was no pub and we bought our provisions from the travelling shop, which

called once a week, or we cycled to Portree. Gordon had brought
his bicycle and I'd bought another for ten shillings.

The next four months were quiet and happy. Not completely
happy; we were both sensitive, possessive and demanding, but on
the whole we slipped into the easy rhythm of the life and when
we quarrelled we would go our separate ways for a few hours and
come back more peaceful.

There was always something to do. At first we idled the days
away exploring and finding out to what extent we could live off
the land. We lived amazingly cheaply. A hundredweight of coal
lasted us four months. Gordon had brought an axe and a saw
with him and we collected great baulks of timber from the shore,
tree trunks and hatch covers, and brought them home for firewood. There was a peat hag behind the house with dry peats already stacked, and we cut more. Although they didn't have time
to dry out sufficiently, they made a good fire with a few knobs of
coal.

The old garden was neglected, but in their season there were
rhubarb, raspberries, currants and gooseberries. We found wild
garlic in the gullies above Loch Harport and I made delicious
soups from cheap vegetables and stinging nettles. Butter, milk and
eggs came from the farm and I baked my own bread.

Then there was the fishing, but not in March – that came later,
when the spring gales were over.

The weather that spring was true Skye weather: mist and rain
and wild gales roaring in from the south-west. Occasionally we
had rain for three days at a stretch, when we would slip out of
the doorway in a momentary lull and look seawards to judge if
we had enough time to fetch water from the spring. The opaque
grey curtain would be coming into the bay, blotting out the
islands as we watched, and when it struck the cottage a soft whisper filled the house as it swept the tin roof. Hail was terrifying; it
sounded as if we were being sprayed with machine-gun bullets.

We spent the wet days lounging by the fire and reading. We
had joined the Students' Library: an extremely useful organization which enabled us to borrow any book we wanted merely for
the price of the return postage. The classic writers of fiction were
termed 'reference' by the Library, and I had become very interested in the Russians. Whereas in the cottage on Cader I had been

consciously trying to improve my mind by reading Lorca and Rilke, now I had a genuine craving for the classics. I read a lot of Dostoyevsky and Tolstoy, interspersed with natural history.

Sometimes, after hours of reading, we drove ourselves out into the storm for exercise. Gordon had brought a pistol – a Colt .45 – with him, and we would go down to the shore for target practice. It was a heavy, powerful weapon which fascinated me against my will. I loved firing it, and we often talked about shooting rabbits, but decided against it as they came out only on quiet evenings and the sound of the shot would be heard for miles if it weren't stormy.

The rabbits gave me a lot of heartache. I convinced myself that we would be justified in killing them for food if they died instantly. Everyone assured me that wire nooses were fool-proof; the victim was strangled immediately. So next time we went to Portree I bought six wires and placed them in runs behind the house. I visited them morning and evening for days with no result, and then friends came and I left them for twenty-four hours. The next morning I went out early and found a dead rabbit in one noose, very bedraggled. I stared at it, trying to convince myself that it had died instantly, but the grass was torn where it had kicked . . . then I heard something flailing in the undergrowth, and looked, and found another, dying in the noose. Frantically I searched around for a weapon, and, finding a stone, battered it on the head. then I dissolved in a wild fit of weeping, picturing them lying there for God knew how many hours, strangling in pain and terror. After a long time I collected the six wires and the two dead rabbits and returned to the cottage.

I put the wires on the fire and, tearfully practical, cleaned and skinned my victims and started making a rabbit stew.

The friends who had come to visit us were George and Desmond, from London. I had met George the previous autumn when I was with Ian at Glen Nevis youth hostel. He had just been demobilized from the Royal Army Medical Corps, and, like me, he was trying to find his feet in civilian life. He had an absorbing interest in everything imaginable and his capacity for understanding, for sympathy, was, to me, phenomenal. Superficially he reminded me of the artists on Cader, with the great difference that he was sincere. But, as with them, I thought I was just a little bored with him; I wanted to live more on the surface than he did. Mentally he was far more mature than the rest of us, but that didn't stop his taking as much, if not more, delight in our explorations.

For some time Gordon and I had been attracted by the big island in the bay: Wiay. It was protected by great cliffs except for a break on the western shore (the side away from us), where the crofters told us there was a landing place. Uninhabited now, sheep were once pastured there, being ferried across in flat-bottomed boats. The rotten hulls still lay on the shore.

Wiay was about two miles from Skye; its landing place farther, so we chose a calm day to visit it. We borrowed a dinghy from one of the neighbours and set out in the early morning. On our way we passed a great stream of coloured jelly fish, floating idly shore-ward, and about a mile from land we were joined by a large grey seal. He followed us right to the island. We sang to him and occasionally he would rise, head and shoulders, out of the water to listen.

We rounded the northern tip of the island and found the landing place: a little cove with a ruined bothy standing on the shore. We beached the boat carefully, watched by the seal. He was still there when we left the shore, but after that he must have decided we weren't going to sing any more and we didn't see him again.

The island was alive with birds. This was before we'd started on natural history and we could only identify gulls and terns. It was the nesting season and we had to be very careful how we walked, because there were eggs everywhere on the ground, mostly the big, olive coloured eggs of herring gulls, splotched with darker brown. Above us wheeled the parents, stooping occasionally to dive-bomb us, some coming so close that our hair rose in their slipstream. There were a few black-backed gulls and several pairs of buzzards. The latter got an easy living because there were rabbits everywhere. Probably the old shepherds had introduced a pair to provide them with food.

When we returned to the boat there was a good breeze coming in from the sea, but we wanted to make the round of the island before going home. Once we had pulled away from the landing place the shore line became very wild. Black cliffs dropped straight into the sea, while – at water level – vast caverns, blacker than the cliffs, gaped like mouths, and the swell thundered in the subterranean depths. We rowed into one and, as we drifted beneath the roof into a mysterious fluid twilight filled with the sound of water, little black things detached themselves from the walls and dived below our bows. Astonished, we looked seaward and saw the cormorants come up in the sunlight. They were nesting on ledges inside the entrance. I wanted to see a nest, so we edged into the side, and while the men tried to hold the boat steady, I waited for the lift of the swell and then jumped for a foothold. I climbed to a ledge and saw the nests with white eggs gleaming in the dimness.

The others were gesturing wildly; they were having difficulty holding the boat. I retreated gingerly and we drifted a little farther, the crash of the waves in the back of the cavern growing deafening. Then we were suddenly seized with panic and, almost too late, turned the boat and rowed strongly for the open sea.

Outside we blinked in the sunlight and then realized, uneasily, that the wind was rising fast. There were white horses running now, and the rocks at the foot of the cliffs were ringed with foam. Occasionally we glimpsed wicked fangs just below the surface, lying too far out from the cliffs for comfort.

We rowed round the rest of the island, giving it a wide berth, but it took a long time to regain the shelter of our own little bay and lights were showing in isolated crofts before we tied up below the cottage.

Sometimes we went fishing in the evenings. We seldom came home with anything, but it was then that I think we caught the true spirit of the islands. The sun would be slanting low across the water, intensely bright. We drifted idly, staring over the side at the rocks several fathoms below: a black, empty sea bed with weeds growing like a fungus. It was a desert of rock and weed with, occasionally, an oasis of deep jade sand. Then the tide would carry us over a great hole, bottomless and black where, said Gordon, cod would lie in the season.

Gannets loved the calm evenings; they dived like white arrows and the spray rose behind them in gleaming fountains. They ignored the boat, flying almost overhead in great widening circles, heads stooped as they watched the water above the patches of sand. The circles widened and spiralled upwards, then suddenly the bird, in the middle of a plane, seemed to stop dead, slip sideways, turning a somersault too quick for us to follow, and then he was hurtling straight for the water, which rose behind him as from a depth charge.

There were other evenings when I went away alone, to spend long hours at sunset sitting on a rocky point with fishing lines dangling from my toes. Often I caught vivid sea urchins which I threw back, but once, to my amazement, the hook caught in the shell of a large crab. Once landed, I hadn't the remotest idea how to deal with it, but in the end I tangled its pincers in the line and bore it home in triumph.

They were wonderful, colourful evenings. Isolated on a point with the sea on three sides and the land falling away behind, when the sun dropped below the hills of Duirinish and the sky was flooded with colour, the whole world became fluid and rippling. You seemed to be swimming in light, to be part of the water, sheening silver, and the Long Island floating like a mirage far to the west. And through that glittering world would sweep a flight of oyster catchers piping shrilly as they went. Past the oyster catchers went the cormorants, winging home to the uninhabited islands like little black devils.

As the colour faded, the moon rose above the mountains, and I'd hear, as I came slowly homeward, snipe drumming on the marsh, or a lonely quack from the eider ducks which nested below the house.

I did a lot of writing on Skye, mostly at night when there were no distractions. Sometimes, on midsummer nights, I would be deep in a story, writing by candle light, when I'd hear singing. I'd stop and go to the door, to find that the air had grown thin and cold, and larks were singing in the darkness.

We had to work, of course. We picked winkles for Billingsgate. All we needed was a sack and two saucepans – and the right tides. Right, in the sense that work did not interfere with our leisure. We compromised to the extent of getting up early on occasions. Sometimes early enough to see the porpoises playing in our little bay, their big backs glistening as they leapt, and so close you could hear their splashes.

After breakfast we carried the sack and pans down to the shore and waded in to work. I picked automatically, thinking about plots and rejection slips, then slipping into a happy day-dream of acceptances and the money rolling in. We wanted to buy a ketch, but I needed a typewriter and neither of us had any shoes, only climbing boots. We went barefooted.

It was Gordon who called my attention to the exciting things in the pools, so that a puddle of water became a world of colour and beauty. There were deep blue mussels on rocks creamy with fungus, and anemones waving delicate frills with the movement of the water. Most of these were maroon or wine coloured, but one had a system of turquoise spots, and there was another growing, green and tan, on slate grey slabs. There were hermit crabs living in empty winkle shells and lovely little fairy fish left behind by the tide. Sometimes they were crimson and mauve, sometimes green and brown, with feelers like catfish and lacy orange fins. There were prawns too, and shrimps – darting like tiny X-ray plates into the shadows.

As we worked, the oyster catchers scampered all round us on the weed, running up and down the rocks, slipping sometimes, their wings flapping frantically as they lost their balance. With their scarlet legs and long red beaks they looked like medieval clowns.

When the tide came in we left the sack in the water and tied the top. It would stay there until it was filled, when the lorry called to take it to Portree for shipment. Then, pretending we had done a good day's work, we would lie on the sand and sunbathe, or swim in warm water where young flounders raised tiny sand spurts ahead of our shadows as we drifted.

Our winkles brought us twenty-five shillings for the bag, which must have weighed about a hundredweight. We wondered how much a pint cost in the shops.

*

We were so enthralled with our surroundings that we were at the cottage a month before we went climbing. The Cuillin were a day's hitch-hike away and the thought of packing a rucksack was tiresome. So we stayed on the shore and ate lotuses.

Then Whitsun came with a heat wave and we could resist no longer. We decided to go to Glencoe for a fortnight. Why we were going back to the mainland when we had the Cuillin twenty miles away, I cannot think, except that I had climbed on the Cuillin in summer, Glencoe I knew only under snow.

It was an astonishing heat wave. We camped above the Pools of Etive, and on the night we arrived I lay awake for hours staring at the stars and knowing that happiness is not always in retrospect. My happiness depends on weather and surroundings, seldom on people; I can be happy if I know I'm in for a good spell of weather in the mountains even if I have no feelings for my companions, but bad weather, storms, mist, wind and rain, can make me miserable, uneasy, or inordinately depressed even if I'm with someone I love.

My impressions of that holiday are suffused with an aura of heat and light shot through with a memory, more remote, of water sparkling through the high corries where we bathed.

The first morning I woke before the dawn, in time to see the summit of the Buachaille catch the sun, and then to watch the shadow line slipping down the buttresses towards the moor. I lay and dozed and woke again with the sun hot on my sleeping bag, and went swishing through the dew-wet heather to swim in the Pools of Etive.

That day we did Crowberry Ridge with its Severe variation. We sprawled lazily on Abraham's Ledge, where the climb split into its three variants, and agreed that we should do the Severe. My eyelids were heavy; smoke from my cigarette rose straight in the air; I felt like sleep. But eventually I managed to drag myself to the side of the ledge, to peer for the route, find it, and step on to the wall.

Suddenly I realized that there were no holds on the wall, that there was a big drop below, in short, that it was one of those little sneaky Severe pitches that lie in wait for people who think they are happy leading Severes. I wouldn't have minded if I'd woken up sooner, but I woke up almost too late. Halfway up this smooth scoop I realized that since I had seen no holds as I ascended and therefore had got up by will-power and friction, then I would find it extremely difficult to reverse those few feet. I didn't pause to think this; it was instantaneous knowledge. I kept moving. I daren't stop; the holds, so-called, were too small or too sloping to take my weight except in passing.

I was trembling when I reached the top. It was the first time that I had been worried on a climb and I realized what a fool I'd been not to study the scoop from the ledge, instead of launching myself on it unseen, taking for granted the fact that all Severes were of the same standard, and if I had led one I could lead them all. It was a novice's mistake.

We ambled up the rest of Crowberry Ridge and lay on the summit of the Buachaille. There were no clouds, no wind; a match burnt evenly held above my head. (One is reminded here of New York harbour.)

The next day we tried to climb again: Alan and Bell's route. It was too hot. Halfway up we retreated and went down to swim in the Pools.

*

As a contrast to the glorious Whitsun in Glencoe, we made an epic traverse of the Cuillin Ridge at the end of June.

The main ridge is seven or eight miles long with about sixteen peaks of over three thousand feet strung along the chain. The average time taken for the traverse was ten to thirteen hours, some parties took twenty-four, others were bringing the record down to fantastic times, as on the fourteen-peak walk in Snowdonia. We hated records; we decided to be different. We would take our time, sunbathe, enjoy the views, carry food for two days, sleep out on top of the ridge; we would set up the record for the *longest* time spent on the Cuillin traverse.

Our enthusiasm had waned by the time we came to eat breakfast at four o'clock on the first morning. Apart from the obvious reasons, I didn't like the sunrise. Across the western sky, lying lightly on the peaks of Rhum, stretched a great band of cumulus; its underside was a straight line cutting the pale sky like a knife, while the top billowed in puffy golden clusters which deepened to orange as we watched.

We ate Grapenuts and bread and jam moodily, but it was June, and Skye was notoriously inconsistent in its weather; we wouldn't let a brassy sunrise deter us.

Five o'clock saw us on the road, carrying one sleeping bag, a torch, compass, map, and one twenty-four-hour Pacific pack. The latter was a flat tin about six inches square, containing two tins of concentrated food, a biscuit or two, a mouthful of dehydrated oatmeal, five cigarettes and some lavatory paper. It was supposed to contain provisions for one man for twenty-four hours. With a tin of sardines it kept us alive for forty.

Although the corries were clear, the mist hung about the peaks. We said it might move as the sun got up, but already the sun was up and the moor between Loch Eynort and Glen Brittle was green and gold. Too gold.

At nine o'clock we stood on the southernmost peak of the ridge – Gars Bheinn – and looked down its seaward slopes to where two pitiful figures, like inhabitants of another inferno, toiled up thousands of feet of unstable scree. They were guests from Glen Brittle House also attempting the traverse. (Gordon and I had climbed to the ridge direct by way of the Sgumain stone shoot, thus we had already done one or two mountains over which we must retrace our route, but we preferred that to the Gars Bheinn screes – and had proved it faster, as the others had started out from the house a little before us.)

We rested on the top and looked seaward. There was a tacit decision to delay the work as long as possible and we had not yet looked along the ridge. The sea, three thousand feet below, was seamed and laced with silver shallows, but farther out the band of cumulus was still stretched across the sky – white with blue depths – and Rhum brooded in the shadow. Still farther, the outer islands were a long grey frieze on the horizon. Visibility was excellent. Soay lay below us: an island of rough moorland with a few trees on its eastern shore and fishing boats moored on the loch like flies on a looking glass. Eigg's steep cliff was gold against the hazy background of the mainland, and farther north, between the openings, like fiords, of Hourn and Nevis, stretched the shining Sound of Sleat.

As we turned to look into Coruisk we saw that the weather was building up in the north. There was mist on the nearer peaks and, behind it, a wall of cloud holding rain – or even snow.

We looked and wondered, and looked away, seeking consolation in the peacock colours of Loch Scavaig. Both it and Coruisk were green and blue: emerald and sapphire and all the shades between, set in a corrie that was pearl-grey in the sun and black under the cloud. Mist played lightly about the summit of Blaven like a kitten teasing an old cat.

We started at nine-thirty a.m. and four hours and three mountains later we ate a biscuit, a piece of cheese and half a fruit bar each, on top of Sgurr Alasdair, and called it lunch. We had climbed into the mist, and now it was snowing. We crouched under an overhang for about twenty minutes while we waited for the others – who had been a summit behind us from the start. There was no wind; we could hear the whine of a tractor far below in Glen Brittle. I pictured the soft greenness of the trees, the laburnum drooping in the heat, birds singing in the rhododendrons . . . strange contrast with our own position in the middle of a snowstorm, but a situation which was to become familiar with alpine seasons, when people, sipping wine on café terraces, stare, unaware of its significance, at a cloud 'no bigger than a hand' on the mountain, while you – in the cloud – climb cautiously through the storm, or wait under an overhang while the abandoned axes sing with electricity on the crest of the ridge.

It was an electric storm that day, too, on the Cuillin. After we'd left Alasdair (and seen an eagle take off from the crest of Sgurr Thearlaich – a tantalizing glimpse of a huge grey shape in the mist launching itself into space) we came down off Mhic Coinnich and I felt something happening to my head. My hair was, or should have been, shoulder length, but the outer layer was standing up vertically; I could feel it waving about like Medusa's snakes. That was before the rain started.

By the time we reached the Inaccessible Pinnacle we were drenched. In mist the pinnacle was not so awe-inspiring as I had found it on other days, for mist hid the exposure. I don't like these two-dimensional climbs at the end of the day. Exposure can be frightening when it's just behind, but the mountain is taking unfair advantage when you get drops on either side and then, when you reach the top of a pinnacle, in front as well.

We were both growing tired now. Lack of food, rain, wet rock and poor visibility were taking their toll. It was five-forty p.m. and we had been climbing for eleven hours. But the fatigue was psychological at first. I kept going at the old pace for another two or three hours and two more peaks. The rock was good enough on

Banachdich and Thormaid to make me forget the weather in pleasure at the scrambling, and even if the holds had to be cleared of
half-melted hailstones, the exertion kept all but the tips of our
fingers warm.

Then suddenly, standing in the gap between Thormaid and
Ghreadaidh, I knew I was exhausted. Gordon was plodding up
the slope ahead, oblivious, and I followed slowly, realizing after
a while that it was only my legs that were tired. They felt like
lead. Every step was an effort.

We rested on the summit and felt better, and in thirty-five minutes we were on the last peak of the day : Sgurr a' Mhadaidh. At
nine-thirty p.m. we stopped on the ridge above a scree shoot and
Gordon lowered the rucksack to the ground. This was the bivouac
site, chosen by reason of a little spring a few hundred feet below.
It would have been an important consideration on a normal June
day, but this evening we had only to place a cup under an overhang and it filled in a few minutes.

We descended about two hundred feet, found a large overhang
and ate our supper : a tin of concentrated yellow stuff optimistically labelled 'Ham and Egg', one and a half biscuits, some of
the dehydrated oatmeal and five lumps of sugar. Then we spread
our oilskins on the ground, placed our anoraks on top for insulation, and prepared to sleep.

The ground sloped at an angle of thirty degrees and we had been
too tired to clear it completely of stones. They were very sharp
stones. Soon the hail started. Our overhang gave no shelter. All
through the night, as the drifts piled up and tickled our nostrils,
we made sleepy dives for the interior of the bag. Unfortunately it
was a single bag, and although we were both small, we weren't
that small. There was only room for one person at a time inside.
Chivalry was thrown to the winds by Gordon, common sense by
me (I knew that with my lower metabolic rate I stood a better
chance of survival than he) and I spent all my time and energy
perfecting methods of keeping inside that bag and leaving Gordon
outside. Gordon was doing the same thing. We were both telling
ourselves that there wasn't *really* any danger in being exposed to
the elements – but it was damned uncomfortable. The idea was to
wait until the other person was asleep, when you moved slightly
and slid, with the bag, of course, about a foot down the slope –

the other being left out in the drifts. You weren't exactly snug even now, but at least the hail wasn't stinging your face, so you went to sleep, only to wake a little later to find that the manoeuvre had been reversed.

In the morning the snow was knee-deep, but it had started to thaw and the water coming off the mountain above us was draining – every pint of it – down and under our overhang. It had found the holes in my oilskin and our anoraks were a sodden mass. We dressed, snarling.

Breakfast was a tin of sardines, two biscuits and a fruit bar between us. It was very cold despite the thaw.

It wasn't raining when we started up the ridge, and despite our soaked clothing, we were warm by the time we started climbing.

Visibility was worse than the previous afternoon. On either side the sound of flooded burns rose from the hidden corries. Every hold had to be cleared of slush and the rock streamed water.

We left the bivouac site at ten-fifteen a.m. and we finished the ridge seven and a half hours later. All those hours I thought of food. We had finished the Pacific pack for breakfast. I remember more and more rain, chimneys streaming water, slabs streaming water, myself getting lost on An Caisteal and climbing up a waterfall in a gully, but most of all I remember my hunger.

We came down off Sgurr nan Gillean – the last one – and at two thousand feet we emerged into daylight, after twenty-four hours in the mist. The sun was shining on the Red Hills, the pink screes running down the slopes like strawberry sauce on a pudding. My mouth watered. Miles away we could see the gables of Sligachan Inn.

We had taken about thirty-nine hours on the trip and established our record. Perhaps I shall break it myself, but in good weather, for out of those thirty-nine hours my most vivid memories are of that sly progress down the scree slope in the sleeping bag, of hunger, and, lastly, of the raised eyebrows when we sat down to dinner in Sligachan Inn and asked for second helpings.

When we returned to Glen Brittle we found that the two men from the House had abandoned the traverse when they reached Sgurr Alasdair.

9. The French Alps

After our traverse of the Ridge we came back to the cottage to bask in idleness for a while – but not for long: the Ridge had jolted us out of our lethargy and I, at least, was eager to be away again. When David Thomas wrote to say he was off to the Alps and why didn't I go too? we packed our rucksacks and started hitch-hiking to Chamonix.

To go abroad had been my ambition since I first realized that other countries existed. The fact that this ambition was formed in my early years before I had seen a film, before we possessed a radio, was significant. A wider knowledge of life might have led me to believe I could be satisfied photographing wild animals or climbing mountains, but it wasn't until the middle thirties that I heard a radio programme on Everest or heard of Cherry Kearton, and already I knew that only one thing could give me adventure and that was Travel. I was impatient with people who called me a tomboy; I wanted more than trees to climb and orchards to rob (although I did these as a matter of course): I knew without a shadow of doubt that in the wild lonely spaces of Central Asia, in the Waingunga jungles where I would live with Bagheera and Kaa and Akela as easily as Mowgli, there I would find what I was looking for. Kipling and Ella Maillart became my gods.

In bed at night I could cry with the intensity of my craving to travel in remote places. I don't think anyone, either teachers or parents, realized my feeling in this matter. Had they done so, they would have helped by recommending ways in which I could achieve my ambition – at least to travel. Even to me, the exploring part was a dream. However, the situation did become known, for it was then that journalism was suggested: a step in the right direction even if it meant, to me, an interminable and boring apprenticeship in this country. It was after three months in a newspaper office that I went into the Land Army. There was more chance of going abroad in the fighting services, but the parents put their feet down here (I was just seventeen) and it had to be cows. When I did reach the A T S, still I didn't travel. I tried to – all through the war – but then it was the fighting that attracted me: I wanted to be as near as possible to the centre of things.

Now, hitch-hiking south to the Alps, I realized that the old craving had gone. I had no interest in travel as such; it would be interesting to see how other people lived, to note different customs, but as far as adventure went, I was satisfied. I had adventure – better than any jungle or desert – every time I put my foot on rock. Travel now was new mountains: not sand or swamps, but ice couloirs and frontier ridges, glaciers and crevasses and before-dawn starts.

We had scarcely any experience of snow and ice, Gordon and I. We didn't expect to do any big peaks together, but we hoped that if we were out there for long enough, perhaps working at a climbing centre, someone would take pity on us and take us up a real climb.

We left the cottage towards the end of June, carrying almost everything we owned except the tent, which we sent to Chamonix. We were so ignorant of Abroad that we were quite convinced we should never see it again.

The cheapest way of crossing the Channel was by the Newhaven–Dieppe boat, so first we went to Sussex to see Mother in Hove. We must have looked odd tramping Brighton promenade that summer evening in all our climbing gear, including nailed boots (we had to cut down on weight so we wore it), trying to hide our ice axes, almost bent double by our packs ... We nearly missed the bus because, at the penultimate moment, I was being sick under the Palace Pier. The excitement preceding each successive alpine season has produced the same reactions. First, the long build-up of anticipation resulting in a climax a few days – perhaps only hours – before the actual journey: a physical climax when I feel ill. After this I am empty, devoid of emotion, apparently oblivious whether I go to the Alps or stay at home. (But experience has shown that I'm heartbroken if I don't go.) Once on the boat or in the air I am a balanced person again and can take an intelligent interest in life. I suppose it is the reaction of the child who thinks everything is too good to be true.

We were both subdued on the drive to Newhaven and we didn't sleep much that night – on the floor of a deserted Army hut outside the port.

Next morning we crossed to Dieppe. I shall never forget that first close sight of a foreign town: houses – ordinary houses (one has seen a million photographs, why does one expect something utterly unrecognizable?) but with odd little differences that made them French. They were taller, narrower, and the balconies and shutters looked natural, not self-conscious as they would at home.

We walked out of Dieppe, staring – at least, I did; Gordon was trying to be blasé, he had been to Paris. The country was similar to Sussex, rolling downland; it wasn't very interesting, just the little things were strange.

We came to Paris by way of Rouen – mostly on lorries – and from Paris we headed south-east until, forty miles beyond the capital, we had our first stroke of luck. The previous night we had slept in a dutch barn and the farmer who found us in the early morning was definitely hostile. I hadn't been surprised. The evening before, while walking – rather wearily – through flat arable land, I had been possessed by a raging thirst. Some farm buildings were brilliantly lit at the end of a track on our left.

'I'm going to ask for some water,' I said.

Gordon demurred, suggesting we push on to the next town, but I mistook common sense for timidity and walked towards the lights.

The entrance to the farmyard was closed by enormous solid gates, but I could hear voices beyond and sounds as if a lorry were being loaded. I knocked on the gate and called but no one heard me. Feeling rather silly, I shouted. They heard me that time. For a second there was dead silence, then a whole pack of dogs (chained) started to bark with those terrifying angry bays that are full of snarls. I could hear the chains rattling as they leapt and lunged. A voice on the other side of the door told me to go away. By this time I didn't want the water, but politeness insisted I should explain myself. I took too long struggling to translate 'had only wanted' and the man shouted to someone to loose the dogs. I went quickly.

Now here was another farmer making a fuss about his dutch barn, but he had no dogs and we showed a little more dignity.

Once we were on the road, telling each other what we thought of French hospitality, we saw a small Renault coming and, automatically, we hitched it, still complaining bitterly.

The Renault stopped and the driver, a large, bewhiskered young fellow possibly attracted by Gordon's splendid beard, beamed at us and, without asking our destination, started to crawl out from the wheel. From the back two more large blond boys emerged – Swedes this time (the driver was French). The Swedes' rucksacks and tent were beside the driver. We set to work redistributing the gear. We tied it on the wings, on the boot and on the roof. Then, with some difficulty, we all got into the car (really needing a passer-by to close the doors on us) and we drove on – very fast and not very safely. Until now our lifts had been on the backs of lorries and I had not yet had the terrifying experience of seeing traffic pelting towards us seemingly on the wrong side of the road. At the last moment I expected oncoming cars to swerve back to the correct side of the road (to an Englishman) which would mean disaster, because we were on the wrong side anyway. It was a long time before I was convinced that as long as the two lanes of traffic were both wrong nothing could happen.

We stopped for lunch and we stopped for dinner. In between we stopped for petrol and coffee – and none of the passengers was allowed to pay a penny. Some time during the day we were all shepherded out of the car and taken to admire a magnificent church – or it may have been a cathedral – built by one of our driver's ancestors.

At Lyons we ran out of petrol. It was early morning by now, and our friend was suddenly and inexplicably in a hurry to get home. While the other three pushed the Renault through the empty streets, two of us ran ahead to locate an all-night garage. Then we discovered the fruit market on the banks of the river and sat on the kerb gorging ourselves on peaches.

Dawn was breaking as we came to a wide and rolling country where we left the main road and ground in low gear up a neglected car track, the valley opening out below us, golden with wheatfields. When the trees thinned ahead a crumbling château was revealed, sleeping peacefully in the sun. We dismounted slowly, stretching ourselves, and suddenly the great door flew open and a very lovely young girl threw herself into the driver's arms. She was wearing pyjamas and peep-toe mules and her toe nails were deep magenta. I was greatly impressed.

We were taken inside and shown our rooms. Ours was huge, shabby and comfortable and lined with books.

I got into bed.

'Gordon,' I said, 'this bed's *warm*!'

They had given up their beds for us.

Next day, or, rather, later that morning, we met the old mother and father. They were overjoyed to see their son again (we never found out what he did or how long he'd been away). The family seemed to be extremely poor. The old gentleman took me to see the empty stables and the kennels where one hound was left of the pack they used to keep.

Lunch, where as much reverence was done to a roll of spam as if it were a sirloin, was splendid and pathetic. There was no servant and the old lady and the girl waited on us. We felt most uncomfortable eating their food, but I reflected that perhaps the young man, who had treated us so royally on the journey south, had now brought home some money.

After lunch we proceeded slowly to the drawing-room where the enchanting little grand-daughter of the house was presented to us, curtseying with great dignity to each, then we were shown a collection of faded photographs of the château in the early years of the century. The one I liked best was that of an elegant and beautiful woman mounted side-saddle on a magnificent hunter. It was the old lady who had waited on us at lunch.

We were pressed to stay another night but we said we had to meet friends in Chamonix. The Swedes, too, thought of excuses to leave. We were not allowed to walk away. The car was brought round and we were driven to the nearest town – and beyond – to 'put us on the road'.

*

Hitching went badly that afternoon and towards evening I suggested to Gordon that we separate and meet again in Chamonix. Our treatment of the last day had dulled my sense of caution, or I would have been more wary about hitching on my own, at night and in a strange country.

Gordon slipped up a side track and in a few minutes a car

stopped for me. Two men were sitting in the front seats. I got in the back and we drove on, talking desultorily in French. Occasionally they spoke, rather impolitely, to each other in a dialect which I couldn't understand. They came from one of the big Swiss towns: Lausanne or Zürich, I forget which.

After a while they said they hadn't eaten. Would I have a meal with them? I agreed reluctantly. They were going through Chamonix and I was tired of hitch-hiking. If I stayed with them I would finish my journey that night.

When we went into the café I found that the 'meal' was to be brandy. I refused a drink and watched them. That was when I should have left, or, at least, stayed in the café. Trying to convince myself that I was being very provincial, I returned to the car when they'd finished their brandy – and the younger of the men squeezed in the back with me. Before the car had turned on to the road he had started to maul me.

Fortunately I was wearing trousers. I struggled, carefully at first, reluctant to hurt him seriously because then I would have the other man to deal with, but when he hit me the first time, I lost all reason and started to fight. This went on for an eternity: being hit and lashing out, gasping for breath and all the time desperately trying to think of a way out. The worst moment came when he was shouting at the driver to get off the road. But it was still comparatively early; the older man drove on cursing. It didn't strike me then that he could be looking for a lonely, safe place to be rid of me. Every time he slowed down I thought he had other ideas, and although I was just holding my own in the restricted space with one, I had no doubt that outside, with two, I would be overpowered immediately.

Once we went through a town and I was held rigid with a hand over my mouth. I could see people staring into brilliantly lit shop windows. I saw traffic lights ahead and prayed that we might have to stop, when I would make a supreme effort and break a window. Perhaps we jumped the lights, perhaps they were green, I remember only the dark country on the other side and again the vicious blows. He had control of himself: after he'd hit me once with his fist there had been a quick remark from the driver; after that, it was the flat of his hand for my face, but the back too – heavy, stinging blows. I wasn't afraid any longer. I just wanted it to stop.

Then suddenly the driver pulled the car into the side of the road and I was pushed out on the tarmac. I was frantic: my rucksack and ice axe were in the car! I heard the engine revved. The car pulled away, stopped suddenly, then reversed fast towards me. I rolled away and into a ditch. My rucksack bounced after me, then a man appeared, wildly brandishing my axe. Suddenly I realized that he was very clear: he was lit up in a car's headlights! He realized it at the same moment, threw the axe at me and leapt for the car. With a spurt of gravel they were away.

I lay still as the other car passed (trusting no one at that moment), then I got up, slung my pack on my back, picked up the axe and started up the bank.

They'd shouted that the wolves would get me. That meant I was in mountainous country. Then I was safe. They wouldn't get me on my own ground if they decided to come back.

The hill was very steep. I went straight up for a hundred feet or so and then crouched in the undergrowth waiting for the cars to pass, straining my ears to hear if one stopped. After a long time I thought that they wouldn't come back, but just to be sure I put a good distance between myself and the road before I stopped again.

I got my sleeping bag out, and lay down, and after a while I slept.

I could find no water to wash in in the morning and I had a raging thirst. I had no looking-glass so I couldn't see what my face was like, but it was very painful. My jaw wasn't broken, anyway.

I went back to the road and walked until I found a café. It was empty except for the waitress, who stared at me in amazement. 'I fell in the woods,' I told her. 'Please show me the lavatory.'

My face was a mess. Swollen and bruised and my lips were badly cut. I reflected that he must have been wearing a ring. I washed carefully and wondered what I ought to do. I dismissed the idea of going to the police. Instinctively I knew that French gendarmes would have little sympathy with me. And failing the police there was nothing I could do – expect to stop hitch-hiking. But I had to get to Chamonix and I wasn't going to spend money doing it. I compromised. I would get off the road long before dark.

After a frugal breakfast I left the café and waited for the first hitch. To my disgust I was trembling. A big lorry stopped with

three men in the cab. Big, jolly working men. I had to sit on some
one's lap. They roared with laughter and then burst into song.

'Come on,' shouted the driver, 'sing, mademoiselle, we won't eat
you !'

I smiled weakly. I felt like collapsing in tears and pouring out
my story.

I arrived in Chamonix very subdued. The clouds were down
almost to the roofs of the town and it was raining. I went to a
café in the square and a sweet little waiter brought me a coffee.
Yes, he knew where I could find a room. He bustled off to attend
to another table. I watched him eagerly. He was a friend. He
came back.

'Now if you wait until we close, I will take you to my friend
who has a room . . .' he smiled, staring deep into my eyes.

I started to get up. He followed me to the door, protesting.

'Look, here is my address. You come here after we close . . .'

But I was fleeing across the square.

I found a modest hotel with a woman at the desk. I could see no
male staff through the glass door of the dining-room and the men
visitors all had women attached. I went in and booked a room, and
that night I locked the door.

*

The following day was Saturday and when I woke there was a
market in progress below my balcony. When I went to the window to see Mont Blanc I was lost. I forgot my geography and
stared in bewilderment up a long valley glimpsed between the
roofs of the neighbouring buildings. By craning outwards I
caught sight of dense forests rising steeply to a serrated skyline.
There was no snow, nothing to be called a peak. I felt vaguely
cheated.

I dressed, had coffee and rolls, and then went out into the town.
The place seemed to be full of souvenir shops: postcards, cow
bells, ice axes in racks. Everyone was wearing climbing boots. I
strolled down the street, taking everything in, mildly amused, and
then I looked up as I turned a corner – and saw the snows.

First the gleam of them, with the sun full on the vast fields,
no shadows, and brightness which, in that first great moment,
seemed cloud above. And then I realized that it wasn't cloud, that

it was all snow, solid, tangible matter reared upwards, so unbelievably high that, for an infinitesimal moment, one had the
sensation of physical effort as the eye struggled still higher to
reach the summit. To one who had never seen a peak higher than
Ben Nevis, Mont Blanc, in that first awakening, was perfection.

I went to a café (not the one of last night) and, sitting outside,
ordered coffee. Slowly my knowledge came back to me as I stared
upwards. For now the great Aiguilles were revealed. I recognized
the Grépon, the Grande Charmoz, the Blaitière. Shadows were
beginning to seam these northern faces, adding to their height,
their amazing sharpness which pierced the sky.

Later that day I met Gordon. He stared at my face and I told
my story. When I reached the end he said nothing. We started
talking about something else. It wasn't until a year or so later
that I raised the subject again.

'Why did you say nothing?' I asked.

'Because there was nothing to say.'

And I was dying for sympathy! I never forgave him.

                              *

The first thing to do now was to find work. Despite that first
glorious morning the weather didn't remain settled and we
weren't tempted to climb.

We moved down the valley to a village near a hydro-electric
scheme. The work was being done by Italian contractors and they
had just received a consignment of machinery from Canada –
with assembling instructions in English! Gordon – who was an
electrical engineer, and a very good one – was given a kind of
foreman's position directing the labourers who were assembling
the plant. One of the office girls found us accommodation in Old
Servoz, a little unspoilt village standing back from the main road,
with enormous chalets where the family lived on the ground and
first floors, the cattle lived in the basement, and the loft was used
for hay. We had a loft all to ourselves. We had a balcony too, looking out on to Mont Blanc. We slept there on fine nights, to wake
with the dawn and see the snows flaming in the first of the sun.

In the village I met a friendly English couple: Tom and Mary
Lees. They were very interested in us and told us their young
nephew had just started climbing. From the heights of my three

years' seniority I should have been astounded had I known how closely I was to become associated with John Lees in a few years' time.

One day, contrary to all our expectations, my tent arrived, and we left the chalet and went to camp in a clearing in the forest.

It was a lazy time for me. I couldn't find permanent work in the district and I had nothing to do except prepare Gordon's meals and lie in the sun.

It was very hot. All day the avalanches came thundering down the side of Mont Blanc, while near at hand the grasshoppers shrilled and lizards basked on the warm rocks. There were snakes too, little pink ones, lying in the thick dust of the paths. When I picked the wild raspberries for dinner I would glimpse a gleaming tail slipping through the grass, and one morning I woke and lay, idly staring at the coiled climbing rope beside my face and wondering why it was wet. After a time I realized that one of the little pink snakes was staring back at me. I lifted him gently on an ice axe and put him outside. They might be asps.

The monotony of the long days in the glade began to pall and I started going to Chamonix as soon as Gordon had left for work. So I found that my friends were in town: David Thomas and George Dwyer – the latter raw and bleeding from the consequences of using glacier cream too late – and Toni Nicholson.

I had met Toni at Idwal Cottage. He was a Civil Servant and quite an important one, I believe, but we were not allowed to see anything of this respectability. What we did see was a large, unshaven bear of a man with irregular teeth and a hairy chest. He was surrounded by fantasy. It was said that he never washed, that he was an atheist but came of a Catholic family and had been intended for the priesthood. He was known to have caused an international incident, having been arrested by carabinieri and thrown into an Italian cell. He told this story himself with gusto. He had a certain physical attraction. A well-known lady climber – a formidable tigress – once trailed him through the Oberland after being benighted with him on Scafell. This last can be fully appreciated only by climbers, for Toni was no tiger.

My most vivid memory was also my introduction. We were lying above the Slabs one hot afternoon.

'Listen!' they said.

I listened, and heard from far above, roaring and guffawing through the golden air, a great voice pealing *La donna è mobile*. And, staring up at the Upper Cliff, we saw a figure moving up the sunlit edge of Central Arête.

'That's Toni,' they said.

I met him for the last time outside Chamonix station on his way to do a climb. A day or two later we heard that he had been killed. He had unroped for the last easy snow slope, and slipped.

We followed him to the cemetery. It was difficult to suppress a smile (now the shock was dulled) as one pictured his glee at this ponderous procession : it was vintage Toni right down to the four black plumes which nodded on the hearse; and this fantastic equipage was drawn by a black horse draped in sombre velvet.

On one of my sorties to town I met Vicki Russenberger – a young man of mixed Swiss, English and American parentage who had been born and brought up in Paris. He was a typical member of the French school of climbing : superficially gay (but only in the valley) and deadly serious above the snowline. One never quite felt that they *enjoyed* their climbing. At the same time I met a young Scot who was just starting to climb and seemed rather lost in Chamonix. David and Vicki decided that Hamish MacInnes (the Scot) and myself should make up a four and go to the Requin refuge to attempt the Dent du Requin.

I rushed back to the tent in the afternoon, packed my rucksack, grabbed my axe, left a note for Gordon and was back in Chamonix the same evening. The following day Gordon stopped work and came after me, but by then I was well above the snowline.

*

The Requin was my first alpine refuge. After Scottish youth hostels the common-cum-dining-room seemed quite familiar, but the sleeping quarters were a revelation. They were large rooms with an aisle down the middle, bordered on each side by a continuous wooden bench. Behind the benches were palliasses on the floor, forming two communal beds. But the wild and sinful orgies conjured up by these conditions exist only in the minds of laymen. You sleep in all your clothes except boots, and when you are going to rise at any time between midnight and dawn for a day's pleasure harder than most forms of manual labour – with the risk of breaking your neck if tired – then the atmosphere of an alpine dormitory is as innocent as a night nursery. Innocent, but hardly congenial.

There are the Englishmen who will keep getting up to open the window, and the Continentals who keep getting up to close it. There are the late arrivals coming to bed about nine o'clock when you have to get up at midnight, and there are those who get up at midnight when you don't have to rise until three. There are people who go to the lavatory quite unnecessarily, and those who curse you when you *have* to go . . .

I thought the Requin was crowded that first night, but I did have the advantage of an end place so that I could brace myself against the wall when Thomas turned over. The following night it was really full. We stayed the second night because the weather had been too bad for the Dent du Requin on the first day. However, we had climbed the rocky point behind the refuge: Pointe 2,784 (metres), putting up two new routes which we graded Very Severe. I saw no reason why, on beautiful sun-warmed rock, I shouldn't follow my usual custom and climb barefooted. I left my nails at the bergschrund, creating some astonishment among the Frenchmen who were watching us.

That night we went to bed early and, not realizing how fortunate I had been in my end place the night before, I stretched out luxuriously in the middle of the huge bed. The others spaced themselves variously about the dormitory. Gradually the room filled up. The pressure increased on either side until, in desperation, I turned on my side. Once there it was impossible to get back, least of all to turn. Had I been next to a member of my own party I would have kicked, but I was rather uneasy about the strangers on either side, so I was stuck. I slept fitfully.

A strange sound awakened me. I looked at my luminous watch. It was three o'clock. I lay still, trying to identify the intermittent rushing noise with the low musical note running through it. Wind! It was eerie to project oneself into space and look back at the hut, shuttered against a wild alpine night, all its occupants, except me, secure in sleep and unaware of the beast that prowled outside. I shivered and burrowed thankfully into my blanket.

Someone was pulling my foot steadily.

'Time to get up,' Vicki hissed.

Like a sick, vicious cat I hunched my shoulders and snarled, but he was away. I rose without a word (my actions setting a pattern for all alpine starts to come) and padded downstairs after him.

He looked up from the petrol stove he was fumbling with. 'The Requin is impossible but we will try the Plan if you like.'

I would have cut my throat rather than demur.

Whether Vicki wanted to give me a proper peak, whether he already had ideas for another season in my company and wanted to try me out, or it was merely that he felt energetic I don't know, but I have never since started on a climb in such conditions – and not turned back.

As soon as we rounded the corner of the hut we were caught up by the wind and flung from the path; we stumbled among the moraine of the glacier, falling over loose rocks, slipping into holes, and all the time there was this incessant buffeting of one's body, and hair stinging one's eyes. Words and breath were torn away by the wind. I groped after Vicki in such confusion that, after a while, movement became simple, mechanical. If he could move, then I could; if he encountered no obstacle then I wouldn't if I followed in his footsteps. As it grew lighter we could see the grey ice ahead, under the cliffs of the Dent du Requin.

Dawn was a wonder of colour. Almost unnoticed, as we plodded upwards (bent against the wind) the grey twinge of twilight faded and a flush of pink came stealing down the snowfields from the highest ridges. Rock flamed gold as the sun caught it, and one thought of the burnished lances of a great army; but the valley below, with the shadowed Mer de Glace, was still deep in night.

We stopped and put on snow goggles.

As we climbed, the snow grew thicker and softer. It was merely a case of following Vicki's footsteps. There was one steep snow slope before the ridge but even that was deep and soft.

When we reached the top I looked over and down – and stopped. It was like looking over a wall, but the ground on the other side was seven thousand feet below.

For several hours we had been moving in a white world where the eye couldn't focus unless a rock broke the surface, and here the eye leapt downwards to the valley – a dark green floor with cloud shadows passing slowly over the forests – and again one could not focus. All scale, all sense of proportion was lost; and still the wind tugged and slammed at our two insignificant bodies. The rope swung in a wide horizontal arc between us.

It began to snow and Vicki shouted that we should move fast. There was no time to identify the peaks. I had a confused glimpse of the Caïman, the Crocodile, and the Blaitière – and the Midi, unfamiliar and unrecognizable, if Vicki hadn't named it, away to our left.

Then we were hurrying towards the summit, the snow stinging our faces, frozen hair whipping about our eyes. The final rock-pyramid was only a moderate scramble under good conditions, but to me, exhausted by speed, exertion and excitement, every movement required an effort. The last few feet seemed a succession of mantelshelves: no exposure, no overhangs to push one off, yet just beyond my strength. On the summit I managed one weary glance at the whirling snowflakes now obscuring everything, and then I was peremptorily ordered to retreat. By now I was intensely cold and my hands and feet were numb. I fell and slithered down the mantelshelves, and then, without a backward glance, we set off hurriedly for the refuge.

The snow slopes which had been so laborious in ascent were descended by running and glissading. We were in the refuge by eleven o'clock. No one else had left the hut except to return to Montenvers. I began to feel elated.

There had been no time for any emotion on the climb. In fact, I don't think I fully deplored the wind until afterwards when I realized what a hazy recollection I had of the view from the summit. Even coming down, when we saw the debris of avalanches covering our ascending tracks, I had felt only surprise. When we had to cut across the foot of the glacier to the refuge, we ran the gauntlet of scattered stones and boulders which came whizzing and leaping down the ice with a malicious, sibilant sound in the air, a dull thud as they bounded. Vicki cursed and shouted at me to run. I didn't answer: I was running as fast as was humanly possible. I was doubly annoyed because two Frenchmen were sitting on the moraine smoking, and watching our life or death race with benevolent amusement. They weren't excited enough to be making a book on our chances.

We spent that night at the Montenvers hotel above the Mer de

Glace. The following day we took the railway down to Chamonix to be met by David and Gordon, pregnant with disapproval. But I was caught up in the whirl now, and the next day Vicki and I were off again to try the Mer de Glace face of the Grépon, one of the great classic routes on Mont Blanc.

In those days the Refuge d'Envers des Aiguilles had not been built and this route was done from the Refuge de la Tour Rouge on the Grépon. 'On the Grépon' was what Vicki said, a phrase which I couldn't understand, as I visualized the Grépon as an unbroken two thousand feet of cliff with several hard routes running up it. I asked a few questions but the answers were all of the 'wait and see' variety.

It is indeed difficult to describe the position – and more – the atmosphere of the Tour Rouge refuge. It is on the Grépon. Seemingly on the whole of this face there is one small ledge large enough to carry a hut about fourteen feet by eight. To say it is large enough implies, perhaps, ample space round the outside. This is not so – the four corners rest on supports, the outer ones being visibly essential because the hut is slightly larger than the ledge. One support has fallen away. Six hundred feet below is the Trelaporte glacier. The building is of wood and it moves when there are many people inside.

When the rocks are icy one ropes to fetch water, but the traverse to the secluded ledge where more private operations are performed is equally delicate and exposed. Fiercely defending my privacy (and, incidentally, being very British) I traversed alone.

The roof of the hut slopes from five and a half feet to four. The building, states the guide-book, accommodates six. We managed ten, sleeping in two rows of five.

The approach route is also distinctive. From the Mer de Glace you ascend a good two thousand feet of scree and dusty earth by way of a tortuous path zig-zagging upwards through the dwarf rhododendrons. You emerge on a gentle slope, littered with boulders, below the steep little Trelaporte glacier. Away to the left, diagonally upwards above the bergschrund, is the start of the rock route to the refuge. The hut, to unaccustomed eyes, remains invisible.

When we were on the glacier the bergschrund was in triplicate, so we took longer than usual crossing the ice and dusk was falling by the time we reached the rocks. Then the rain started. I was not unduly alarmed. Vicki seemed quite unperturbed that we should be starting a six-hundred-foot climb in semi-darkness with the rain sluicing down the rocks and the temperature only a little above freezing. We started to climb. Fortunately we had brought only one ice axe, but I, being second man, had the heavier ruck-sack. It grew steadily darker. Waiting for the leader to work up his pitch, my hands became numb and I could feel the rain slipping down my back. When I moved, my shirt moved clammily on my shrinking flesh. Vicki said nothing. On a severe chimney pitch, when I was being rather slow, I felt one or two steady pulls. I emerged at the top breathless. The silence was eloquent with understanding. The Grépon was very big that night . . . and very black. The hut, for all we could see, might have been an illusion.

We went on climbing by our headlights. The rain sent golden spears flickering down the beams. When we had been climbing for what seemed hours, we were suddenly – and fantastically – hailed by a voice, and simultaneously I was aware of a beam of light (other than our own) slicing the darkness away above us on our right. This is delirium, I thought, but it was the Tour Rouge refuge.

We came out of the darkness and the driving rain into that tiny patch of light, and, peering in, saw that the hut seemed full of people. In reality there were only three men, all French who, like ourselves, were hoping to do the Grépon the following day. We unpacked our gear and found that we had some clothes still dry. While we rested, snug and warm, on the palliasses, the others cooked their supper. When they had finished we changed places. There wasn't enough room for us all to cook at the same time.

We ate almost silently, being intensely hungry, and the others were sleeping. With our eyes on weight, we had brought just enough food for five meals – for the next day and breakfast the day following. Reluctantly we stopped eating before we were satisfied, pushed the dirty pans to one side, and lay back on the palliasses to lose our hunger in sleep.

Confused murmurs of 'neige' awakened me early. In my ears-laid-back mood I awaited the order to rise, but there was no active movement, rather a subsidence, a sinking-back. There was pal-pable relief in the atmosphere. I, too, succumbed.

At eight the door was flung open. Someone unshuttered the window and sunlight flooded in. White wisps of cloud floated round the peaks, and snowfields gleamed, but near at hand every ledge and pocket on the Grépon was white with newly fallen snow. It was melting rapidly, but far too late for us. We ate breakfast gloomily, thinking of our dwindling stock of food.

After the meal we tried to lose our forebodings in work. We slung ropes from rock to rock above the precipices and aired the blankets. Every ledge and pinnacle was festooned with drying clothes. I sunned myself in pyjamas and duvet jacket while the others took photographs. We made an ascent of the Tour Rouge itself, perhaps an Easy Severe route, and then abseiled and traversed back to the hut, to sit outside on the boulders and watch fly-like figures slowly coming up to the Trelaporte glacier below.

That night five more people arrived. We were cramped but warm.

Next morning I was wide awake as Vicki went stumbling over sleeping bodies to the door. His language was an improvement on that of the previous morning. And the word that mattered – 'neige' – was prominent. We five oldest inhabitants were all awake, muttering and grumbling, and knowing that nothing could be done.

We settled down again, for once reluctant.

When daylight came we crowded to the door as we wakened and murmurs of astonishment brought the laggards, curious. And for August the Grépon was an unusual sight. Every ledge was plastered a foot deep with soft, dry snow. The sun glittered, but down in the valley mist was creeping up the Mer de Glace. It was rapidly obscuring the Drus, the Droites and the Courtes while we watched.

A few flakes of snow began to fall but changed to rain almost immediately. The Grépon was hopeless, everything was hopeless. We turned back to breakfast.

Rain was falling fast and steadily by the time we'd finished eating. The snow was no longer dry; it was wet and slushy. The rocks were running water and Vicki said it was near freezing. With the rocks ice-covered it would be almost impossible to descend to the Trelaporte. We had eaten the last of the food so we decided to retreat immediately. The others said they would risk the temperature dropping and come down later in the day when the weather cleared.

With all the food eaten our packs were light, and in warm, dry clothing we were feeling quite happy as we left the hut and started the descent to the glacier.

Scarcely had I lowered myself over the edge and was peering for the route below, when there was a terrific explosion overhead. It was like the close discharge of very heavy artillery, but with no echo or rumble afterwards. The rain increased. I knew the explosion must have been thunder but it was like no peal I had heard before. There seemed to be no lightning; I suppose – the storm being directly overhead – the flash and the explosion were simultaneous and one drowned the other. For some distance as we descended, there was no sound but the sweeping of the rain across the rock face and these sudden exhilarating crashes that filled the world with sound. The Grépon seemed to shake under the impact.

We were moving in a gleaming fluid world. The snow on the ledges was wet as we brushed the holds clear with our hands. Very soon we abandoned climbing down and started to abseil. We calculated we had just enough pitons to enable us to reach the glacier. Once or twice we were able to economize by using spikes of rock, but finding the projections meant too much time sweeping the ledges clear, and we reverted to pitons.

After the first hundred feet I felt my skin grow clammy and knew the rain had penetrated. Gradually we grew colder; our hands became numb in an instant sliding down the rope; there was a moment to warm mine while Vicki pulled down the rope and inserted the next peg, then came the long slide again, the swing out over space as bootnails scraped rock and slipped, wondering how numb fingers could grip the rope – the welcome feel of the arrival ledge, and the wet, clinging nylon still cutting painfully into the thigh.

Halfway down I was standing on a ledge waiting for Vicki to finish a traverse away to the right, when, with a swish and a clatter, a muddy cataract of stones and snow came pouring down the overhang beside me. I watched it curiously with an interest that was quite objective. I felt more awe when, safe in a café in Chamonix, I heard the unseen avalanches roaring down the slopes of Mont Blanc.

Soon afterwards Vicki picked up the rope curiously and, running it through his hands, paused at an almost unnoticeable flaw. He jerked – and the plaited nylon snapped like a piece of cotton !

As with the thunder, this was too much for words, except to remark that our abseils would now be half as long.

We continued, fifty feet at a time, removing pitons when we could (sometimes Vicki climbed down), hoping the rest of the party would bring down the remainder. After what seemed an eternity of sliding down the streaming rocks, we came to the glacier, negotiated the chasm between the rocks and the ice, and came to the bergschrunds proper.

We found a bridge over one branch but the others were more complicated. At the second I was told to slide and fall in. I protested half-heartedly, but obviously it was the only alternative, and common sense (felt dimly by a brain sodden and numb with wet and cold) told me that Vicki would not deliberately kill me. But logic is prone to desert one at the penultimate moment and so, as I slid out of control down the ice, I felt one sick moment of regret as I shot over the lip and started to fall.

I landed on a solid snow bridge twenty feet below the upper lip, and Vicki followed. His leg went through the bridge and stuck and we had to excavate him with the ice axe. Then we climbed out, found a bridge across the next crevasse, and came running and sinking down the snow-covered ice to the rocks and the zig-zag path above the Mer de Glace. The two-hour trip to Montenvers took us eight hours.

We changed at the hotel and rode down to Chamonix in our remaining dry clothes: pyjamas. Gordon and David were again in town awaiting our arrival. We collected in the old Biolay refuge outside the town and made gloomy prophecies about the weather.

The following morning the snowline had crept down into the forests. The season was over.

Gordon wanted to go home. I didn't but I recognized the futility of looking for work here in the off-season. Reluctantly I packed my rucksack and, with our remaining money, we bought train tickets to Dieppe.

10. Boats and Babies

The Grépon was my last fling for a time. Very soon I married and settled down to housekeeping in a cold, damp tin shack in Llandudno Junction. Gordon found work at a garage in Conway. By December I was pregnant, and, dreading the effect of the unheated shack on my health, had managed to find a cottage in Ro Wen, in the Conway valley.

The village stood at the foot of Tal y Fan – practically the last of the Carnedds: that great whalebacked range of Snowdonia where sudden cliffs block the ends of long radial cwms and you can walk for days and never see a soul: a high, empty upland belonging to the sheep and foxes and the wild Carneddau ponies.

With a comfortable place to live in, my state of health improved temporarily and we climbed most weekends. I would leave home Saturday morning and, walking slowly and exploring as I went, make my way up the cwms or the subsidiary ridges to a point on the main ridge, where Gordon, moving fast along the tops, would rendezvous with me about dusk (having left Ro Wen at midday) and we would continue together over the rest of the range and down to Idwal hostel in time for supper. On Sundays we climbed, sometimes walking back in the evenings, more often being driven home by John Hammond: a very promising climber who was with the Food Office at Colwyn Bay. John seemed to be in charge of a kind of research establishment, and every weekend he brought large and delectable Continental sausages to the hostel and submitted them to the occupants, gravely recording their reactions. His voice was a joke among his friends: supercilious, inordinately loud (so that you were embarrassed in bars) and it carried like a buzz saw. Yet he talked well and was a delightful companion. He was unusual in that he took up climbing later than most people and from that point developed very slowly but steadily. I don't think he had been climbing long when we met him, but in a few years he was one of our leading alpine climbers. Eventually he went to New Zealand and, to the astonishment of his friends, who had watched his late flowering with admiration, he was killed on Mount Cook.

The hostel had changed since the previous year. There was a new clientele. Some of the old crowd had disappeared completely; no one could tell me what had become of Pete Hodge or David Nott. There were rumours of marriage and babies. Attention was now shifting to the cliffs in the Llanberis Pass which were short and steep and strenuous, and people went up to the Pen y Gwryd on Saturday evenings instead of the Royal or the Bryn Tyrch. I felt that the old spirit was lacking, unaware that I had changed as much as anyone. I would have refuted the accusation indignantly, insisting that it was physical and superficial – it was primarily physical but it had far-reaching consequences.

At Christmas George Sneed, who had rowed round the uninhabited islands off Skye, was visiting us and we all went to Idwal and bivouacked in a deserted machine-gun nest on the shore of Llyn Ogwen. On Christmas morning I crawled, heavy and lethargic, to the summit of Craig yr Ysfa and watched the Climbers' Club (trailing balloons behind them) make their annual ascent of the Grimmett. John Lawton, trotting along the quartz ledge of Pinnacle Wall, shouted to me to come down and join on the tail, but I felt sick and went back to lie on the bracken in the pill box.

Now I embarked on an orgy of self-pity which lasted for weeks. I became quite ill, and then, one blustery March day, I packed my rucksack and started walking down through Wales on one of my old-style expeditions. The first evening I spent in a barn outside Maentwrog and it wasn't until I'd washed in the cattle trough the following morning and was well on the road to Trawsfynydd that I realized that, for the first time in months, I had not been sick.

After this I improved almost hourly. I stayed away for two weeks, visiting Cader again, traversing Plynlimon and walking round the wild coasts of Cardigan and Pembrokeshire, swimming in the icy sea, eating like a horse, and sleeping, all the time, in barns or the open air.

I returned to Ro Wen glowing, and ready for the upheaval of moving house. The owners of our cottage had let it only on the proviso that we should be out by Easter. We moved to Conway where, owing to Gordon's connections with the yachtsmen and fishermen, we were able to live on a succession of boats, moving from one to the next as they were required by their owners.

Since I was being forced to settle now and become domesticated, I had felt for some time that I would like to join a climbing club, and my choice, rather naturally, lay with the Pinnacle Club. The members are all women: mainly professional women; as an aspiring writer I felt that this was my milieu. I had been invited to attend the Easter meet as a guest.

The club has a cottage in Cwm Dyli, right under Snowdon. The nearest large cliff is Lliwedd, a crag which has become – perhaps mainly from propinquity – an old friend and a favourite with most members. I had done only one climb on it: the unnamed route with Tom three years before, and it was this Easter which saw my true introduction to a cliff which, for its complicated lay-out of climbs, its *difference* (in strata mainly; all the holds come towards you in tiny riblets) and also for its very lack of popularity generally, has become one of my favourites as well.

Although the weather at the start of that weekend was kind, it wasn't long before I was to see Lliwedd in one of its most impressive aspects. On misty days, particularly if the weather is clearing after a bad start, a band of cloud may stretch across the face above which the twin summits loom menacingly, so that you have the uneasy feeling – walking towards it – that the whole mountain is leaning forward, about to fall into the cwm.

On Good Friday I led through on Roof Route, an easy, pleasant Difficult, and at the top I was asked if I would be attending the alpine meet that July. When I said it was impossible my companions tried to persuade me. My husband could look after himself for a fortnight, they said. I told them I was having a baby in July.

Consternation! Most of the club were on the cliff (including several doctors) and messages were relayed from climb to climb, and up and down the ropes, to the effect that Moffat was having a baby and which was the quickest way to get her off the cliff?

One would have thought I was about to be confined on the Great Terrace (one pictures with awe the Pinnacle Club coping with such a situation).

I refused to be stampeded. I had come to the meet to join the club if possible and I was going to lead my climb to qualify. Besides, since we were on the Great Terrace, I pointed out that the easiest way off was to climb. So I led Red Wall and Longland's Continuation – barefooted, of course – while a frieze of Pinnaclers sat on the top and watched critically. I felt like a cripple who rediscovers his body while swimming. Here on the airy slabs of those two delightful climbs, where the holds are one-toe holds in places and the run-outs are long, I could forget for a while my pear-shape and feel the old elegance. And, not illogically, there flashed through my mind the hope that the baby would be a girl.

Escorted back to the hut by solicitous Pinnaclers, I ate all my own dinner and was given the first refusal of everything left in the pans, and in the evening was elected to full membership.

When I returned to Conway after a welcome three days' climbing, I found that Gordon, mindful of his responsibilities, had bought a boat. At least, a hull. He had borrowed ten pounds, subsidized his wages, and paid the owner twenty pounds. The scrap merchants had refused to give as much.

She was called the *Lady Kathleen* and she had once been a fishing boat : a ten-ton nobby, forty feet long and power driven. The last owner had used her as a houseboat. He had also cut off her stern, forming a transom and completely spoiling her lines. When he and his family went to live ashore, the boat fell over on her side (she was on the hard and floated only at high water) and, with large holes in the hull, quickly became water-logged and full of harbour mud and refused to rise.

Then the harbour authorities demanded her removal and the desperate owner sold her to Gordon. The fishermen and yachtsmen were idly amused but not very much. He'd been too much of a sucker to merit interest. A few took the trouble to tell him how many experienced people had tried to lift her and failed. All this happened while I was climbing, so I missed seeing Gordon and his friend, Victor – off one of the yachts – raise the *Lady Kathleen* with a home-made block and tackle and shore her up on a makeshift cradle, the legs of which were tree trunks filched from the Council woods.

When I returned she was floating, rather sullenly, bow on to the Marine Walk: a dirty shell of a boat reeking of mud and sewage, most of her ports and skylight broken, a great hunk of rusted iron in the engine-room and two rotting bunks in the fo'c'sle. The floorboards disintegrated underfoot. When Gordon and Victor told me with great enthusiasm that 'otherwise' she was as sound as a bell, I believed them, but I didn't see how it helped to make us a home.

We thought the baby was due in July (but the doctor was a month too soon in his calculations). It was now April. A lot of work would have to be done to make the boat habitable in two months. And because we had to live, Gordon must continue working at the garage, even overtime if possible, for there would be materials to buy. He could work on the boat some evenings and at weekends. I could work all the time.

The first job was to remove several hundredweight of mud.

We stripped the whole boat below deck: the old engine went over the side and the rotten floorboards and bunks followed. Then we heaved out load after load of foul mud and I got down to the job of scraping the timbers (even the deckhead – which I persisted in calling the ceiling – had its veneer of slime). Then we started painting. At one time tar had been put on the inside of the hull, and I must have applied about six coats of paint before I had a surface to take the final coat. The deckhead was the worst part, particularly in the fo'c'sle, where I had to stoop to paint, and all the stuff ran down the brush and my arms, and my whole body ached.

In the evenings Gordon filled the bilges with cement and laid new floorboards, both below deck and in the cockpit.

We had the bright idea of making the boat into a sea-going fishing vessel again, and, as soon as the baby was born, working her with Gordon as captain and me as crew. But the first essential was to make a home; the owners of the boat on which we had been living needed it themselves, and we didn't want to be thrown out on the beach. We were lucky to have good weather. It was the glorious summer of 1949. I swam every day and was growing very brown.

Once the boat was clean and painted inside and the floorboards laid, I moved in, sleeping on the floor in my sleeping bag, but it was only a matter of days before Gordon had made new bunks, bought Dunlopillo mattresses and bedding, and then we had real beds. I made curtains for the ports and in a locker up forward I began to accumulate a layette.

Victor came in the evenings to help build the wheelhouse, and now, well into July, I started to feel tired at the end of the day, and while the men hammered and sawed and fitted glass, I sat quietly below and knitted by the light of the oil lamp.

With the wheelhouse finished, Gordon started on the old engine-room, which was to be our saloon. With a loan from my mother we had bought a petrol engine which had started life in a launch on Windermere. It was very small, but we planned to have a sailing boat with an auxiliary engine instead of the other way round, as she had been before we bought her. Over the engine we fitted a large crate and we had a table.

We used fibre boarding for lockers, bulkheads and the tiny partition behind which we installed the lavatory. This was an old conical receptacle Gordon found on the beach. I enamelled it, and he fitted two pumps salvaged from the junk heap. It worked beautifully and was our showpiece.

We had retained the tiny coal stove and bolted it to a platform at the side of the saloon. It was connected to the smoke stack by a long interior pipe which provided us with central heating. Because a boat has to be weather- and water-proofed it is, of necessity, draught-proof as well, and on winter evenings we were to swelter in the saloon in shirtsleeves.

As the summer wore on I became increasingly lethargic. Most of the fittings were in position and we had started caulking the deck seams. This was a job which Gordon liked to supervise, or, rather, he didn't like me doing it on my own, so I spent a gloriously lazy month – at least, in the daytime – lying in the sun in the cockpit doing nothing but read. I couldn't be overlooked because the boat was bow-on to the Marine Walk and we fixed canvas wings to the sides of the wheelhouse so that I was completely hidden. If people called they banged on the hull at the bows (where we kept the ladder) and I had time to throw on some clothes before I received them.

The District Nurse and the Port Medical Officer were most alarmed about my decision to have the baby on the boat. I had them aboard and showed all my preparations, trying to convince them we were clean and healthy and efficient. Privately, I wanted to have the baby on my own. By roundabout ways I'd learned that Barbara had had her first baby in the cottage on Cader with only her husband present, and I was determined to do the same. Gordon was fiercely protective and very rude to the authorities. I don't think we made a very good impression. Of course they were worried about something 'going wrong', particularly in view of my strenuous activities.

I had stopped climbing now, but kept fit by swimming. When the tide is ebbing or flowing at Conway it is very swift because of the narrows at the bridge. It is awe-inspiring to watch the yachts straining at their moorings in the fairway, and the first time I swam from the *Lady Kathleen* I was aware of the fishermen watching from their boats, and guessed that, below the gunwales, their hands were clenched on boathooks.

Because of my unusual shape my Bikini hid nothing, but I was able to slip over the stern of the boat into the water unobserved, and once there I was in my element. No weight to carry, hardly any swimming to do; there was a back eddy with an ebbing tide, and I would swim lazily upstream close to the shore, then strike out into the fairway where the tide was racing for the open sea. Once I was in the current it was tremendously exciting. I streamed past the moored yachts at high speed, judged my distance and then struck out diagonally for the shore, finishing up at the stern of the *Lady Kathleen*, having given the visitors a nasty few minutes.

We attracted a lot of attention. I still wore slacks and fisherman's jerseys but my condition was obvious. We had to carry all our water two hundred yards from a tap, and elderly gentlemen stumbled along the slippery beach spilling most of the water while I was too polite to refuse their offers of help. I had to watch their retreating figures through the ports and then nip out and get another load.

Although carrying the water wasn't so bad, it was awkward lifting the buckets up the ladder and I was very glad when we had water tanks installed. We bought a dustbin then and rowed to the quay for water at high tide. Gordon made a dinghy out of galvanized iron. Even with a pair of oars it cost only six pounds and out of the scraps he made a sink, draining boards and shelves.

I cooked on a Primus stove or the fire We had electric light from batteries, and we'd made navigation lights out of jam jars.

Gordon fitted a new and larger skylight in the saloon and covered the coach roof with old sailcloth After I'd given it two coats of paint the cabin was finished and weather-proof, and we turned our attention to the rest of the deck We put Bitumastic compound in the seams and then started painting.

It was late one evening in August and I was casually slopping red lead on the deck and wondering idly if I'd swum too far that afternoon. My heart wasn't in painting and although usually I loved working on the boat, that evening there was no satisfaction in it. I untied the dinghy and went for a row I was fairly efficient at the oars by now, and I drifted gently upriver past the quay and under the bridge to idle quietly along the shore beyond the castle. After a while I turned for home, only to find that the tide was flowing too fast and I couldn't pass under the bridge. I waited an hour or so until the tide slackened, then rowed home.

I tied up the dinghy and returned to the painting, but after a while I gave up and went below to bed.

The big difference about having a baby on a boat and having one in a sensible place is that when the inevitable happens and you've given in and said, yes, you will go to hospital, things have gone rather far and you have to climb into a tossing dinghy, and climb out of it again, and crawl up a ladder on to the Marine Walk. Then somehow – in this particular instance – you have to get to the ambulance (which can't get to the boat) with all the summer visitors looking on, and a little girl saying, 'Mummy, what's wrong with that lady?' Then they suddenly realize what is wrong and are overcome with embarrassment and you see the ambulance waiting with its open doors . . .

I remember the bell ringing as we rushed through Conway, seeing a sheep feeding on the cliffs above Penmaenmawr and wishing I were a bloody sheep, trying to avoid the eye of Nurse John and asking Gordon to hit me on the head. That journey was agony, but once inside the hospital I abandoned myself to convention and let others take the responsibility. The windows of the labour ward were wide open. It was a hot afternoon. I could see the Carnedds through the heat haze.

Two astonishing things happened. The first was that it all seemed so ordinary. It shouldn't be, I thought, it's a Wonderful and Uplifting Experience. It wasn't at all. I felt like a cow calving. The other amazing thing was the way the pain stopped. Suddenly, in a second, and it was forgotten completely.

A girl, they said : six and a half pounds. No deformities and all the parts were there.

They took me to a small ward where I gossiped for an hour or so to another new mother, got up to look at the Carnedds – rather elated that I could still walk (I had always wondered if those Australian aborigines really did drop out of the line of march to have their babies, then caught up with the tribe in the evening) – went back to bed and slept.

After five days the hospital had had enough of my vegetarianism and my lectures on how to rear babies with particular attention to Nature Cure in the event of illness, and no one was sorry to see me go. An ambulance took us to Conway (passing Mother in the bus en route, who had come to fetch me) and dropped me on the quay. I went down to the boat but no one was there. I didn't like to climb the ladder with the baby (I soon learnt to, though), so I laid her on the beach and, keeping a wary backward eye on her in case of dogs, I went aboard. Then Gordon arrived and handed her up to me, so, when she was a few days old, Sheena came to live on the *Lady Kathleen*.

Gordon had made her a carry-cot out of sailcloth and in the daytime she slept on deck. I had been worried about the gulls but they showed no interest. There was a seat on the Walk at the bows and that seat was always tenanted by people attracted by the nappies fluttering in the rigging. I could hear their comments through the ports.

When she was a week old, Geoff Sutton – then an officer-cadet in Chester – came down to the boat and insisted that we should all go climbing. I had done nothing since Easter, Gordon for longer. We decided we were justified in taking a day's holiday. I attracted some attention on the road and still more in Llanrwst where we were waiting for a bus and Sheena grew so hungry that I had to turn aside to a convenient surgery and feed her in the doctor's waiting-room. I was wearing climbing gear and carrying the rope.

At Idwal Geoff and Gordon went trotting gaily up the Slabs while I fumed at the bottom until a walker came along and I sent him to sit on the rock below which Sheena lay asleep, while I ran up Hope solo and joined the others on Holly Tree Wall.

*

Now that we had made the boat habitable, Gordon was anxious to put into execution his plan to make her into a fishing vessel again. He had had the engine running. He had done some tricky work here adapting it from petrol to paraffin, and making a new universal joint because the couplings on propeller shaft and engine were of different sizes and set at an angle.

I was making sails. We had bought a set of head sails from a yachtsman and acquired elsewhere an ex-W D tarpaulin. This I sewed, double-sewed, and patched; we treated it with Cuprinol and red paint and we had a very fine mainsail.

The mast was varnished and stepped, then the boom went up and a length of timber was trimmed for the gaff. We fitted new crosstrees and started splicing wire rope and hemp for the rigging.

One morning at high tide we started the engine, cast loose the cradle and reversed into the river. It was a nasty, squally morning with the tide flowing just before the turn. The wind was in the south-west. We took the nobby upriver towards the bridge, Gordon up forward, myself at the helm. Sheena was asleep in the fo'c'sle.

Opposite the quay we came round in a wide circle, hoisted sail and cut the engine. What went wrong I've no idea; everything seemed all right until we were level with the Perch – the point at the mouth of the estuary. Then Gordon decided it was too rough outside and we must come round and back to our beach. But he had some trouble with the sail and, although I had the tiller hard over, the bows wouldn't come round The tide was ebbing now and we were almost on the mussel banks below the Perch. The boat was pitching like a mad thing and I could hear Sheena screaming below. I was very worried – so were the watchers on the quay who had gone to telephone for the lifeboat Then her bows came round and we were pointing up the fairway Gordon started the engine but we could make no progress against the current. He rushed on deck and ran forward to throw the anchor out. The boat was falling about all over the place like a sick animal. The chain ran out (I was in agony at the thought of Sheena's terror – the chain locker was beside her head) and we waited. Waited for the anchor to grip. The chain tautened, a few more links slipped out, and she held, straining powerfully, her back end swishing resentfully, but in a few minutes she'd settled, and lay there quietly with the tide streaming past.

I rushed to Sheena. She'd been sick but I quietened her. It was the only time I sailed in the *Lady Kathleen*.

One advantage of living on a boat is that you have all your possessions with you in an emergency such as this. It was Sunday so there was no hurry to get home; I had the food aboard for lunch, and after we'd washed up we settled to odd jobs and the papers just as normal families do on land. On deck the wind howled in the rigging and rain slashed the skylight, while below, with all doors and ports tightly closed, the little stove roared merrily and Sheena slept soundly up forward.

We came back when the tide turned, chugging quietly upriver and slipping, rather shamefacedly, into our berth. Of course, we came in for a lot of criticism. I took the wind out of people's sails by agreeing that – with a baby aboard – we had been foolhardy and wouldn't do it again. Alone I would have loved sailing the *Lady Kathleen*, but not with Sheena.

November came and the river fogs. Coming home from our afternoon walks I would brood over the long white band lying up the estuary and wonder about the effect on our health. Bedding was always damp. I had neuritis in my arm which prevented my sleeping.

I went home to Sussex for the winter, but at Christmas Penny and Bill Condry (who had been the wardens of the youth hostel in Nantmor and were now living in Cardiganshire) found me a furnished cottage next door to their own. So Sheena and I moved again.

Nothing happened in Cardigan except that Bill asked me on one occasion – after I'd read them an article about the cottage on Skye – why I didn't write for the BBC.

For a year now I had been writing regularly for a naturist magazine – articles of a thousand words or so which fetched the amazing sum of three guineas! I wrote on sleeping out, having a baby the simple way, swimming and camping. In one issue I ran my own correspondence column, writing all the questions and answers. I had met the editor: a harmless little man with spectacles and a suburban air. My first article had been illustrated with a back view of myself on Buachaille Etive Mor and one of a member of the Climbers' Club beside Llyn du'r Arddu. My editor told me that, in response to this article, he had received letters addressed to me which he had decided not to forward. One had been from a sergeants' mess in the British Army of Occupation of the Rhine, the other from a group of men on a ground nuts scheme in Africa. Then there was an Anglesey nudist who wanted my address and a public schoolboy who had designed his own tent. These letters were passed to me. I answered the schoolboy's letter in good faith, gravely reviewing the plan of the tent. Back came an enthusiastic reply asking if he could come to see me. There was no mention of the tent but the letter was interesting. I wondered what the sergeants had said and the men on the ground nuts scheme.

I pondered over Bill's suggestion of the BBC and dismissed it. I didn't think I was up to the standard required for radio scripts. I shelved the subject for a year.

At Easter I went back to the boat and found it changed. Not the boat, but the life we led, or perhaps it was I who had changed. Last summer I had had the boat to work on and the baby to look forward to, but now the boat was finished and life was a dull round of shopping, washing, cooking and mending. Sometimes climbers came and talked about Idwal. Sutton had written to me when I was in Cardigan and asked me to go and climb Mount Kenya. (His elegant writing-paper confirmed the old rumour that he was in the Somaliland Scouts.)

I hadn't climbed since Sheena was a week old, only taken sad little walks about the foothills of Plynlimon pushing a pram and wondering how long it would be before I would feel rock again. I had one or two weekends at Idwal during the summer of 1950 but I felt very guilty about leaving Sheena with Gordon, and he was intensely jealous of this passion for mountains, which he knew meant more to me than anything else except Sheena.

In the autumn, both feeling that a change of surroundings

might benefit us, we moved north, back to Gordon's aunt on the Gareloch – she who had welcomed us when I sprained my ankle nearly three years before. I stayed with her until Gordon returned to Conway. He meant to bring the *Lady Kathleen* north to the Clyde; he had tried to persuade me to crew for him but, remembering our lucky escape a year ago, and thinking of Sheena, I refused.

Soon after he'd returned to Wales I borrowed some money and rented two rooms above a stable. They were furnished after a fashion. I had nothing to do now except look after Sheena and read. What contributed to my moods of depression almost as much as the absence of friends and the lack of climbing was the lovely weather of that autumn: the changing moods of the mountains of Argyll which reminded me so vividly of past winters when I'd been free. Gales came raging in from the south-west and alternated with still days of fog. I used to take Sheena for walks on a little hill above the village from which we could see the sunsets over the western hills, when great purple cumulus clouds towered above the mountains with all their tattered fringes blazing, and the high snows gleamed like silk in the light. Snow would be everywhere, even in the ravines; there were no cliffs on those hills – it was only in the thaw and under new snow that I could trace the line of the burns. The afternoon would be all purple and white except for those bright flakes and shafts of gold in the western cloudbanks.

There were frosty nights when, unable to bear the flat any longer, I would walk down to the shore where the air was so still that I could hear a bus on the other side of Loch Long. At midnight you could see Arran under a full moon with all the snows lit up.

Some days the fogs crept up the Firth and the horn of the Cloch lighthouse blew all day and night, the echoes moaning among the mountains until the next blow. Washing hung damp and deadstill in the garden, and I would dream of a remote cottage hostel in Wester Ross. I applied to the Scottish Youth Hostels Association for a job as warden at one of these hostels and in the middle of February, leaving Sheena with my landlady, I went to Glasgow for an interview. They must have been interested to send for me, but my application was refused. I was told that the life would be too rough for me. I considered telling them something about my life, but thought better of it; they wouldn't believe me. Perhaps I should have worn my climbing clothes instead of tweeds and nylons.

Gordon came back to the Clyde before Christmas. He brought Geoff Sutton with him and a stranger – Pat Browne – who was starting to climb. I was embarrassed and ashamed that I should be seen like this: reduced to domesticity, babies, real poverty. Poverty without responsibility is amusing and unconventional, but to a woman with a family it is squalor. They stayed at the flat for a while (Sheena screaming for her meal), and then left for the north. After they'd gone, Gordon said they had wanted me to go to Glencoe with them – an invitation which, by its timing, didn't ease the situation.

I followed them two or three days later when Gordon had got used to Sheena's routine and I felt I could safely leave her.

*

On a Sunday morning, very bright and cold, I was alone with Pat on the Aonach Eagach: the crest of that great wall which bounds Glencoe on the north – a wall over two miles in length and seldom dropping below the three thousand foot level. It is easy to reach at either end, but once on it, in winter, it is very hard to get off except in two or three places, which are difficult to find unless they have been studied from a distance beforehand. Pat and I hadn't the remotest idea where these escape routes were.

The long months without climbing had taken their toll on the ascent. I felt very unfit and allowed Geoff and a fourth member of the party (who had joined us from the youth hostel) to go ahead. Pat and I plodded behind.

Once the crest was reached, we sat down to admire an incredible view of hundreds of peaks: Schiehallion, Cruachan, Nevis, the Cairngorms, Ben More on Mull and even the Cuillin far to the west. But it was too cold to stop for more than a few minutes, and we were soon hurrying along the ridge towards the Chancellor.

About five o'clock we ran into trouble. The daylight was almost gone but I wasn't uneasy as there was a full moon. We had been climbing on the north side of the ridge and I was leading back to the crest. Pat was belayed below me at the head of a gully. When I reached the crest and went to take in the slack the rope was jammed. I shouted to Pat to let it go, but nothing happened. Eventually he climbed up to me with his rope hanging behind him. Apparently all the slack had fallen away from his feet into the gully, and by the time I had climbed down to investigate it seemed to be frozen hard, and without another rope with which to abseil there was no way of freeing it.

We anchored the end of the rope and went on. We came to a nasty little ice-covered slab where we could see the marks of Geoff's rope. A knife-edge of snow ran into the bottom of the slab and below its crest, on either side, the cliffs dropped away for several hundred feet – to gleaming snowfields on the south, and black depths on the north. I sat down at the top of the slab and started to slide, gathering momentum. I struck the knife-edge, swayed, plunged in the axe, and stayed there – trembling. Pat followed, virtually into my arms. I knew we were committed now; we couldn't go back. We had to go on, or be stuck on the ridge.

We went on a little way, across a tiny col where we flogged down another snow arête with our axes, up and along the crest and so to a gap. Beyond was a rocky step about sixty feet high, with ice-covered slabs on its northern side. Some years before I had done the ridge with Gordon and I remembered that the route lay up those slabs. I stared at the step, and then looked down, following in my imagination the line of fall – a long way – perhaps a thousand feet? Fascinated, I stared through the moonlight and calculated, trying to make it the good round figure of a thousand so that I could turn back with an easy conscience. I made it a thousand and we turned back to the little col.

We retreated quietly, in that strange, relaxed mood when the decision to bivouac has been taken and before the disadvantages of that decision have been realized.

It was nearly seven o'clock now. We wondered when Geoff would come back. We knew he would. I felt guilty about the uneasiness in the valley; the first thought down there would be of an accident, but we were powerless to do anything about it.

At first we didn't think of deliberately spending the night out. It was our first experience of benightment, and where now I would accept the situation and make meticulous plans for the spending of those hours until dawn, then we thought only of rescue. I was thinking that someone had to come, because, even in daylight, those slabs would not be feasible unroped and with a novice.

We took up our position on the little col. There was nowhere to sit; we made a sort of path about eighteen inches wide and fifteen feet long and we stayed there for ten hours.

The night was clear and very cold. Occasionally a few snow-flakes drifted past and mist played rather ominously about the higher sections of the ridge.

We could see the lights of cars three thousand feet below and the tiny yellow glow that marked the croft at the head of Loch Achtriochtan. Behind that glow people were sitting comfortably reading the Sunday papers perhaps, or darning socks, completely unaware of ourselves staring at the light. For a while I signalled with my torch but no one answered.

When we had been on the col for about an hour we were astonished to see a fire on the north face of the Aonach Dubh, directly opposite us but much lower. It flared for a few moments and then went out. We stared until there were spots in front of our eyes and then we saw it again – only a tiny fire, but definitely flames, too red for a torch, and they flickered. Then a bus came up the glen; we had been waiting for this – a climbing club going home to Glasgow. The bus stopped below us and we watched lights start to move away from the road and up the Aonach Dubh! We learnt later that someone was stranded on a ledge, and burning his guide book to attract attention.

I signalled occasionally after that, but never had an answering glimmer, and after a while we gave up and turned to the difficulties of staying awake and keeping warm. Pat had no gloves and at intervals he had to put his hands in my pockets to ward off frostbite (but in the end it was his feet that were frostbitten). Trying to keep our feet warm we stamped all night, swaying dangerously on the brink as we tired, taking little fifteen-foot promenades along our path, turning and stamping back.

We watched Achtriochtan freeze far below; we saw the shadows advance on the great cliffs as the moon moved round, and we watched the mist. I talked continuously – of anything – just to keep awake. We sang. We worked through all the climbing songs, opera and ballet, and came to the Psalms, and when we got to 'death's dark vale' we stopped.

It was some time about two or three in the morning when, staring dully northwards, silent for a moment, I saw a ladder with white rungs and went to move forward – and woke up. It was a gully wall several hundred feet away, black in shadow, with evenly spaced ledges, snow-covered.

At half-past four we thought we saw lights coming along the ridge, and a little later we were certain. It was Geoff and one or two others; fortunately not an official rescue party. They brought all we needed : experienced leaders and a spare rope.

There was a little good-natured chaff which we were still able to return, a sip of whisky, and then we were off. Although I didn't mind the steep slabs with the security of a rope, I knew I had been justified in turning back without one.

It was light when we reached the end of the ridge and started down. We seemed quite fit and competent and the descent was only soft sloping snow on steep grass. We had dropped down about two thousand feet and the others were running on ahead. I was floundering in their wake, my ankles giving under me, and taking headers downwards which I was too tired to stop. I was so weary of being on my feet.

Then I took the last toss and felt something crack. My foot seemed to be up around my chest somewhere. The pain was excruciating for a moment. I lay there sweating and wondering when the others would look back. They were several hundred feet below but I didn't care. I knew that my leg was broken and no more could be expected of me. I lay back in the snow and waited.

Pat woke me up, a pale round face like a younger Orson Welles peering anxiously. I sent him for the stretcher and relaxed again.

The cold numbed the pain but I wasn't aware of it. I lay in a blissful stupor, staring at the Aonach Dubh. Thin cloud had descended and through it the rock walls showed in green patches – why green I have no idea. They were a giant's footsteps on a vast snowfield. I heard shouts in the distance and knew they were bringing down the other injured climber.

After three hours the stretcher arrived, by which time I was as happy as a drunk. Pat had come back for the last hour to keep me company. It was a general service stretcher (the other one was on the Aonach Dubh) and they roped me on it carefully because of the angle, but I kept slipping and my feet hung over the end. The stretcher bearers were in agony because of the pain I must be suffering, but I felt nothing. Nothing, that is, until they traversed steep slopes and I glanced sideways and downwards straight to the road. I was terrified.

They dropped me on the tarmac and I sat up and started to shake. A nice strange man rubbed my back. It was all very pleasant but I couldn't stop shivering. They took me to the Clachaig Hotel where the proprietors, the MacNivens, rose to the occasion with soup and drinks all round. I was put in the residents' lounge in splendid isolation except for an enormous Labrador and even he walked out after a while. A painful trek to the lavatory disclosed Pat and my rescuers having a party in the bar. I was disgusted.

It was Mr Duff at the Belford in Fort William who put me in plaster. I had been worried about my reception; I hadn't realized that the surgeon would be a climber. So, instead of censure and hostility, I had sympathy and humour and the assurance that I would be climbing again in a few weeks.

*

If I had been depressed in the months preceding the Aonach Eagach incident, in the time that followed my mood was intensified out of all proportion to my disability. I no longer found beauty and sadness in the flaring sunsets, but savage rebellion. The long weeks of idleness with a plastered leg, drinking parties with the yachting community and reading too many sombre books – all fed the fires. I tortured myself by attending a lecture of Tom Weir's on his recent expedition to the Himalayas. There were slides of peaks with the sun shining on ice walls and ridges, and puffs of cloud girdling their buttresses. Gorges and narrow tracks. There were shots of mountain villages which seemed, to me, very familiar, the roofs great slabs of stone like Horsham stone, pitched very wide and shallow, more so than those of alpine chalets. I think that the fact that the monsoon was imminent, and then arrived during the expedition, improved the pictures. They had a rain-washed clarity, and the flowers were so vivid it was as if the last drops of rain were still falling as the sun came out. There were some rhododendrons: palest pink with faint maroon specks in the centre of each floret. And there was a close-up of crimson blooms on a dark green branch, and through the leaves – the sun on far peaks.

*

When my leg healed I started climbing again. I climbed on the Cobbler with Betty Starke and other members of the Ladies' Scottish Climbing Club, and I went to Glencoe again and led my first snow climb.

One night in Glencoe youth hostel I met a man who said he had climbed Clachaig Gully in winter. This was a formidable undertaking and I looked at him with great respect. When he suggested that we should climb together the next day I was overwhelmed. We added a novice to the party and set out on the Sunday morning for Stob Coire nam Beith. When we reached the foot of the cliff the Clachaig Gully man suggested that I should lead. 'Where?' I asked, not troubling with the guide book. He should know.

'Anywhere,' he replied, 'it'll go anywhere.'

Obediently I tied on, well aware of the great honour this tiger was conferring on me in allowing me the first lead of the day, more – in leaving the choice of route to my judgement. I dabbled rather ineffectively at the rock, and then started up. About twenty feet above the ground I began to doubt his assurance that it would go anywhere. I traversed here and there, chipping away ice from the holds, clearing snow, until suddenly I was very tired and climbed down, shaken. They said nothing, but Bill – the tiger – moved back from the face and stared, rather meaningly, at another section. Meekly I tried this new route with the same result. By this time – tiger or rabbit – I had reached the all-right-you-lead stage, but Bill was literally very deaf and mistook my meaning. He sat down and pulled out his sandwiches. We ate. Afterwards I took them round into Coire nam Beith and straight up the back towards a break in the cornice. Although the (one) novice understood a bowline at the first demonstration, Bill had so much difficulty that I had to tie it for him. Myself I find it impossible to tie a bowline back to front, and standing behind Bill, reaching round his enormous frame to tie the knot, I reflected that this indeed was a far cry from Clachaig Gully in winter

As we approached the cornice I lost my irritation in that world of white snow and dark sky, and the knowledge that it was my first true winter lead. The snow steepened as we neared the top until it was snow ice below the cornice. Here there was a large rock and I brought Bill up and belayed him. A little to the right was a vertical wall of good frozen snow. I cut steps up this and when my head was level with the top, discovered, to my astonishment, a ledge about two feet wide running along under the cornice. Right at the point where I wanted to gain the ledge was a large overhanging bosse of snow which was pushing me off-balance. I looked back at Bill and shouted to him to be ready (in case of a fall) but, of course, he couldn't hear and only stared inquiringly. I turned to the bosse, muttering. I managed to clear away the outer covering of snow to discover a hard core of ice. I encircled this with my left arm, drove the pick into the ledge and heaved myself up. Then I snaked along under the cornice on my belly to where there was a break, and in a few strides I was on the ridge.

The next day I climbed alone. I thought it was safer.

The weekends were not so enjoyable as they should have been because I dreaded returning to the flat at the end of them. I climbed in a kind of angry dream. I thought poverty and the tiny flat were at the root of the trouble. If Gordon could find work, I thought, and we could move into a certain high, lonely cottage that looked down the Clyde to Arran, things would be different. Or there was a good job – with cottage – on Arran itself, but Gordon failed to get it. I wrote to estate agents in Lochaber, trying to rent a croft near Fort William where he could work in the aluminium factory, but all with no success.

We had a stroke of luck financially when I sent an old manuscript about the Skye cottage to the BBC in Glasgow. Not only was this accepted but I was asked for some short stories when I went up for my audition. I hadn't written a story for years but when I went home I dashed off two in the following day, and to my amazement they were accepted immediately. I began to think I might become a writer after all.

The odd climbing weekend and the sale of manuscripts were not enough, or, rather, they emphasized the frustration of the rest of my life. I felt trapped.

Mother came in the summer and saw what was happening, and when she wrote on her return, 'If ever you feel you need a home . . .' I was off like an animal bolting for its hole.

Sheena and I went south to live in Sussex.

11. The Swiss Alps

Shortly before I left Scotland I had received a postcard from Vicki. He was looking for a second for the Alps and Dolomites. I had declined this glittering opportunity, but now – in Hove – I realized that there was nothing – and no one – to stop me going. Mother was positively urging me to take a holiday.

I wrote to Vicki and waited for his reply in agony. I felt sure that he would have found someone else by now. In a few days' time came a terse message: he would meet me at the barrier of the Gare du Nord in Paris off a specific train on a specific day. Then we would drive in his car to Zermatt.

Zermatt! Big snow mountains: the Matterhorn, Monte Rosa, the Dent Blanche, the Weisshorn! I was in Heaven.

I was determined that this was to be a very different season from the first. No more hitch-hiking and struggles with the language, no more sleeping in barns awaking to the hostility of strange, frightening farmers.

I went into Brighton shopping for the first dress I had bought in nine years.

On the boat at Newhaven I hid my axe and rucksack and whiled away the crossing drinking with a Scottish student from the Sorbonne. In my lovely new dress, bare-shouldered and high heeled, I was my own dream of a *femme fatale* on my way to meet a man in Paris. The Scot and I did a canny deal with the porters at Dieppe and, having dodged the Customs – for no reason but that it was fun – and feeling very worldly, sat down to afternoon tea attended by waiters who kept an exquisite balance between boldness and deference – with no help from me who, drunk with excitement and sun, and the sudden shock of realizing I was still young (which I had forgotten during the last few months), found amusement and delight in everything.

Vicki was astonished when he met me, having never seen me

clean nor out of trousers. I was rather shy of him, too: this scrubbed, handsome youth (but he was my own age) in the casual Continental tweeds and the woven tie. We blurted polite greetings at each other, and he picked up my rucksack and led me to the car. As he packed my gear away, I stood and watched Paris whirling by, glittering in the sun. It was unbelievable to think that in another twenty-four hours we would be at the foot of the Matterhorn.

*

The journey across France had a dream-like quality due partly, perhaps, to the unaccustomed speed and ease of travelling in your own car, partly again to the golden summer day with the heat hitting us like a blow when Vicki cut the engine and we stepped out to stretch our legs while waiting for petrol.

That first evening we came, after dark, to a village where we turned off the main road and found an empty *place*. Here yellow street lamps shone on cobbles and heavy trees sighed in the breeze. There was an old, old inn where we were served chicken and wine in a dim café, and uneven passages and low beams, and always, everywhere – even after midnight – that caressing heat which set the seal on the difference, on the start of an adventure, on the way to the Alps.

I woke before dawn and sat down at the open window watching the mist dissolve above the river as the sun came up. We breakfasted at six and before seven we were on our way. The little Renault went speeding down the long, poplar-lined roads and river valleys still full of mist, while far hills trembled in the heat. At mid-day we came to the Jura, unknown country to me, a country of great limestone cliffs and walls, and black firs friezing the skyline. There was a little village called, I think, Meutiers, where Vicki turned off the main road and climbed through narrow streets shadowed by old, tall houses. I had glimpses into sunlit courtyards lined with byres and stables, where sleepy horses – all strawberry roans – dozed on three legs in the midday break.

We lunched in what seemed to be an old manor turned into an hotel: lunched off trout with a sauce of melted butter and roasted almonds. Again there was wine and I emerged into the sunlight mellow and sleepy. I sat in the passenger seat and stared at the country through half-closed eyes, fascinated by the higgledy-piggledy roofs of Besançon: great russet tiles plastered with yellow lichen – and I started to calculate how soon we would be in Zermatt.

Lausanne was clean, modern and prosperous. There were streamlined cars and sports shops that were very sophisticated and Continental. I bought a pair of Swiss boots.

Speeding along the shore of Lac Léman, I thought that Italy must be like this, with the villas and vineyards, the intensely blue sky and water, and – on the south shore – limestone crags dim in the haze. Little white sails dotted the lake and bronzed children were diving along the shore. Far to the south a long line of cumulus marked the Alps.

Then came the Rhône valley, less wooded but wilder than the Jura; we were actually in the foothills now. Excitement mounted. At Visp we turned right, up the side of a gorge which would end at Zermatt. There was no fence, only little stone posts set apart, much farther than the length of a car, and several thousand feet below – or so it seemed, perhaps it was several hundred – the green-cream of the glacier torrent.

The slopes were too steep to be more than sparsely wooded. Occasionally a little alp appeared with chalets. We saw no snow but the presence of that glacier stream below, the scent of pines, the very air – were like coming home. Vicki was exuberant. I sat calm and subdued and cried a little. So we became quite hysterical when we met other cars where it was too narrow to pass. There was much shouting and gesticulating.

Cars were not allowed in Zermatt in 1951 (very few are allowed now, and they belong to local inhabitants and can be driven no farther than the outskirts) so we had to finish the journey by rail. We arrived at Saint Niklaus one minute before the train was due to leave – it was already in the station – but all the passengers descended to heave our luggage aboard. I collapsed on a seat while Vicki hung on the platform at the rear of the carriage shouting at a boy called David, of all things, what to do with the car.

As we rattled up through the avalanche sheds, twilight descended on the valley although it was only seven thirty, yet on the curves we caught tantalizing glimpses of a great sunlit bulk of ice at the head of the valley – the Breithorn. And then came a lot of lights on the valley floor, and – leaning far out from the platform – trying to see what lay ahead of the train, I saw the Matterhorn.

It doesn't matter how many ash trays and table mats have that shape stamped upon them: they may be ignored. Although I remember a cheap jeweller's in Halifax and a trinket tray, with the familiar shape – stark white – rising from emerald forests into a cobalt sky, and I stopped and smiled, seeing the reality behind the souvenir.

That evening I was reminded of seeing Mont Blanc for the first time, but the Matterhorn was not only unbelievably high, it was also (unlike Mont Blanc, which is rather lumpy) the traditional mountain-shape: a splendid isolated spire. It was my dream of beauty. In ensuing years I came to look beyond its aesthetic qualities: to gauge the difficulties of its faces, to wonder where were friends benighted on the Furggen, to calculate the possibilities of the Föhn building up from that direction; but still it takes my breath away to see it for the first time in a season.

We were taken to the Bahnhof that first evening. This was the nearest hotel to the station. We had been met by an English friend of Vicki's: Geoff Holmes. (Vicki had arranged that we should make a four during the first part of the holiday; he would climb with Lucien George, I with Geoff.) The latter was staying at the Bahnhof and he said there were some spare rooms. The landlady didn't live there, but they were very casual and we could take possession now and see her in the morning. Meals were not provided; you had to eat in the town.

So we left our equipment and went to a restaurant for steak and music. Afterwards, still excited, we practised traverses on hoardings in the *place*.

*

The following morning I awoke to a cloudless sky – and a storm of impatience from Vicki who, rather than wait for Lucien to arrive, decided to go and do the Furggen ridge with Geoff. This was the ridge that formed the left-hand skyline of the Matterhorn seen from the town. It is by far the hardest of the four ridges; Alexander Taugwalder – whom I met later – told me that he would do the north face again, but not the Furggen. To anyone who has seen the stonefalls and the avalanches coming down the north face, this comparison is a revelation. The difficulties of the Furggen are concentrated in the last few hundred feet, where the ridge steepens abruptly under the summit. The route-finding is tricky and there is the constant danger of falling stones. A bivouac at that altitude, in bad weather, could be disastrous. I didn't know all this at the time, and was so bemused with Zermatt and my instructions on meeting Lucien that I scarcely noticed their departure.

I was to meet Lucien off the train – any train, Vicki didn't know which one – and take him to the hotel. Then explain where the others had gone, and keep him at Zermatt until they returned. This was less easy than it sounds because I had been given no idea what Lucien looked like (Vicki was possessed by the Furggen) and he spoke no English. So I raced to the station every time a train came in and accosted all climbers who looked French, and, as a last resort, those who didn't. I was kept busy rushing from climber to climber frantically trying to see that none escaped through the crowd and got away into the town.

Surprisingly, I found Lucien – and took him back to the hotel. Here things were rather complicated as I'd given up our accommodation after Vicki left, and moved into Geoff's room. Lucien wasn't bothered (he had just come from the Dolomites with numbered [1] ascents on the Civetta to his credit) and we went out to eat and talk and, inevitably, to look at the Matterhorn. For all of us, it was our first visit to Zermatt.

We came back after Madame had left, and Lucien could find no place to sleep, so automatically I proffered my floor space, and – with the thought of a training walk tomorrow – we went to bed early. Some time during the evening I heard voices in the passage and the door opened. The light was switched on but I pretended to be asleep, straining to hear what was said. Madame sounded incensed and I caught the constantly reiterated word: 'concubinage'. Lucien woke up then and there was a long argument in French. Finally Madame departed for the gendarmes. We hung out of the window, giggling, noted that she really did go up the street towards the police station, and eschewing valour in favour

1. That is: his routes had been done so seldom that the number of ascents could be counted.

1. The *Lady Kathleen* at her moorings at Conway
2. The cottage in Skye

3. Ben Nevis from the air with the peaks of Glencoe in the background
4. The author in Glencoe
5. The author in the Lake District, Little Chamonix, Borrowdale

6. Climbing in Snowdonia

7. Ben Nevis, The Great Tower (from the west) of Tower Ridge

8. The author climbing in North Wales

9. Abseiling in the ice fall of the Grenz glacier

10. Aiguille du Chardonnet: the Forbes Arête

of discretion, threw all his gear out on the landing where he bedded down on a wooden settle.

Madame returned with the gendarme but Lucien was a barrister and no action was taken. But it was maddening that he should have to rent a room on his own when there was floor space in mine (and he had very little money left), so next morning we moved. But first we had a pleasant trudge up the Mettelhorn – about ten thousand feet – with splendid views of the whole of the Oberland and the Valais, and two amiable Germans we met on the summit identified the peaks for us. About midday clouds appeared and increased throughout the afternoon. We began to wonder how Vicki and Geoff were faring on the Furggen, and then remembered that they should have done their climb and be back by now, so we ran down to Zermatt but there was no sign of them, neither in the Bahnhof nor the cafés.

That night we slept in a tent beside the river outside town, but it was an uneasy sleep and we were back in the main street early the following morning, anxious for news. We telephoned the Hörnli refuge, for they would have left their unwanted gear there, but drew a blank. We hung about on the outskirts of town stopping people coming down off the Matterhorn, but with no result. No one had seen them. For something to do we moved our campsite closer to town, camping on a strip of ground beside the river and below the Matterhorn track.

At seven o'clock we were sitting outside the tent, no longer making any pretence of hiding our uneasiness, when we heard shouts from above and there were Vicki and Geoff waving frantically to attract our attention. (The river was very noisy and only a few feet away.)

They had failed on the Furggen. The previous night, when darkness fell, they'd still been trying to find the way up the last few hundred feet. They had bivouacked – precariously – and abseiled in the morning, to traverse the east face and reach the summit by the easy Swiss ridge.

We had a reunion dinner in the Walliserkanne and I drank my first Chianti. This had a disastrous effect on me, and the following morning, waking late in the tent, I was aware immediately that Nature was making extreme and urgent demands. Above me a frieze of curious tourists leaned on the fence watching Vicki and

Lucien cooking breakfast on the grass. Not a square inch of our camp site was hidden from them. But the Chianti was driving me frantic, and the eye of desperation found a tiny building at the end of our strip of land. I made a dive for this, my only cover, realizing, too late, that it was a little house for fattening cockerels. The birds must have been in there for ages. They were completely wild and flew at me in a pack as I opened the door. For a moment or two we were all berserk: I frantically trying to get in, the fowls equally frantic about getting out. They got past in the end and I dragged the door shut viciously, aware, as I did so, of Vicki and Lucien squatting over the stove and staring in astonishment at the cascade of cockerels erupting from the pen.

We spent the rest of the morning rounding them up and carrying them, squawking shrilly, back to captivity. Even then one eluded us until late that evening. Sitting on a café terrace in the sun, or dancing to the Harry Lime theme in the Walliserkanne, he would be remembered suddenly and, flushed with confidence and Valpolicella, yet another sortie would be made. We caught him in the end but, of course, we had to move from that camp site too. We rented a room on the top floor of a chalet. There were windows in two walls: the Matterhorn on one side, the Dom and Täschhorn on the other. We were not allowed to cook in the room, so when we did, everyone sang at the tops of their voices to drown the noise of the petrol stoves. I washed the dishes in the bath. There was no hot water.

Next day Vicki and Lucien left to try the first ascent of the east face of the Strahlhorn – a route they had been dreaming of all through the previous winter. Geoff and I went up to the Hörnli refuge to try the Z'mutt ridge of the Matterhorn. That afternoon, strolling above the hut and reconnoitring the descent to the glacier which we would have to do in the dark the following morning, I saw my first stonefall. A great chute of stones came clattering down the east face, spreading out on the glacier below in a wide fan. There was a cold spot somewhere deep in my stomach.

We didn't do the Z'mutt. The weather deteriorated during the night and we retreated to Zermatt in the rain. I felt sorry for Vicki, baulked of yet another great route.

The rain continued the following day and in the morning they returned. They had climbed the lower two thirds of the face – in rain and snow – until a really bad storm drove them off. They retreated by way of a great ledge which cuts across the face, rather spoiling its value as a classic climb, but a godsend in bad weather. They were returning the following day to finish the route – and I was going with them !

Sunday started poor but around midday it cleared, although clouds still hung about the Furggen. We rode up the side of the valley on a chair lift – as effortless as movement in a dream. No sound, no energy expended. I just sat there, my rucksack on my knee, swaying gently above the pines, while the Matterhorn loomed higher and whiter, and more and more dazzling, until it dominated the valley.

At the hut I tried to eat a good supper but the spaghetti defeated me. We turned in early and I cat-napped until midnight when we were called, and crept down through the sleeping building to breakfast.

Outside it was cold, with stars gleaming above the dark bulk of the mountains. We moved along the moraine by the light of our head torches and then started the long plod up the glacier.

We reached the pass – the Schwarzberg Weisstor – just before dawn. We looked over – and down into Italy : an Italy covered by a great cloud sea which washed right to the foot of the mountains, lapping the east face of Monte Rosa, so that all the peaks stood out pale pink and clear in the sunrise. It was bitterly cold. As we adjusted our crampons, our fingers stuck to the metal. We put on duvets (Vicki had lent me one of those lovely eiderdown jackets) and their warmth was like a benediction.

We roped up and started climbing to reach the end of the Great Ledge. Below us was the face they had climbed two days ago, invisible now, but above we saw its continuation : a cliff eight hundred feet high, clear of snow, every detail bright and hard in the early morning light. It was appallingly loose.

Climbing to the ledge was fun. The snow was fairly steep – at about fifty-five degrees, but hard and firm. The two men led through round me, and I was lulled into a sense of false security, letting others do the work while I merely ran the rope round the axe and admired the picture Vicki made in his red anorak as he swung his axe against a vivid blue sky.

We reached the ledge and moved along it to the point where the climb had been abandoned two days ago. Vicki took the lead and, because there were no belays, tried to insert a piton. But the rock was like chalk; it crumbled and flaked under the hammer blows. Pitons were useless and there were no rock belays. We would have to climb without. Suddenly I realized why the face hadn't been climbed before. Apparently the rock below was firmer although technically harder than that on the upper part, but the whole of this upper cliff was constantly shedding its rubbish, so that any climbing on the face was, as far as this danger was concerned, unjustifiable.

I had never been in such a position before, but I would have followed Vicki anywhere – still trying to use my own methods. Fresh from British climbing, I started slowly and carefully. It wasn't Vicki's scorn that made me accelerate but the first stones coming down the face. Some came fast with a whine like a bullet. Others fluttered down like birds as they rotated at high speed. But there was a peculiar exhilaration in the sounds. Like men in battle I knew that *I* wouldn't be hit . . . However, I needed no encouragement to hurry. On one occasion, following Lucien (who had narrowly missed one fusillade, and was shouting to me, 'Vite, vite, Gwen! VITE!'), I started to *run* up the rocks, came on a steep bank of dirt which started to crumble away under my feet. But, like a mouse on one of those toy wheels, I went on running, then grabbed the rope with both hands and ran up that. Vicki, peering out from his sheltering overhang, was helpless with laughter.

Lucien now led a very tricky traverse. I had a psychological belay, that is, the nylon was passed behind a small block perched on the ledge which moved under the friction of the rope. I belayed the leader; it would have made no difference had he been belayed by the stronger man because neither Vicki nor I could have held him had he come off.

The traverse led round great blocks, each one separated from the mountain by continuous cracks. 'Distribute the weight,' Vicki said, but this was no help, for the blocks were so large that one's weight was merely distributed on the same one. I did the traverse trembling so much that I'm sure the blocks trembled in sympathy, and I saw below me Vicki's eyes widening with the cracks.

Then we were at the top, and Vicki built a cairn while we lay and dozed in the sun. I felt very lazy. It was my first high mountain for three years and I had found, to my horror, as I sat on the stances on the way up, that several times I had slept lightly instead of watching the rope.

We had to descend the whole face to the glacier as the men had bivouacked down there the night before they started the climb and had left their equipment behind. We had a long way to go and the cloud was dropping. Already the outliers of the great cloud sea were pouring over the pass where we had been that morning, rolling down into the valley of Saas.

The descent was a long snow couloir at one side of the face. There was a steep snowfield at the top. Naturally the couloir was an avalanche channel and a stone shoot. The snow slope, softened by the sun, was hair-raising. To belay in it would have been like anchoring in butter. So we all moved together, and fast.

We came to the top of the couloir and the glacier seemed miles below. In the middle of the gully was the chute made by the avalanches; I could see the debris spread out on the ice at its foot. I wanted to turn and run. Vicki and Lucien looked down the couloir, poker-faced, and motioned me to start.

I started. At the top it wasn't so bad; we kept to the easy rocks at the side for about six hundred feet, then the ground became steeper and we were forced into the bed of the gully. Here we would have no chance if we were caught. We were on the alert all the time for the soft, sinister rumblings from above; the sound of tons of snow sweeping down the gully with the speed of water. My fear and fatigue made me clumsy. I slipped constantly, sometimes checking myself, often held by Vicki, and all the time they urged me to go faster.

The mountain was very kind. No avalanche fell while we were in the couloir, but I was so exhausted when I reached the bottom that, tramping across the glacier to the bivouac site, I didn't give a damn that I was still walking on the fans of rubbish, when I should be hurrying for the safety of the bare ice away from the foot of the cliff.

The bivouac was on a little island of rock in the middle of the glacier. They had built low walls of stone as windbreaks. When we reached it we lay down and slept immediately.

I dreamt that someone was approaching with crunching foot-steps and awoke to the stonefalls coming down the great face above, and as I stared upwards, half asleep still, an avalanche dripped like lazy lace down the route we had climbed that morning. I had only been asleep an hour but in that hour the cloud had come down. Mist was forming and dissolving about the site and it was cold. I woke the others and we started the long plod to the Schwarzberg Weisstor. The upper part of the glacier was snow-covered and the snow was knee-deep. I felt that the Antarctic must be like this: the cold, the mist and the fresh snow, the others glimpsed vaguely ahead, and the feeling – past fatigue – giving an air of unreality to all movement so that, blessedly, lifting the legs through the snow, became, not agony, but purely automatic. We were unroped now. One feels very vulnerable without that thread of nylon uniting the members of the party, particularly in mist or darkness.

I plodded on, peering for the tracks at my feet, but in that pale light, without shadows, they were almost indistinguishable from the unbroken snow. Then I heard talking, and, looking up, saw the men moving at right angles to their original line. I veered to inter-cept them, checked in snow thigh-deep, and wallowed back to the tracks.

The bergschrund barred further progress. It was a nasty rift: wide and deep with soft snow lips. Vicki and Lucien were moving carefully along the edge. I followed, suggesting diffidently that we should rope. There was no colour in the bergschrund, only the wide black slit, quite bottomless. They found a snow bridge and I relaxed in my tense creep along the lip. Here we would have to rope. The bridge looked as if it were made of cotton wool. As I tied on, I felt brave and strong again, a mood which lasted quite a while – during the uneventful crossing of the bridge, up the knee-deep snow beyond, to the pass and down the other side. It lasted until we were on the dry part of this morning's glacier. Unroped again, the men moved ahead. It needed only one crevasse for them to jump, one a little wider than usual, where I paused and jibbed, and backed, advanced again, breathing through my nostrils like a frightened horse, and then trotted up and down the lip looking for a narrower place while their figures drew farther and farther away without a backward glance – only one crevasse like this and I was

resentful and frightened again, and each crevasse became bigger
than the last. Some I forced myself to jump, and then cursed myself afterwards for taking unjustifiable risks.

Once I was on the moraine I kept going hard and caught them
up. Vicki had sat down to remove his boots. He had some bad
blisters. I passed, almost at a trot, ignoring his demand that I
should wait.

We reached the Fluhalp at eight in the evening after nearly
twenty hours' climbing.

*

The summer of 1951 was a season of storms. The same storm had
driven Vicki and Lucien from the Strahlhorn, and Geoff and me
from the Matterhorn. You could squeeze in climbs by going up to
a hut in bad weather and waiting for the occasional good day.
Where we went wrong was waiting for a good day and then going
up in the hope that it would stay fine for tomorrow.

So we waited through two days of bad weather: eating and
drinking, talking and dancing. The first day (the day we came
down from the Fluhalp) smouldered sullenly along after an argument with Vicki as to who should have the first use of a bath in the
chalet of a friendly guide. I, on the strength that the guide was
my friend, not Vicki's, won. Relief came late that night after a
very sudden, very dramatic scene in the chalet (with Lucien and
Geoff delighted spectators) and I walked out into a thunderstorm.
I hadn't realized it was raining as I made my theatrical exit, and it
was impossible to go back. So I strode through the sleeping, bright,
streaming town to the barn at the camp site, where, soaked and
frozen, and without a sleeping bag, I shared the hay with the rats.

Arthur Dolphin and friends were camping by the barn. Having
breakfast with them the following morning, I saw Vicki walking
down the other side of the river. With superb poise he withdrew
me from the circle, apologized like a gentleman – and laid himself
open to a day of retribution. We ate cream pastries, peach mel-
bas, ham rolls, fondue, and drank lots of red wine and he was sick
all night and breakfasted on Vichy water.

It was a lovely day. Grim and pale, he left for the Rothorn hut
with Lucien. I waited in the main street to trap some unwary and
unattached person whom I could interest in the Z'mutt. I was

still there when the goats came home. These are one of the attractions of Zermatt. Every morning they pass solemnly in procession down the main street to graze on the outskirts, and every evening they return, heralded by their tinkling bells. They are driven by diminutive children, and followed by the road sweeper. They are well-conducted until they reach the centre of the town where the old buildings close in above the road to form a bottleneck. Here, in fine weather there is always a dense throng of tourists, and here, inexplicably the small goatherds disappear. The goats, left to their own devices, trot among the people, accosting anyone with a bag, while timid people jostle and laugh a little self-consciously as they dodge the horns. Now and again a child, almost a baby, will materialize, seize a goat by its collar and lead it away, but others remain, and once I saw a white nanny standing in the shoe shop, gravely watching an embarrassed member of the Alpine Club trying on new boots.

In the end I found companions – but not for the Z'mutt – and before dawn next morning Geoff Holmes, Valerie Stevens and I were moving up the glacier behind caravans bound for the ordinary route on the Zinal Rothorn. Vicki and Lucien had left hours before to look at the east face of the mountain. We had left our departure too late. By the time we reached the rocks below our ridge the sky was indigo over Italy and the wind was in the south. But the Rothorngrat was bare of snow: a castellated crest of strawberry rock rising to the summit. We went on.

For over an hour we climbed happily, absorbed in a route that was hard enough to make us think, but well within our limits. There was the summit ahead, a visible goal, the sky above, and nothing between our boots and the glaciers on either side but a thousand feet of air. Then I felt a strange chill in the air and, turning, saw that we had company.

The mist was creeping up the ridge behind us, drifting up the gullies and slipping round the towers; even as I stared the first snow began to fall.

In another moment we were in the cloud. The temperature remained high, fortunately. At first the snow melted and the rocks streamed water, then the holds filled with slush which we had to clear before we could move. We climbed as fast as we could, and as we neared the Gabel – the great notch in the ridge below the summit where the ordinary route comes up the couloir on the right – we heard voices. Then we glimpsed figures through the mist, moving very slowly downwards from the summit.

We all arrived at the Gabel at the same time, the other party ensconcing themselves a little below the crest to eat lunch. We stood and shivered in the raw south wind which came sweeping up from the glaciers, flattening our drenched clothes against our backs, and whipping frozen hair into eyes already red and sore from the driving sleet. Valerie said she had no feeling in her hands.

At last we started to move down the couloir – an easy route normally, but now plastered with new snow as soft as flour. There were no belays: all the rocks were hidden and an ice axe belay was useless. It was slow, laborious work, but we knew that we had only to descend this couloir to the snow ridge a few hundred feet below, and we were virtually home. We would *stroll* down to the hut from the snow ridge, they said . . .

We crawled down carefully, lost the way, abseiled, went on crawling, edging our shrinking bodies down the face above the invisible drops. We were still in cloud but there was that uncanny feeling of space below that warned us that the gently sloping snow slope on our right was convex, and we were reminded that new snow lay on old. My legs felt stiff and clumsy, my fingers reluctant to leave the security of a good jug handle and feel their way across the next slab on mere wrinkles.

We came to the snow ridge and relaxed (it must have been quite wide then; I've known it too sharp to hurry down as we did that evening). Happily we trotted downwards, thinking of soup and tea and the welcome cigarette as we changed into dry clothes in the security of the dim dormitory.

Chattering and laughing we bore right through the mist, finding rough ground, which grew rougher and steeper, and we didn't talk so much because we were watching our feet, and we stopped laughing. The ground grew still steeper, and we started to traverse leftwards. It was hard to see, and most reluctantly, and incredibly, we realized it was dusk.

After an hour or so of this wandering, with the ground becoming ever more hazardous, we had to admit that we were lost. At least, not *really* lost – we knew where we were: on a nasty face above the Upper Trift glacier. We were, we calculated, not far from the hut, but by this time it was too dark for any more wandering. We found an overhang and, with Valerie and I looking on, the men started to level a shelf.

Slowly it was borne in on us girls that they were deliberately taking a long time in order to keep warm. We shivered on the edge, and occasionally one of the workers would back into us, to be grasped ardently round the waist as our heels teetered on the brink. We stuck this for a while, then pushed under the overhang and squatted on our axes, only to be hauled out again to rope ourselves to a piton. We had all been roped originally, so now we had three long ropes and six short ones. Fortunately no one was wearing crampons, and soon few people were wearing boots, for most complained of frostbite and the fit started rubbing the extremities of the afflicted. I persevered with Valerie's hands until I was worn out, but with no success. I wish I had known then that rubbing was injurious; I could have had a pleasant rest merely holding feet and hands instead of beating unresponsive flesh.

As with the night in Glencoe, we talked. Perhaps it might be considered an advantage to be able to sit in a bivouac, but seven or eight hours on an ice axe shaft leaves a groove which takes days to fill out again.

We sat in a semicircle with our feet in sacks or in other people's laps, being rubbed. Eventually everyone developed cramp. We took it in turns to stand up and stretch the affected part, but it was agony to disturb the set of one's clothes and feel the wet wool on shrinking, clammy flesh. The worst part of a bivouac – for uninjured people – is discomfort.

About midnight the cloud cleared and the stars came out. Vaguely we could see glaciers and cliffs. Gradually people dropped out of the conversation and dozed. I think Val and I were the last ones talking. Then she dropped off and the bivouac was silent. Only the wind came hissing down the crusted snow. Above the Italian frontier the soundless lightning ran along the sky. The two men on the edges of the circle were in silhouette, their heads resting on their knees, the taut ropes holding them inwards . . . there were drifts of snow on their shoulders.

Valerie, beside me, grumbled a little, half-asleep. She said it was getting lighter. I took no notice.

I felt terribly tired. My eyes closed. I couldn't be bothered any longer . . .

I don't know how long I slept. I became aware of movement, of the pain of the ice axe shaft, of an eagerness in the air. I looked out at the mountains and I could make out, very faintly, where the glaciers ended and the cliffs began.

It took us an hour to sort out the ropes, to retrieve socks and gloves from the trampled snow beneath the overhang. It was the most unpleasant – and definitely the coldest – hour of the long night.

As I waited for the other party to descend, I looked up and, for the first time since dawn yesterday, I saw the sunlight. It had just touched the summit of the Matterhorn and the new snow was like gold as the light slipped down the north face. It must have been very lovely, but at the time I wanted only to *feel* the sun.

The way down was easy to find in daylight. After descending from the bivouac site, we had only to traverse a snow slope and we were on the rocks of the ordinary route – and in the sun. And there we met our 'rescuers': Vicki and Lucien and others, setting out from the hut to retrieve our mangled bodies from the glacier – the picture that had haunted them all night. As is usually the case, with the survivors haggard and exhausted after the night, we weren't upbraided (although we shouldn't have lost ourselves so close to the hut) but given cigarettes and studied solicitously for signs of frostbite, and then shepherded closely down the glacier.

Vicki and Lucien, caught in the bad weather, had retreated from the east face the day before.

By the time we reached the refuge I had recovered my spirits, so, after breakfast, we left the others to go to bed, and Vicki, Lucien and I started down for Zermatt. We slept for a while on the short grass above the Trift Hotel, while sheep moved slowly about the hillside, their bells tinkling through my dreams, and the sun penetrated to my tired bones. Then on to the Edelweiss, leaving the men walking slowly down the track, deep in conversation. At the Edelweiss I lay on a chaise-longue on the balcony and ordered red wine and stared at the Breithorn, idly planning a route up a great ridge. (I didn't know there was a route: I was studying the Younggrat.)

Then Vicki and Lucien arrived still talking. I was too lazy to follow their French carefully. Almost asleep, and already half-drunk, I knew they were talking about me. The Breithorn was mentioned and they stared at its mass across the Vispthal. Then I heard the Santa Caterinagrat and heard it dismissed. *Face nord*, they said. Which *face nord*? *Du Cervin. Cervin, Cervino*, Matterhorn . . . I played with the names. They were staring at me. I stared back owlishly through a haze of sunlight and Burgundy. Any climb would do for me . . .

They pulled me out of my torpor, countermanding my order for a second bottle of wine and drove me, protesting, down to Zermatt.

We ate and danced the rest of the day away in the Walliserkanne and the following morning we left for Italy and the Marinelli.

*

The Marinelli couloir is on the east face of Monte Rosa. Roughly four thousand five hundred feet in length, it is the perfect avalanche channel. The route is simple : you traverse into the couloir from the refuge on its left bank, and then you go straight up the ice for four thousand feet until you reach the Silbersattel at the top – that is the summit ridge of Monte Rosa. I knew nothing of this when we left Zermatt. In fact, owing to my laziness in trusting the leader and never reading the guide book nor questioning Vicki in advance (he wouldn't tell me anything, anyway), I knew nothing of any route until I was on it. The whole of that journey into Italy and back over the frontier into Switzerland was a string of surprises.

We had left Lucien at Saint Niklaus and Valerie at Brigue – the latter nursing revolting water blisters on her fingers (I was the only one to escape frostbite after the night on the Rothorn) and both on their way home. The first surprise was the Italian Customs officers at the frontier, who locked the carriage doors on the train while our papers were examined.

'Vicki,' I breathed. 'Italians at home don't have eyes like these.'

'It's the climate,' said Vicki.

Domodossola was odd with no cheap rooms, and a dull meal of cold beef and Gorgonzola. It reminded me very slightly of a Welsh country town on Sunday evening, except for the radios blaring from colonnaded courtyards as we went to bed.

In the morning we found a bus in the station square due to leave for Macugnaga at nine-thirty. We had eaten no breakfast, but when the bus showed no signs of leaving, Vicki went away to buy food. We left at ten a.m.

It was a delightful journey. There were no other tourists. The passengers seemed to be local people who had come into town for the weekend. They watched with amusement as Vicki sat on the floor spreading butter on rolls with the can opener. I sat on the knee of a large, perspiring gentleman who tried to terrify me by miming our probable fate as we drove along the lip of fantastic gorges. But I'd graduated from a hard school. Having driven up the Vispthal with Vicki, the Val Anzasca held no terrors for me.

It was raining when we reached Macugnaga, with the cloud ceiling just above the village. There was nothing to indicate that the finest face I'd ever seen lay behind the mist. I'd had an oblique glimpse of it from the Strahlhorn, but it is from Macugnaga that one sees the real glory of it, draped in the ice of its hanging glaciers whose séracs totter above the long drops, and, from the valley, one hears the echoes of the avalanches growl among the hills.

The rain poured down. We stripped behind a barn, put our anoraks on again, rolled our trousers up to our thighs, and started up through the weeping forests. There were words at a glacier torrent which was bridged by a fallen fir with the bark removed. The water was dashing over it. Vicki stood on the other side and stamped and swore, and I stood on my side and stamped and swore, but after he had shouted that I could go home if I didn't come NOW, I did it, mincing along those few yards of fear with the rucksack swaying on my stiff hips and me moving in a cloud of terror that was almost tangible.

We came – at about the tree-line – to a café: the Belvedere Albergo, where we understood there should be a view when it wasn't raining, and where we met Togliatti, who glared at us. (Vicki speaks English with a strong American accent.)

There were a few guides about and, as always, when our plans became known, we were warned off. We agreed good-humouredly to retreat – and continued, only to be lost on the moraine a little later.

At last, in worsening weather, and after a pleasant scramble up the Marinelli spur, we reached the refuge, to be welcomed by the avalanches careering down the couloirs.

The refuge was a one-roomed cabin, but far more luxurious than the Tour Rouge hut. The sleeping quarters were a raised bench, and there was an oil lamp. We didn't go to bed until ten o'clock, when it was still raining. We had to be up at eleven to start the Marinelli at midnight. Every nerve in me rebelled at the prospect of only an hour's sleep before a hard climb and after a long approach march. I prayed for the weather to continue bad.

Vaguely I knew that Vicki was up during the night, vaguely I remember the words, 'Two thirty, too late,' and I knew nothing until nine o'clock. The weather had been bad at midnight, he said; by two thirty it had improved, but this was far too late. We had to be at the top of the couloir by nine – before the sun started the avalanches.

Avalanches! After cleaning the hut, I sunbathed on the roof and listened and watched, completely awed. At midday I counted them as they poured off the face. They averaged one every three minutes. Quite a few were in the Marinelli. You heard them coming, swishing fast down the green ice channel, and – just on our level – there must have been a rock below the middle of the trough, for the snow leapt up and over in a big wave, for all the world like water, but heavier, thicker, far more sinister than water.

All day the Föhn fought the north wind from Switzerland, and in the end the Föhn won and we were driven off the roof by mist and cold. Then we saw two climbers coming up the spur below and we started putting our things together. By the time they arrived we had turned in for an hour or so until supper time.

We had a superb meal at four o'clock, with noodles and tomatoes and an opened tin of corned beef, which we'd found in the hut and which still smelt fresh. The newcomers were Austrian and, thinking we knew no German, clucked to each other like old hens about our foolishness in being on the east face. They referred to us as 'die Kinder'.

We went to bed at five-thirty p.m. and slept well, although

some time later two more Austrians arrived and had to be told all about 'these children in the Marinelli'.

We were awake at eleven-fifteen and off at midnight. The night was very warm. My headlight was almost finished, so the rock traverse to the couloir was rather tricky, but once we were on the ice, lights were no longer necessary. As we left the hut an avalanche fell somewhere on the face. We paused momentarily, silent, listening; then we moved off.

The snow-ice of the Marinelli was in superb condition; for nearly three thousand feet it was consistently hard and pleasantly steep. We were able to move together, and quite fast. We rested every hour, on the hour, and these were the only times we paused, except when Vicki crossed the actual avalanche trough, and I waited, belaying him at the side while he cut down, across, and up the green ice. I don't know how he felt, working in such a place, but when I stood in the bottom of the trough I felt an intruder, and a very vulnerable one at that, in the gleaming empty furrow waiting for the avalanches.

At three o'clock we began to strike soft snow, which deepened rapidly. It lay insecurely on the old, hard stuff, and interspersed amongst it was tough ice, the whole masked by these new falls and the constant clouds of spindrift now streaming down the face from above. We realized that it was colder, that the north wind was blowing from Switzerland; that we would have fine weather for the descent. But it was cold, bitterly cold. The sun came up but it was only a little warmer. My nose ran continually and there was no time to stop and put on cream, no chance to take my hands off the rope as Vicki laboured above me, clearing away the new snow, cutting into the ice underneath. I was wearing fingerless mitts and my hands froze to the axe head.

As the couloir ran out into the level of the Silbersattel I felt little relief, for the climb hadn't been hard (and because no avalanches had fallen in the couloir, I had forgotten the danger) and I preferred the comparative shelter of the east face to this beating, bitter wind which met us on the ridge. Stumbling and sick with the cold (yet with the sun shining brightly in a cloudless sky) we turned south and ascended the Dufourspitze, the summit of Monte Rosa. We went straight over the top without a pause, hating every second of it, hating the verglas on the rocks which slowed us down, hating the coils of rope catching on projections, numb, bitterly resentful.

We took a short cut below the Dufourspitze, slipping down an untracked snow slope to the head of the Monte Rosa glacier which basked in the sun below us. I was certain there was no wind down there. Perhaps it would be so hot we might experience glacier lassitude . . . The snow slope was convex. I went down first and found a bergschrund, but there was a bridge too, right where we needed it.

In a few minutes we were running – heedless of hidden crevasses – the rope dragging shamelessly in the snow, running down to the sheltered warmth in the middle of the great white bowl.

It seemed too late to put on glacier cream then. The price of the east face of Monte Rosa was a face like raw beef and fingers slightly frostbitten. We won some little notoriety at the Bétemps hut, where we earned the title of *Monsieur et Madame Marinelli* from the guardian's family, and later – much later – when the Austrians plodded in, having followed us up our route (and used our steps) we, *die Kinder*, were scolded for going too fast.

Vicki talked about the north wall of the Lyskamm that evening. We had passed it on the way down and it had looked very tempting. But the weather was poor again in the morning and, with one of our snap decisions, we went running down to Zermatt to catch the train for the Dolomites.

12. The Dolomites

We reached the town at ten-thirty a.m., having raced the train down from Rotenboden. The other train – the one down the Vispthal to the Rhône valley – left at ten-fifty. We had exactly twenty minutes in which to collect all our gear from the attic in a six-storeyed chalet and to drag it down to the station at the other end of town. Suddenly, as we trotted towards the chalet, Vicki shouted, 'Meet you at the train,' and disappeared.

My immediate reaction was to follow and drag him back, but I didn't know the reason for this sudden and overwhelming urge to leave me, although I had the feeling that if he could put a twenty-minute time limit on his business, its primary importance was as a dispensation for the baggage job. So I smouldered passionately as I banged my way up and down those six storeys accumulating enough equipment to load a hand cart. Then, of course, I had to manoeuvre the cart down the cobbled alley and into the *place*, and I was too inexperienced to risk doing it myself and using the handle as a brake (you pull the cart, and push the handle back when it starts to lose control). With about a quarter of a ton of gear aboard, the cobbles assumed a terrifying angle – in the same way that ice steepens by twenty degrees immediately you start to lead through. I was almost in tears beside my trolley at the top of that vertiginous slope when two American college boys came to the rescue.

The train was making impatient noises and people were shouting good-byes as we came galloping down the main street in front of a belated horse taxi. The horse and I swung round the corner into the station square neck and neck, the Americans straining grimly on the back of the hand cart. Climbers – people we'd danced and wined with in the Walliserkanne – leapt down from the train and hoisted the luggage aboard in a few moments. The Americans retired, dragging the hand cart. They passed Vicki, who turned and stared silently, glanced at me, ran his eye over the baggage, and remarked complacently that it was good and we'd just made it. Since I abhor public scenes I had to wait until we were in the car heading down the gorge from St Niklaus. I was defeated again by the road and the glacier torrent so many hundreds of feet below, and Vicki's terse, 'Don't talk on this stretch, please !' – out of the corner of his mouth.

By the time we were heading for the Simplon Pass (after he'd craftily bought me everything I wanted for a picnic lunch) I felt calm again and, lolling drowsily in the car as we sped up the long, long gradient towards the Italian frontier, I felt really good.

Neither of us spoke. The breeze swished past the wide-open windows, and a cicada shrilled. After a while I bestirred myself to hunt for it. It was muddling work searching among Vicki's legs, the steering column and the gear shaft, and trying to work my way up behind the dash-board after a very heavy lunch. When I withdrew, puzzled and hot, the cicada was silent. I settled down, muttering, and the monotonous shrilling started up again. I caught Vicki's eye. He was burbling with suppressed laughter. He was wearing a new and very expensive wrist watch.

'That's what you were doing when you left me,' I said quietly, 'buying a new watch?'

'Oh yes,' he answered, waving his wrist to see the carats catch the sun, 'very good, don't you think? With an alarm, too. Excellent for midnight starts.'

Cars are bad places for violent scenes, because one cannot pace and rage and throw things. One has recourse to verbal venom. We hissed at each other all the way into Italy, stopping only to stare at the handsome frontier guard with such hostility that he waved us on after a glance at our passports. Fortunate, as we had a load of Swiss food in the back. Vicki took his revenge on me by saying we had no time for wine with our supper that evening (which was dull, and so unmemorable that I forget in which town we ate) and drove fast until two in the morning because he knew that I was terrified of speed on strange dark roads.

We slept on the grass verge of a drive somewhere on the flat plains of Northern Italy. The drive led to a convent with a tinny little bell that chimed the quarters and woke us every time. Cars sped by at long intervals. It was a peculiar night, rather like a night in a bivouac or sitting up beside a sick animal. One was half-asleep: dreaming yet aware of the cars that passed; one was half-awake: hearing the bell, and seeing the shining metal rocket by a few feet away. It was half-light all the time, with a moon some-where about. Everything was hazy, never quite complete, and the basic cause of our uneasiness was the fact that we were very much in transit, poised – even on our air beds on the grass – for a moment between one range and the next. The night was a dream between realities.

*

When you are travelling across plains towards the mountains you think that the first hills must be incredibly dramatic, but, in fact, often the transition is so gradual that you are unaware of it. Per-haps the line of demarcation is marked by a town, and you drive towards it over flat ground, seeing nothing but the buildings ahead (although there may be high blue shapes above and beyond the roofs if you look for them) and then, on the other side of the town, you realize suddenly that you are in the hills.

So, at one moment during that hot morning, I awoke, meta-phorically, to the fact that the country had changed. Suddenly we were among gorges and cliffs and rocky torrents. We were in Dolomite country, but as yet there were no fantastic towers, thou-sands of feet high, nor even a proper climbable crag.

At midday Vicki nosed the car into the empty sun-baked square of Listolade. He switched off the engine and immediately we were aware of heat, and silence.

Listolade is only a tiny village. There wasn't a tourist to be seen, and all the local inhabitants must have been drowsing in their dim chalets. Not even a cat stirred in the hot shadows. Only the cica-das shrilled (genuine ones; Vicki hadn't dared to test his alarm since the frontier). Between the gaps in the houses we could see the blue-green vines climbing the slopes and above them – dark forests of firs. Still no towers.

An hour or so later we had sorted out the equipment. We had sat in the dim wine shop and drunk Chianti, lain in the shadows and toyed with some salami and rolls, and packed our gear. Now, in the full heat of the day, carrying – in addition to our normal packs – a week's supply of Swiss food and another sack literally full of carabiners and pitons, peg hammer and étriers (I had this sack) in that heat, when every breeze was like opening the oven door, we started up the mule track.

It was purgatory. Not only was the sun hot on our backs, it was reflected from the naked white flints underfoot as strongly as from snow. Normally I don't have to stop on a trudge such as this, and if a flower or a bird does halt me for a moment, it doesn't disturb my rhythm, but on the way to the Rifugio Mario Vazzoler it was all stops and no rhythm. Vicki was sympathetic, which shows it was bad; in fact I had the impression, from his attitude, that it was an emergency. Perhaps I looked pale. At each stop he dashed down to the stream to make Nescafé with cold water in a thermos flask. I watched him return, skipping over the shining rocks with the crystal drops flying in the sunlight, and knew it would make no difference.

Still there were no towers.

The crowning humiliation was the tigers descending from the refuge. At least, I had thought of them as tigers, but as one lithe blonde swayed past, Vicki remarked that she hadn't the legs of a climber. And I, surveying my own, covered with dirt and old scars, agreed. So we struggled on, rising all the time, with the water rushing below us, useless as a mirage, and the undergrowth rustling occasionally in the hot breeze. I kept my eyes on the dust and the toes of my boots.

When the refuge was very near, I saw a deck chair in the shade on a flat terrace. Stiffly and carefully I worked the rucksack off my back, sat down and closed my eyes. It was unbelievable: cool, comfortable, still . . . Vicki had gone to find the guardian.

Very slowly I started to surface. With my eyes still closed, I listened. To the hum of insects and the vague, distant sound of voices . . . it was drowsy, beautiful, peaceful.

I opened my eyes and saw the tower.

It was about half a mile away. I looked straight across the tree tops to this wall over two thousand feet high: two thousand feet of rock with a golden tinge about it because it was early evening

The refuge stands at the entrance to a great cirque: an elongated horseshoe, with Monte Civetta – like a large-scale Snowdon – at the head, and, at the terminal points of the horseshoe, twin towers, the Trieste and the Venezia. The first was the Trieste. The Venezia was just behind the refuge. I saw it when I stood up and walked to the edge of the terrace. There, above the roofs, above the chimney pots, loomed this other spire – with gigantic overhangs chiselled out of its wall very, very faintly reminiscent of those neat oblong overhangs on the gentlemen's face of Gimmer.

There was no conventional beauty in these shapes but a strange and fantastic splendour that overwhelmed me. Between the two towers, as the crow flew, there was scarcely three quarters of a mile across the entrance to the cirque. Between them, if you followed the ridge that connected with the Civetta at the back of the great cwm, was mile upon mile of fretted skyline, interspersed with leaning pinnacles like a dozen Bhasteir teeth, and soaring spires and plunging gaps.

We ate in very boisterous company that evening. There was, I think, a sprinkling of Austrians, but otherwise, and with the exception of ourselves, everyone was Italian. There was one young Roman who spoke English and who was delighted to practise on us. So they were quick to learn our plans, particularly as Vicki was laboriously trying to translate the Italian description of a route into French. They were very polite, but, as usual, there was an air of surprised disapproval in the atmosphere. By now we were used to it and were not intimidated.

*

Vicki woke me at five-thirty a.m. Armando, the warden, said the weather was bad (there was mist about and it had rained during the night), but we ate a quick breakfast and started for the Torre Venezia.

To start from the refuge in daylight along a beaten earth path that was level was a forgotten luxury – and a poor preparation for what lay ahead. Vicki lost the way before the foot of the tower and we had to battle through acres of dwarf fir which masked great holes among the boulders. Everything was soaked with the night's rain. By the time we emerged at the foot of a dry stony couloir we were both bad-tempered, a situation which was not improved by my determination to climb barefooted. Vicki was furious and, indeed, I found the going rather painful and quite chilly. We weren't in the sun at first and we climbed in sweaters and anoraks.

The route – the Via Andrich – was one of those climbs with the hardest pitch first : only mild Very Severe, perhaps (Five Superior in the guide), but for the first pitch on strange mountains I found it rather demoralizing. But soon I recovered my poise and began to revel in the rock and the steepness. The good climbing was on firm, grey limestone, but occasionally there were intrusions of loose yellow stuff, and on one pitch a hold came away in my hand and I was left with my feet firm but held inwards only by the rope. Fortunately we weren't on a vertical pitch then, and Vicki (who stood no nonsense) gave a good heave and landed me, gasping and cross.

The cliff was as bare as concrete except for tiny blue and yellow flowers growing in crevices; exquisite things lost in that desert of stone until we discovered them.

Tendrils of mist floated around us as we climbed, but then the sun moved round and we began to feel its warmth. Now it was neither too warm nor too cold but just right. The wall dropped away below our feet : sometimes I could see no more than a few yards, then the mist would eddy, and peering down for a foot-hold, my glance would slide past my feet to the screes over a thousand feet below.

Cattle were grazing down there, on the green pass; the sound of their bells followed us almost to the top, until we climbed into cloud. Then there was only the gentle rasp of the rope sliding up the rock, and the occasional click and clatter of a dislodged stone.

By the time we were nearing the summit we were tired. Above us rose a formidable crack with five pitons in it. We looked at it rather half-heartedly and then traversed away to the left, to an enormous chimney. This was quite safe but rather strenuous. After the extreme exposure of the last few hours I found it great fun, but Vicki (who ignores exposure) hated it. So much so that he was quite bad-tempered again when we arrived at the top and said rude things about my climbing. They were justified : the Dolomites are not suitable for bare feet.

We sat, a little apart, on the summit, and sulked. There was nothing to improve our tempers. No view. The tower dropped away on all sides; one felt as if one were suspended in space. After a while I left Vicki without a word and started looking for the way down.

He followed, and we prospected in different places until I found the obvious descent and spitefully left him searching somewhere else. I relented after a hundred feet or so and talked him down.

The descent was easy: little more than Very Difficult with two pleasant abseils. Soon we were in the sunlight again, and we arrived back at the refuge about three in the afternoon.

Vicki, still silent, but not sulking on the return, was very kind that evening. It appeared that I was the first woman to do the Andrich; it appeared also, from an overheard conversation, that I was a veritable tigress! The Italians told us that the crack which we had left undone wasn't the most difficult part of the climb; that we had already done the most severe pitches when we reached that point. I basked in a pleasant atmosphere of honour-restored and Chianti.

After supper we were invited to a party. A party, we thought, up here? Sergio – the man from Rome – told us that there was a chalet at the foot of the Venezia owned, I think, by the local mayor; his wife and children were staying there, and we had all been invited for the Saturday evening. Each person was to bring a bottle. Would we come? Would we!

Armando, the warden, went, and Sergio (who had done his first climb that day), Titi and Licia: a gay pair of students, a grey-haired sunburnt lady from Milan with her niece – and ourselves. We were welcomed very warmly by the mayor's family and a kind of *ceilidh* was held in the big bare kitchen. The *pièce de résistance* was an astonishing cake baked 'according to an English recipe'. It hadn't risen, but the thought was there. I was very touched. Vicki was puzzled. We sang and talked (by-passing the language difficulty with French) and we left, regretfully, at midnight.

We walked home through a gentle night of moonlight and shadows. Above us loomed the Venezia, a little aloof now; it seemed odd that we had spent most of the day on that smooth wall, and had sat on the summit, sulking. I looked at Vicki, striding along the track, and smiled.

*

Vicki took his climbing very seriously. His main ambition that season had been to do the Strahlhorn. I don't think he visited any district without having his eye on one of the great climbs, or 'one of the last unsolved problems'. Now that bad weather had driven us to the Dolomites he was contemplating something too hard for me.

On that side of the Torre Trieste which faces the refuge is a route first done by a Signor Carlesso in 1936. It is a little over two thousand feet long and has several pitches of Six and Six Superior. At least three are artificial. The route had not been repeated since its first ascent.

Armando agreed to do the climb with Vicki, not as a guide, but for fun.

The climb is too long and too hard to be done in a day, but a little over halfway is a ledge where a bivouac can be made.

The day after the party Vicki and I left the refuge late and, carrying food and sleeping bags, climbed the most horrible route of my experience – to reach the ledge on the Carlesso. It was an 'ordinary' route, supposed to be easy, technically only Very Difficult, but dangerous. The approach was bad enough, up a steep couloir: a gully of muddy scree with huge boulders balanced delicately on banks of wet earth. Then came the climb itself: a zig-zag route up the tower, here seamed by easy, firm couloirs, but the traverses between each one were long sloping ledges covered with an accumulation of gravel which rolled away from underfoot like ball bearings. Every hold was loose and the rope was quite useless. We built cairns to mark the best way.

When we reached the great ledge we were in mist again. It was a feature of the district while we were there that mist should play about the mountains all day and retreat in the evening to give a clear moonlit night.

We left the gear in the dwarf firs and went back. On the way down I burnt myself rather badly abseiling and a falling stone hit me on the bridge of the nose. Vicki insisted always on abseiling in the classic fashion; that is, with the rope round one thigh and the opposite shoulder. He said that the far more comfortable method of sitting in a sling with the rope running through a carabiner was harmful to the nylon. So we abseiled classic.

That night the atmosphere in the refuge became a little hysterical, but it was balanced neatly by the presence of some stolid

Germans who were above the excitement of Six Superiors. Armando's wife, Olga, seemed very miserable, but I was excited, vicariously happy, and praying for a fine day tomorrow. Armando lent me his powerful field glasses so that I could watch.

The tower was clear when we went to bed.

Despite the night's excitement, the day's holiday was an opportunity too good to waste and I lay in, secure for once from Vicki's disapproval. I got up about seven-thirty a.m. and went straight to the window. Already, through the glasses, I could see them – Vicki in the red anorak – moving slowly above the foot of the wall. I took a quarter of an hour over my lonely breakfast (everyone else was climbing) and then carried a deck chair out on to the terrace and lay back, with the field glasses trained on the tower.

From eight o'clock until nine-thirty Vicki was leading and made very little progress. I thought I could hear Olga and the kitchen staff praying. I felt rather uneasy myself, but at ten o'clock the gap between Vicki and Armando increased visibly, although he was on the same pitch which he'd been on at eight o'clock. I ordered a bottle of Chianti.

During the morning some surveyors arrived on the terrace and I explained what was happening in French. One of them suggested politely that I should look through his instrument mounted on a tripod. I did so – and felt faint! There was Vicki – in red – dangling head downwards on a taut rope! The surveyors doubled up with laughter. Apparently these instruments show things upside-down.

I didn't relax my vigil until they halted together and I saw that they were sitting. Guessing that lunch was being eaten, I snatched a bite myself, and felt remarkably cut off in the dim dining-room.

It was a hot, drowsy afternoon. Again I lounged on the terrace, occasionally looking through the glasses, sipping idly at the Chianti. It was when I was pouring myself a glass that the rock fell. The air was still, and the boulder came crashing down the tower in stupendous bounds that reverberated through the cirque. I jumped in my chair, the canvas gave way and, soaked with wine, I struggled in the wreckage to focus the glasses. It was all right – they were still there – in orthodox positions. Trembling, I went to find another chair.

As the afternoon wore on, people returned from their climbing

– all faces turned to the Trieste as they approached along the terrace. Madame, the mayor's wife, came over from the chalet, and we sat and watched, sharing the glasses, until, at four-thirty p.m. we saw them reach the great ledge and everyone relaxed.

That night Madame carried Sergio and me away to the chalet. We were more subdued this time. Tomorrow we were to climb the Trieste with water to meet Armando and Vicki. We were also to collect the bivouac gear and bring it down. Thinking that Sergio's English would desert him on that wicked 'ordinary' route, I spent an anxious evening learning the Italian for such *cris de cœur* as 'Don't pull!' and 'Give me slack!'

On our way to the chalet in the dusk a fire had been burning on the Trieste, but as we returned the tower was dark. It was strange to think that there, where we could just make out the bulge of the ledge against the sky, two men slept, halfway to the stars.

They made a good start the following morning. They were very high on the tower now and we, who had to pass underneath them to reach our route, were doubtful if they would hear our warning shouts. I remembered, with some uneasiness, the crashing descent of the boulder yesterday. But nothing fell while we were running across the screes and the rest of the morning went well. I found an alternative approach route up the bank of the dangerous couloir, and the second time on the ordinary route didn't seem as bad as the first, partly owing to the cairns we'd built to mark the way, but mainly because I was thinking of Vicki on the Carlesso rather than of myself.

We reached the ledge and shouted to the watchers at the refuge. Very distantly we heard them reply. Then there was nothing to do but wait. It was blazing hot on the wall. We sipped a little of the water we had carried up, then we lay down and dozed for three hours.

Through my dreams I heard shouts – again very faint. I guessed that they had reached the summit. We sat up drowsily and lit cigarettes, then talked spasmodically until the first stones came rattling down the face beside us. Very far above I could see Vicki: a tiny scarlet beetle crawling slowly down the wall. There was no route to the top of the Trieste on this side, the ordinary route ended at the ledge; the descent was all by abseiling.

We moved under an overhang and waited another hour or two. Occasionally we whistled and shouted to each other and in the silences which followed we could hear the lonely tapping of the hammer as they placed the piton for the next abseil.

At last the white ends of the nylon fell with a rattle to the ledge, and then they were down.

We spread biscuits with jam and gave them water, and then prepared officiously to escort them to the foot of the tower. But in no time they were away, leaping down the ordinary route like chamois, and we were left, stumbling and cursing, bringing up the rear.

*

Life at the Vazzoler was intense and colourful. The proximity of the towers and the dark, green forests, the dazzle and heat of a southern sun, all contributed to turn one's head slightly. Snow mountains are potentially too dangerous to allow one to be muddle-headed, even on the off-days, but the Dolomites conspire successfully. I felt a little mad while I was in Italy.

The day after the Carlesso all the inhabitants of the refuge lay on the terrace completely lost in the sun, with the cirque a background to their half-dreams. Tomorrow, said Vicki lazily, I should do the Trieste by the route to the left of the Carlesso – the Via Tissi. I stared at the tower through my eyelashes and agreed.

But in the morning it was raining. I came out on to the terrace to find Vicki and four Austrians deciding that there would be no climbing. I cried and they were deeply shocked. I went back to my room and an hour or so later Vicki came and said we would do the Campanile di Brabante. I was wildly happy and could have sung as we walked along the familiar track under the Venezia. It was an overcast morning but the rain had stopped.

The Campanile is a small tower about three hundred feet high. The first pitch is the most difficult. Graded Six Superior, it has three pitons (which are very welcome as holds). After a lot of photography at the foot, the Austrians – who had accompanied us – started off, Toni, a big, blond tiger, leading . . . and the rain started. I didn't like it at all. The rock became greasy and two of the Austrians made heavy weather of the pitch. I waited a long time in the cold rain thinking that if King Leopold of the Belgians could do it (he was on the first ascent) then so could I.

I did do it, after a struggle with the pitons; it was hard but not excessively so, and then came pitches of more normal severity which led to the summit. Suddenly the rain increased and it started to hail. We crouched on the top, trying to keep our cigarettes dry, until someone decided to move. My spirits revived as we descended; the ground was comparatively easy and below I could see the foot of the couloir leading to the track. Very soon we would be running home to the refuge: to warm, dry clothing and tea with lemon and a blazing log fire. I didn't stop to wonder why I couldn't see the top of the couloir.

I heard the word 'abseil', and saw Vicki tying two ropes together below me. I halted with the last pair of Austrians and watched. Two ropes? Our own was a hundred and fifty feet long. So this abseil was over seventy-five feet? Ah well, it would be quicker than climbing down . . .

Two of the Austrians disappeared over the edge, then Vicki. We in the rear moved down to the piton. Resignedly, and careful to avoid the burnt shoulder, I wrapped the rope round me and stepped to the edge. I peered over.

There was one blank moment while I took it in, and then my knees started to shake. Below, literally, vertically below, and a very long way down, was Vicki's head. I was out on an overhang and almost the whole of the abseil was free. I wouldn't touch the rock the whole way down and the distance looked well over a hundred feet. (It was – about five feet over.) Below that the ground fell away for another hundred feet or so.

'Vicki!' I called. But it was only a whisper.

I swallowed to lubricate my throat. I called again.

Vicki looked up.

At that distance and through the rain I couldn't see his expression.

'I can't do this!' I shouted.

He looked down and continued unravelling ropes.

I stared at the top of his head. Despair had succeeded terror. I remembered the way we had come up and knew that it could not be reversed. The only way down was this plunge into the abyss, and I couldn't do that. Therefore I was doomed to sit on the top of the Campanile di Brabante for ever.

I looked around, searching for a descent which no one else had discovered, and so I met the eyes of the two Austrians. No one could mistake my look and I must have been as white as a sheet. They smiled at me kindly and held out a spare rope. '*Kommen Sie hier, Fraulein,*' said one. 'Tie' – he gestured with the rope – 'fasten!'

I had never used a safety rope in my life. Perhaps this was fortunate as now it seemed a lifeline. If my arms gave out halfway down, these two Austrian angels would hold me. I was weak with gratitude and relief, but I was still trembling. They had to tie me on, and having two handsome men tie my waist knot was the last thing needed to restore my confidence. We grinned at each other like conspirators, and I hoped they were thinking I was rather sweet and Vicki was a beast to me. Then I went over the edge.

It was worse than it looked. I forgot I was on a safety rope; I remembered only that in a few feet my boots would slip off the overhang and I'd be dangling. I thought of the piton; that wouldn't hold with my weight on it. I wondered where the Austrians were belayed. There was no spike, so they'd be tied to the piton. I felt sick.

One foot came off the rock. Frantically I tried to steady myself on the abseil rope and my arms weakened. The other foot came off. Every muscle of my body was tense and, of course, already aching. I slipped down the rope and started to spin. Rock and air pivoted slowly before my staring eyes. My feet started to rise. God! I would be hanging head downwards in a minute! Below me, in the agonizing silence, I could hear camera shutters clicking, and in my furious resentment I lost a little of the fear and slid slowly and painfully to the ground.

No one said anything. Vicki wasn't there; he had continued down the next abseil. This was nearly as bad as the first, but not so unexpected. I managed it without showing my terror.

In retrospect I've wondered if it really was as bad as it seemed at the time. But the guide book describes the first abseil as 'Excessively airy' which, in the Dolomites, it must be. On this occasion I was already raw from the abseils of the past few days.

But there is a lot of discomfort in climbing; the basic reason why the abseil off the Campanile di Brabante had me gibbering with terror was that I was terrified.

The fact that I'd done another first feminine ascent could not dispel the miasma of shame that clung to me, and Vicki put the finishing touch when he announced that we would not do the Trieste the following day as the abseils were harder than the Campanile and I couldn't abseil anyway.

*

He changed his mind and we did the Trieste.

It was a glorious morning and a wonderful climb. I was wearing Pierre Allain[1] boots now, and found that they didn't lower my standard. These climbs up the great towers are so long that one remembers few details afterwards. There is the diary, of course, written sleepily that evening: technical details such as, 'Halfway a pitch of Five Inferior with a traverse from one solid flake across another – rickety – where I had to leave the piton behind as it meant holding on with one hand (already off-balance) and knocking gently at peg below right foot', but the general memory is of air – very clear and blue – above, behind and below, the quiet tapping of the hammer in the great stillness, and of a red anorak against a cloudless sky.

It was a splendid day. Vicki didn't criticize my climbing and the abseils were not frightening. We descended the great wall from the summit to the ledge where we had watched Vicki, so fly-like, two days before.

There were seven long abseils and I was badly burnt on my thighs and shoulders. However, it was the only way down and I used Vicki's beret to pad my shoulders, but there was nothing I could do about the thighs. I would try to find fresh spots to put the rope at the start of each abseil, but always it slipped back in the old wound. It never occurred to me to ask Vicki if he were burnt.

At the penultimate pitch above the great ledge I had come to rest on a big bollard against the wall. Vicki was coming down vertically above me. I stared upwards, admiring his technique, and

1. Canvas boots with special rubber soles (and a steel plate inserted for rigidity) used for hard climbs.

a stone came down and hit me on the mouth. I wasn't knocked unconscious which was fortunate as I was sitting on the bollard with one leg hanging down the cliff. I swayed inwards and lay against the wall, feeling my teeth gingerly. Nothing was broken, but my eyes kept misting over for the rest of the descent, and when we reached the foot of the tower I was going so slowly that I told Vicki to go on and order supper.

He trotted off into the darkness and I followed at my own speed. I could feel my lip swollen like a wasp sting, and my eyes were still misty. I was stiff and aching, and the new burns were sore, but there were glow-worms about my feet and the two towers rose above the empty cirque. There was a moment of supreme awareness which I might have thought was only the satisfaction which follows achievement, or relief after tension, but I didn't think . . . I knew my moment of truth.

*

As we were leaving the following morning Armando reached up behind his desk and took down an unlabelled bottle. He poured out three measures of colourless liquid. No one needed to tell me that this was a great honour; that I, who never touched spirits, must drink.

I remember reaching for the tiny glass, I remember the trickle of fire in my throat, tears in my eyes, but the memory of the descent to Listolade is dim, for I floated down the mule track in a golden mist.

We sped back across Italy and France to Paris where Lucien joined us on our last evening to hear what had happened after he'd left, and we sat and talked in Vicki's room above the Quai de Passy and played Eine Kleine Nachtmusik and I knew, without a shadow of a doubt, that there would never be a season like this again.

13. The Theatre

Brighton seemed lifeless that September. I was appallingly home-sick for the Continent. For a time I wandered about the town in a mood of resentment and frustration, looking for work. Naturally I found none, for apart from the seasonal dearth of employment in a coastal resort, potential employers were in no mind for my aggressiveness.

Living with my family, Sheena and I were far from starvation, but I had an obsession about financial independence which was strengthened with every evening that I returned unemployed. With the necessity of finding work my resentment had to fade, and, indeed, the memory of the Alps was growing dim behind the immediate reality of buns and tea in cheap cafés, and waiting out-side the newspaper offices for the latest editions. I stood in com-pany with all the other unemployed girls, and when the papers came we hunted frenziedly in the Situations Vacant columns, and little groups would break away, running for buses. The destina-tions were all very similar: seedy hotels or small factories where other women, already there, eyed the newcomers with open hostility.

For a week I worked as a corridor maid in a hotel in Hove. I didn't mind cleaning the lavatories under normal conditions, but one morning they were abnormal and I left.

For another week I frequented the newspaper offices and the employment exchange. Then one morning, feeling a little desper-ate, I went into a pub in a back street not realizing it was near the stage door of a theatre. There I met a stage manager: a young, rather worldly giant who said he needed an assistant. Could I type? I told him I was an excellent typist. (I had been typing my manuscripts on two fingers for years.)

So I moved into the old Dolphin Theatre as they were preparing for the pantomime season.

It was a novel, exciting life and I loved it. My first job was finished in two days; this was typing the pantomime plots and, I think, some scripts. I refused to be sacked afterwards and managed to become property mistress : a title more dignified than the work, but still exciting. Some props I made, others I renovated from existing stock. The rest were borrowed from shops. In return for objects borrowed from a jeweller I took his Alsatian guard dog for walks on the sea front.

The life was a peculiar mixture of sophistication and simplicity. Perhaps not true sophistication, for I found that show people were basically the same as ordinary people. They had the same emotions but they were far more intense. They were jealous, bad-tempered, catty but they were also, almost without exception, astonishingly good-hearted.

The great drawback to working in the theatre was, like pruning in forests, that you seldom saw the sky.

At home I talked of nothing else but the stage. My family were bored to tears. I hadn't the faintest ambition in the theatrical line – when I had a very brief walk-on part it meant nothing to me except that I must do it as neatly as possible. Sometimes I excused the long hours, the hard work and the wage of two or three pounds a week by telling myself it was all Material and Experience and I might write plays as a result, but fundamentally I knew that I would not write about the theatre : I was too much of an observer, not a participant.

The excuse of play-writing came as a result of frequent visits to the Theatre Royal next door where we had free tickets for the matinée – which didn't clash with ours – and could, if we preferred, work back-stage as call-boys. My companion on these ecstatic afternoons (back-stage at the Royal we were silent and wide-eyed, like children in fairyland) was a girl called Mercy who was assistant stage manager at the Dolphin. It was in this way that we learnt the secret of the thuds heard at the Royal when the curtain is down. The work of shifting scenery was done by the Brighton fishermen who wore boots.

My hours were very long. After an early breakfast, with Sheena wobbling and chortling on the rear mudguard, I bicycled to a nursery school in Hove where she created hell until some time in the afternoon when, to the relief of the staff, I picked her up again. The theatre and my home were about three miles apart, and I became quite adept and really fast on my cheap sit-up-and-beg roadster, rushing back and forth between home, nursery and Dolphin.

Not content with spending most of the day in show business, often I moved on, after the evening's performance, to drinking clubs. Sometimes I came home with the milk – literally. It was hectic, but I forgot the Alps.

In the middle of this turmoil came the announcement, during one midday break, of the death of King George VI. We were stunned, as indeed seemed the whole of Brighton. People who were total strangers stopped in the street and spoke to each other. For a while everyone wore a strange expression of bewilderment, of personal loss. In the Dolphin the girls cried in the dressing rooms. The theatres and cinemas closed down, and I went home early through the quiet and empty streets where, behind drawn curtains, the housewives drank tea.

This sudden sense of loss was not completely strange to me. In August, while I was in Zermatt, Pat Browne had been killed in the Llanberis Pass. I saw a newspaper cutting when I returned. Then came the shock of Ian's death in Scotland. It was hard to accustom myself to the fact that he, of all people, no longer existed.

*

The revues went on. Familiar names of music hall came and went. It wasn't a first-rate theatre, and one felt a little sad during some of the performances. But Renée Houston was far too good for us. With her Titian hair, her raucous voice and her terrific energy she captured everyone. Every night was different. I was watching from the back of a box the night she left the script completely and had the audience – and me – literally helpless with laughter. One night, as she was waiting to go on, she told me her troubles. I was astonished at their nature, and at the agony she was suffering, but what put me completely under her spell was the ability to throw it away and stand up, smooth black satin over generous curves, and go stalking on stage with a *gamine* grin and the look of a good-hearted trollop.

There were people who went on stage ill, but were too old or too poor or both to give in. There were others who had been doing their act for so long that one wondered where the sparkle came from. Of course, there were nights when they fell flat and it was sad to hear the old jokes received in dead silence by an audience that was mostly 'paper' anyway.

But there was one night that was superb – looked forward to and enjoyed more by the stage hands and the actors than by the audience. This was the last night of the current revue.

As props mistress I came into my own. There was one sketch (traditional on the music halls, I believe) where the comedian waits on two diners in a select restaurant. In this case the diners were another comedian and the soprano – doubling as stooges. The 'soup' was enamel plates painted orange inside. On the last night, when Jimmie – the diner – remarked wearily that there was a fly in his soup, he froze suddenly and stared with bulging eyes at his plate. The soprano rose and rustled forward. The waiter fumbled – unscripted – for his reading glasses. At the side the stage hands clung to each other, moaning quietly. I had pasted large and piquant photographs from *Health and Efficiency* in the bottom of the plates.

*

One morning I had a letter from the BBC asking me to go to London to give my talk on the Skye cottage.

Mercy and I spent a morning shopping for an outfit, and returned to the theatre with a dull and 'safe' little suit in town tweed and black accessories. It was a far cry from the *femme fatale* of last July.

I came to Broadcasting House one winter evening. Walter Todds was then talks producer. He was very kind. I was allowed two glasses of Tio Pepe before rehearsal and then nothing but coffee.

They left me in a bare room with what looked like matting walls. I sat at a table surfaced with matting, before a microphone. There was a big clock with a red seconds hand, and a dull bulb which would glow green when I was to speak.

I was used to fear and I was prepared for it. I wasn't prepared for the sudden trembling that shook me from head to foot as that relentless seconds hand crept up to the hour. Then, like science fiction, a disembodied voice boomed and I recognized the announcer signing off the programme before mine.

The green light glowed.

I started to read. The script shook uncontrollably so I held my left wrist with my right hand, painfully aware of cadence, of pauses, of emotion that should be felt at the correct moment. After a few pages I realized that I was no longer shaking, and I thought triumphantly, 'I'm not frightened!' knew that I'd made a fatal mistake – thinking – stumbled, picked up the words and went on, sweating. Then I started to enjoy myself, seeing again the rain curtains coming in from the Outer Isles, hearing the porpoises jumping in the bay at dawn, living it all over again.

I came out into the street from Broadcasting House walking on air. I had talked to millions of people! Naturally the journey home was an anticlimax. To my fellow passengers I was just an ordinary young woman on a Brighton train.

*

The novelty of the theatre began to pall towards the end of the winter. In the mornings there was spring sunshine in the streets; the sky was blue and little puffy fair-weather clouds floated above the town. The old, intolerable ache overwhelmed me. I was homesick again.

I packed our bags and with Sheena, my radio, a cot and mountains of luggage, we left Brighton one glorious morning and headed north. I was certain of one thing only: that by evening I would be back in Wales.

14. The Mountain Refuge

We moved into the Pinnacle Club hut just before Easter. I had very little money and no food, but once there was a roof over Sheena's head, the minor anxiety of what was to happen to us evaporated.

The Morins, Nea, Denise and Ian, arrived, and Charles Marriott (Denise's godfather) was in Llanberis Pass reputedly writing a book in Cwm Glas cottage. One damp morning Charles and I went to Lliwedd. It was my first climb since the Alps. Denise had lent me her scarpetti. At the foot of Paradise – an Edwards[1] Very Difficult and therefore a normal Severe in the damp conditions – Charles suggested that I should lead.

I tried it in nails, then in the felt soles, and finally I went up it in bare feet. We followed with Purgatory, and lay on the top in the sun, feeding the gulls and watching the wind whistling through their pinions as they came in to land.

It was Good Friday and that evening, with someone baby-sitting in the hut, I went up to the Pen y Gwryd. The hotel was crowded with old friends, among them all the 'London' people. At closing time I was slipping along a passage to buy one last drink at the back of the bar when a tall and talkative man with legs like a kangaroo blocked my way. Not too polite, I fidgeted, listening for the slam that would mean the bar window had been closed, eyeing him resentfully as he talked on and on.

His name was Johnnie Lees. I remembered him; I had heard his name often from Johnnie Brownsort. He had the reputation of a tiger. Recently he had taken over the RAF Mountain Rescue unit at Valley, Anglesey.

He came back with me to the Pinnacle Club hut. I had thawed by now and we talked a long time and lingered late in Cwm Dyli. He left long after midnight to walk along Crib Goch and down to

1. J. M. Edwards. A hard man who edited the Lliwedd guide book.

his tent in Upper Cwm Glas. He told me the next day that it had been a glorious walk: there was verglas on Crib Goch and he had eaten a tin of marmalade before crawling into his sleeping bag.

The following day he carried Sheena on his shoulders over the Pass to the Three Cliffs. He persuaded some girls from Cambridge to baby-mind and we climbed.

His style on rock was completely unexpected. On the ground, with his long legs and loosely built frame, he looked as if he could scarcely move without knocking something over. Climbing, he was superlatively neat. He hadn't the fast, cat-like grace of George Dwyer, but his movements were smooth and deliberate. Slow, at times painfully so, and steady, he never made a mistake, never advanced where he couldn't retreat. I had been used to brilliant, and sometimes reckless, climbers; now the responsibility of Sheena and the memory of many accidents weighed heavily, and this slow, steady caution made a deep impression on me.

In the days that followed we climbed a little and talked a lot. There was very little to tell me about himself. A good family upbringing in Yorkshire had made him what he was: solid, unimaginative and kind. He had been to school, he had joined the Air Force. He had been in Physical Training and was now in Mountain Rescue. He thought, spoke and lived climbing.

*

I had very little money left now, and towards the end of our stay at Cwm Dyli I was feeding Sheena but eating carefully myself. There was no work in Wales for an untrained woman, with a baby, and in despair I contemplated returning to Scotland. Then I remembered the youth hostel at Ro Wen where it was always so difficult to keep a warden. No one wanted to live up there on a pittance – it was too inaccessible and lonely – no one but a desperate woman who couldn't have enough of mountains.

I applied for the job. While I waited the money ran out altogether and Johnnie, unaware of the true position, brought us food at weekends.

One morning the letter came from the Youth Hostels Association. I was the new resident warden at Ro Wen!

A friend of Johnnie's, Bill Trench, moved us in his van one

evening. I hadn't been to Ro Wen since before Sheena was born, and I was a little afraid of the old associations, but I needn't have worried . . .

The hostel looked straight across the Conway valley to the Denbigh Moors. To the north lay the sea, and to the south – the outliers of the Carneddau : Pen y Gaer, Pen y Gader and Drum, dreaming under the shining sky. The six weeks at the Pinnacle Club hut had been only an interlude. Now, I knew with certainty, I was safe.

*

I kept a meticulous journal of every climb I did from the youth hostel. Nothing else was recorded, only climbs. Every hold on every hard pitch was described in detail, and the hiatus between each written account is now a dim memory of Sheena and running the hostel, and carrying loads up the mountain from the village. When I climbed, Sheena was looked after by the wives of neighbouring farmers, by youth hostellers who wanted an off-day, or by Mother when she visited us. I had no transport, and since I lived at least twenty miles from Ogwen I had to hitch-hike round there after the hostel closed at ten o'clock in the morning, and be back again to open it at five.

I saw a great deal of Johnnie and my original admiration for his technique increased. Until then I had climbed on nerve and natural ability. Now the nerve had failed, and I no longer climbed unconsciously but started to think about what I was doing. I had never known the necessity to think on a climb; I had been supremely confident in myself : a hard move wasn't a problem or a challenge, it was a few feet of rock more delicate and more enjoyable than the rest of the climb.

Suddenly the hard moves had become frightening, and exposure was sharp rocks and excruciating pain waiting below. I looked to the rope for security and remembered Pat Browne and other ropes which had broken : John Lawton on Spectre and George Humphries falling and the nylon snapping as it caught behind a flake on Hiatus . . .

I came back to Wales to find I had something of a reputation from my exploits of five years ago – and then came this appalling realization that I had lost my nerve.

It was Johnnie who showed me another way to climb.

He *thought* on rock. He planned every move before he made it, and one felt, watching, that he could reverse every inch which he had ascended. Once I saw him a little too close to his limit, but never since.

We were on Javelin Buttress one day with Bill Trench. I was at the tiny stance on the wall, and Johnnie decided to lead through from the bottom and try the Blade Finish. This is seldom done and Edwards, typically, says it is 'harder than the ordinary route', which could mean anything but which we accepted as no harder than Very Severe. First they had tried to persuade me to lead it, but I had retreated after one brief glance. It seemed devoid of holds.

I didn't think about my belay until, to my astonishment, I realized that Johnnie was having some difficulty with the Blade. Bill, at the bottom, had gone very quiet. I had scarcely any stance; my feet were flat on the slanting rock. I was held inwards only by the belay. The jerk on my body would be overwhelming if the leader fell. I knew I wouldn't hold him.

He shouted that he was coming off, and my hands were wet on the rope . . .

He didn't fall, but retreated delicately and rested. Then, after a long grumble, he went up again and passed the hard move without causing us more anxiety. Following, I was hard pressed and used the rope as a handhold. The crux was a layback on a huge rounded corner, a step across, and a move to a steep rib using minute excrescences which existed more in imagination than reality, and the pullout finished on a 'jug' which was really only a lump to be used by friction. A hundred feet below, the long sweep of the Slabs flowed for six hundred feet to the bottom. Bill had a tight rope. We all agreed it was excessively severe.

But if Johnnie had been extended on his first attempt on the Blade, his second try was more confident because he had studied the moves and worked them out.

He taught me, too, to look at the rock, to plan my moves; to advance an inch at a time, inspect a hold, reach for it, reverse, rest, and try again. A little farther next time, until the whole sequence of moves was plain, and one went up gently and neatly – not in the brilliant ecstatic dash of five years ago when one had to ask, afterwards, where the hard move was. That was his instruction in theory, but I often forgot – and still forget – suddenly remembering in the middle of a hard move (when it's too late), when one is committed and continues clumsily, grabbing at holds and relying on the rope in the last resort.

I learnt something about rope work. Where before I would run out eighty feet without any protection, now, following Johnnie's example, I used running belays. With my new fear of falling, the thought of dropping only a few feet from the last runner was infinitely preferable to hitting the ground – or flying through space for two hundred feet, knowing the rope would break.

I learnt to climb in nails, and I learnt, shamelessly, from scratch. One wet autumn day before Sheena was born, fresh from bare-footed leads on classic climbs, I took a comparative stranger to Wall Climb on Tryfan and he, artless and astonished, expressed his amazement at my poor lead in nails. Since then, in Scotland and on climbs which seldom went above Difficult in standard, I had been full of resentment at this clumsy form of footwear where I needed great holds the size of soup plates for my boots, and I climbed like a gorilla on my arms and shoulders.

Johnnie would tolerate no heaving on one's arms. I would cry piteously, 'But there are no holds !' and, usually patient, he'd call them out from memory.

'But my nails won't stay on *that* !'

He didn't remind me that I should lean out. I knew it too. I stood on the holds, longing to lean in, to embrace the rock, but I didn't, and I went up, using holds which once would only take a big toe. They took no more than one nail now, and by the time I'd learnt that *that* was enough to support me, I was beginning to take a delight in my tricounis : the small steps upwards with the hands for balance only, deft use of the holds so that the foot was planted firmly on a wrinkle and never budged until you moved to the next hold. That was how Johnnie did it and almost soundlessly (for a good climber in nails makes scarcely more noise than another in vibrams). And how our standard rose when, in warm, dry weather, we reverted to plimsolls !

By July I was leading Severes again, and by August I was soloing with confidence.

I didn't do a lot of climbing from the hostel, for I could seldom find people to look after Sheena. Often Johnnie gave up his own climbing to come and keep us company, cutting down trees for fuel, mending Primuses, emptying the Elsans. In the evenings, with the hostellers baby-sitting, we would go down to the pub for darts and local gossip.

I like Ro Wen. It isn't a typical Welsh village: all slate and gaunt chapels, but one street composed mainly of low cottages, grey stone or whitewashed. In spring the garden walls are draped with purple and yellow rock plants, the air is heady with the scent of wallflowers and a magnolia stands above the bridge.

The village clusters at the foot of Tal y Fan, a mountain only two thousand feet in height but still high enough to have open moor where the wild ponies graze. It is separated from the main bulk of the Carneddau by a pass which is crossed by the old Roman road running from Aber to the Conway valley. This road ran past the hostel, and on lonely winter nights I would wonder if I heard the clash of arms as the ghosts of the legionnaires came trooping down the mountain. Years afterwards I wrote a story about them which was broadcast. I was quite ridiculously fond of it, and still am.

Sheena and I walked all over the mountain exploring, and we followed the course of our little river upstream to its source below the pass where curlews trilled above the heather, and, usually, one of a pair of kestrels would be quartering the moor.

Soon I acquired a cat, and when she grew up, she came walking with us. Mais non! was a dainty tortoise-shell queen of great character. She was fond of me and, indulging her sense of humour, would bring me rabbits and leave their bodies propped against the back door. Then she would retire to a vantage point and wait for me to come out. At night she thought my reactions particularly amusing. The rabbits lived in the Badger Wood well below the hostel. She brought them home by walking backwards and dragging them up the Roman road.

She possessed great dignity; there was a memorable occasion when she lost it – in winter, on Tal y Fan, when the little springs below the summit flooded and froze. Sheena and I, in nails, crossed the steep ice slope happily but Mais non! spreadeagled like a fallen camel, screamed with frustration and had to be assisted. Another time, with her first litter in the kitchen, a large red mongrel from the village trotted gaily into the house. He emerged, a crimson blur, with Mais non! silent and deadly as a cobra, on his tail. Mother and I stood speechless on the lawn listening to the rapidly fading screams. He yelled all the way down the mountain to the village although Mais non! had stopped at the gate.

She carried a certain aura: a kind of potential deadliness. Long before she was old enough to hunt, every mouse – except one – left the house. When she had been with us a week only a pair of rats and this one mouse remained.

I was writing in the kitchen one afternoon – Sheena and Mais non! napping peacefully upstairs – when the door started to shake. I stared at it in astonishment. It went on shaking; I distinctly saw the latch rattling against the socket. Of course, I was thinking of a person playing some kind of trick, and I watched the edge of the door at the level where a face would appear. But it didn't open, and, after a while, I looked down – at the hole at the bottom – and there, panting prodigiously and very cross, was a large rat trying to get his bloated belly through the hole. As he popped out like a cork from a bottle, I grabbed a piece of coal out of the bucket, flew to slam the back door, blocked the hole with the coal, and drew in my breath to shout for Mais non! Then I paused. The rat, racing round the kitchen seemed, at speed, to be two feet long. So I had to kill him myself with the poker. Afterwards I measured him, and then Mais non! and she was an inch shorter. Then we took him down to the farm on a shovel.

'A ve-ry big rat,' breathed old Mr Owen in admiration, 'Ve-ry dangerous she would be!'

I looked at the long green tusks and agreed.

The other rat left that evening and only the mouse remained: the last of the Mohicans. I was going upstairs next day and I trapped him halfway. I called Mais non!, heard the soft plop as she jumped off a bed in the men's dormitory, and then she was leaping lightly down the stairs, ears up and eyes wide in polite inquiry. She reached the last step before the mouse, jumped again, saw the mouse in mid-air, somersaulted, and landed on top of him. She was so surprised she killed him instantly. Later I killed her mice when she played with them, but this made no difference to her delight in hunting.

*

The first summer season at the hostel was quite hectic. The house had to be cleaned properly after the hostellers left in the morning, there was my own housework to do and quantities of sleeping bags to be washed. There were Primus stoves, storm lanterns and Tilley lamps to be repaired almost daily, and all the Elsan closets to be emptied. (I was forced to put up notices to the effect that people should use the latter 'only when necessary' because of the rate at which they were filled.) Shopping was done in Conway and all provisions and equipment for the hostel had to be carried on my back from the bus stop in the valley. Sheena was only three years old, and after a tiring morning following me around the shops she would be a little slow on the mountain and I carried her the last few hundred feet as well.

But, despite the inconvenience, I had a roof over my head and the occasional day climbing. I was, all things considered, well-off. I was paid a pound a week in the summer and ten shillings in winter. The following year I had a rise: thirty shillings in summer, fifteen in winter – but I had no insurance to pay. We could not have lived on this, but it was augmented by a somewhat irregular maintenance allowance for Sheena and the occasional fee from the sale of a story or talk to the BBC. I spent money only on food. My sister kept me supplied with clothes, and climbing boots and anoraks (the latter Government surplus) came as birthday and Christmas presents. The main drawback to the job was the lack of privacy. When friends or relations came to stay we all ate in the same common room as the hostellers and shared the cooking arrangements. When the hostel was full this was very awkward.

When the autumn came the hostel was closed but I stayed on as caretaker. Johnnie was running an extended course for Mountain Rescue in Scotland and we were completely alone. In the evenings I wrote furiously, but now that I was on half wages and the need to make money became more acute, I had a run of bad luck. The rejection slips poured in.

Some time in the New Year I met Geoff Sutton again and, realizing something of my straitened circumstances, he suggested that I should become a guide.

The only guides I knew were the tough, virile men in Chamonix and Zermatt – and George Dwyer – although Sutton himself became a guide about this time. There were no women in their ranks, but both Geoff and Johnnie pointed out that if I had the qualifications sex should make no difference. I didn't know what the qualifications were but I guessed I hadn't got them, for I knew I hadn't got what Dwyer and Sutton possessed. (The latter led me up a good Very Severe that January in snow.)

Meeting George Dwyer that spring I repeated Geoff's suggestion as an amusing Suttonism. To my amazement, George took it seriously and approved. I became subdued and thoughtful.

I began to realize the enormous advantage of possessing a guide's certificate. There were women instructors working during their holidays for the Central Council of Physical Recreation and the Mountaineering Association. With a guide's certificate behind me I could work full-time at what was, to me, a fabulous salary. Sheena, who needed the company of other children, could go to a boarding school. Or I could stay at the hostel and augment my wages by private guiding in Snowdonia.

Deliberately I set out to widen my mountaineering experience, partly by climbing in nails and in all weather, but also by getting to know other districts in greater detail.

With this object in mind I attended two meets in Langdale. My first visit to this centre had been during the previous autumn when Johnnie and I spent a week there. The second time was on the occasion of the inaugural meet of the Alpine Climbing Group. This was an association which had recently been formed 'to encourage mountaineering of the highest standard'. The original members were a group of young climbers who had climbed, and were climbing at, a Très Difficile standard in the Alps or other great ranges. Since I had been asked to become a founder member it was apparent that one qualification for women was to take a part, not a *leading* part, in hard routes. Apart from the usual necessity of being proposed and seconded (which did not, of course, apply to original members), the third qualification was to be below the age of forty. These rather exacting standards resulted in a limited membership. Denise Morin and Nancy Smith were the other women members. Later Nancy retired, which was the Group's loss, for she was one of the finest women climbers I've met. She had done some classic routes in the Alps with her husband, Cym, who was, at one time, president of Cambridge University Mountaineering Club.

Most of the founder members attended that meet at the Old Dungeon Ghyll Hotel. Tom Bourdillon was elected the first president, John Hammond became secretary, and Dave Thomas – treasurer. Sutton was there, and Ted Wrangham (who became secretary after John was killed), Godfrey Francis, Roger Chorley and Dick Viney among others. Sutton led me up Slip Knot on White Ghyll in a snow-storm. He climbed, that day, like Johnnie: slow, steady and cautious, and I was lost in admiration, for it was bitterly cold and the holds were delicate. I found the first pitch delightful, and was starting to think that nails were the best footgear for any standard (even a Very Severe) when I was rubbing my nose on the crux. There was an awkward, off-balance move to the left which was extremely exposed. Here the wind met me and I flattened myself instinctively against the rock. The next move was up a steep little overhang with handholds like Lliwedd's: angular and unsatisfactory; the footholds were smooth and sloping on hard rock which gave no friction to a nail. Sleet swept across the face and the wind roared in the crags. Below there was a sixty-foot drop to the tumbled boulders in the ghyll.

I pawed half-heartedly at the holds with stiff fingers, and after a long time – aware of Geoff's discomfort on top – I shouted for a tight rope. Although not far away, he heard nothing, and the rope stayed just taut, but there were two other members of the Group watching my antics with interest from the ghyll. They relayed my instructions, the rope tightened, and I went up, holding my breath, ready to exhale on the shout 'I'm off!'

The following day I redeemed a fragment of honour leading through with John Hammond on Oak Tree Wall, and lost it again clumsily seconding Bilberry Buttress. Since I had last seen John before Sheena was born I had heard rumours of his prowess at home and abroad. This culminated in his last splendid season of 1953 when, among other classic Très Difficiles, he led the twelfth ascent of the North-West wall of the Olan in Dauphiné: a hard, long route (of over three thousand feet) on poor rock. There was also continuous stonefall in a gully close alongside; which all made it a serious climb. There was only one piton in place. After this season he went to Australia and was killed on Mount Cook in New Zealand in 1955.

Three weeks after the meet of the ACG, I returned to Langdale with the Pinnacle Club, grimly determined this time to make a better showing in nails and despite bad weather. The first evening I had left Ambleside in pouring rain to walk to Langdale but soon my trousers were soaked and I crept into a barn at the side of the road, where I hung the trousers over a cart to dry, and crawled into my sleeping bag. I was wakened in the morning by two elderly farmers coming into the barn. They couldn't see me as I was lying behind a car, but once they moved it, and if they didn't run over me, I would be fully exposed. I had to catch the next bus to Old Dungeon Ghyll and my trousers were hanging on the cart.

I coughed deprecatingly and they stopped talking. I addressed them politely, the sleeping bag pulled up to my chin as I lay on the floor. I asked them to step outside their barn for a moment while I dressed. They went silently. When I emerged and they heard my explanation they were quite upset because I hadn't come up to the house for a bed.

I led all that weekend: not difficult climbs, but they were very enjoyable. We went to Pavey Ark and, with the sun dancing on the water of Stickle Tarn, did Cook's Tour – with its delightful second pitch – a steep, mossy slab made for nails, and descended Gwynne's Chimney and Crescent Climb. On the Sunday I did Bowfell Buttress and Plaque Route. The Buttress is a beautiful route. It is consistently Difficult, but high in that category; it has slabs and walls, cracks and chimneys. It is not greatly popular due to its comparative inaccessibility, and it has the advantage of looking out across the empty upper reaches of Mickleden. In Langdale the roar of traffic is only too often a background to climbing, but on Bowfell one reverts to the more normal mountain noises: falling water and birds.

In Spring Johnnie had leave and we climbed almost every day. It was March now, the rocks were dry and he was in the mood for hard climbs. He took me up Slape – where a hold came out like a tooth from its socket, and I knew nothing until the rope brought me up short still clutching it. We did the delightfully delicate Rowan Tree Slabs with the anti-climax of Balcony Cracks at the top. That was the day I nearly fell off Javelin Buttress, which was scarcely surprising as we'd climbed hard every day for five days.

A few more climbs followed during the summer, but not many, for the hostel was extremely busy, and sometimes when I could have gone away, I didn't because I felt tired. By the time autumn came and the end of the season, I was exhausted, but having thought, and worked, for the guide's certificate through the year, I sent to the British Mountaineering Council for details, signing myself G. Moffat.

In return I was sent two typewritten sheets listing the necessary qualifications. Apart from the expected hard rock climbs and expeditions under snow and ice, a guide was expected to have knowledge and practical experience of mountain rescue, navigation, route finding and loose rock – or perhaps it was just rock. He must have two sponsors, a medical certificate and specialized knowledge of at least one mountain district in the British Isles.

I pored over these qualifications and arrived at the snag: navigation. I had never used a prismatic compass; I doubt if I'd ever looked at one.

Johnnie came up to complete my education one stormy evening when the hostel was full. He tried to teach me about bearings and protractors (yes, we had used *those* at school), grid north, and mysterious things called magnetic variations which altered every year but didn't matter until six (or was it ten?) years had passed, but it was on the side of the maps anyway, so I could disregard the whole business. Just remember the principle. We had a bottle of Chianti that night and this, coupled with the magnificent thunder and lightning, distracted my attention to such an extent that, by morning, I had only the haziest recollection of the night before, and Johnnie, after firing technical questions ('If the magnetic variation was 10′ in 1934 and the true bearing of A from B is 8′, what is its magnetic bearing in 1953?'), left in disgust.

I sent in my application and then forgot about it, for shortly afterwards I was taken ill and carried down the mountain on a stretcher while Sheena – in the throes of whooping cough – was taken away to the Isolation Hospital.

*

A week later, recovering from an operation, I was visited by Mother who brought me a large, flat envelope. There were two grades for guiding: Grade 1, the certificate for rock climbing of a higher standard, Grade 2 for mountaineering. I had been granted them both.

I wired Johnnie and by return came his gift of Stephen Potter on *One-Upmanship*.

15. Toughening on the Ben

I spent six weeks in hospital. Meanwhile Sheena recovered and was looked after by Mother. When I came home it was decided that they should go to Sussex, Sheena to start boarding school after Christmas, while I would end my engagement with the Youth Hostels Association and go to Scotland to recuperate before starting work as a guide.

Johnnie was now stationed with the Mountain Rescue team at Kinloss in Morayshire. Alone and miserable, I started to break up the Welsh home. I found places for the last litter of kittens and, on the penultimate morning, took Mais non! to a farm below the Badger Wood which I was satisfied was the best home I could find for her.

That evening I sat in the empty kitchen and was tortured by doubts. I fancied that I had abandoned Sheena and Mais non! who loved me and were dependent on me. I had given up our home and security in exchange for a life that would be infinitely precarious and, perhaps, even dangerous. This mood was justified during the next few days when, having expected Johnnie to meet me in Scotland, no one was there when I arrived at the station. It was a bitterly cold morning and I waited, surrounded by my luggage, while other passengers walked purposefully into the town, the last taxi pulled away, and a wind from the North Sea howled in the telegraph wires.

I telephoned the camp and learnt that the team had been called out to a Shackleton aircraft which had crashed in the Sound of Mull.

While I waited for their return I stayed with a sergeant's family in Married Quarters. The camp was a bleak, inhospitable place and, more than ever, it was borne in on me that now I had no home, no work, and that Mountain Rescue came first with Johnnie – but how I hankered for a little security !

He came back to find me feeling lost and depressed so, snatching a weekend (the business on Mull was not yet finished), he took me down to Glencoe. We spent two days reaching Black Rock – the hut belonging to the Ladies' Scottish Climbing Club on the fringe of Rannoch Moor – two days in which a cold turned to gastric 'flu. On the second day we sat in a little pub on the shore of Loch Linnhe and listened to poachers' stories. The voices seemed to come from a great distance; I was living on cigarettes and Codeine.

We arrived at Black Rock where I ate a hearty meal and then, quite unexpectedly, after a sortie into the open air, fainted in Johnnie's arms.

He had to be back in Kinloss that evening to wind up the Shackleton affair, so he put me to bed with a hot water bottle and left, very reluctantly.

I slept, and woke late to a blizzard – and the startled recollection that one of my stories was being broadcast that morning. I could eat no breakfast, and I plodded out into the storm and trudged the two miles to Kingshouse rather shakily. Either they had no radio or the aerial was down, and the same applied to Cameron, their next neighbour down the glen. So I hitched the thirteen miles to Glencoe village.

I arrived at the hotel in time to hear the announcer signing off my story. I felt very weak and wondered if I should try brandy, but I settled for coffee and, after two cups, walked out into the storm again, and started hitching up the glen.

The lorry driver who picked me up eyed me with suspicion and disapproval. I swayed drunkenly in the passenger seat, recovered and clung to the door handle, staring blankly at the drifting snow outside. Then I would become aware of fumes and heat and drift off again . . . The driver spoke to me and I couldn't be troubled to answer. I think I said, foolishly, that I wasn't ill. There was only one alternative.

He dropped me at the road end to Black Rock and asked me if I'd be all right. Perhaps he had guessed the truth because the lorry didn't start until I was well along the track. Then he went and left me weaving slowly across the moor.

With my last reserve of energy I lit the wick on a tin of self-heating soup and sat on a bench watching it burn. I sat there a long time and then, leaving the tin on the floor, I went upstairs and lay on the bed.

I couldn't sleep. There was a dimness in the attic as the snow-drifts piled up on the skylight. I wasn't apathetic; I was very frightened: of the snow, of the loneliness, and the growing knowledge that I was very ill (pneumonia?) and I thought I was dying.

But I couldn't die there, alone in the hut. I got up and went downstairs again. I locked the cottage and started back to Kingshouse. Now that I was moving and not lying on a bed, waiting, I was better, but it seemed a long time before I saw the gables of Kingshouse above the heather.

I couldn't get any farther than the hall and they found me sitting on the stairs, a little incoherent, very cold, but no longer frightened.

They put me to bed with hot water bottles, brought me soup, and treated me like a kitten or a child.

The following morning I sat in the parlour reading old copies of the *Scottish Field* and eating prodigiously. In the afternoon, saying I would walk up the road to find my legs again, I went up Beinn a'Chrulaiste and, on the summit, realized that I had done two thousand feet in soft snow without any undue difficulty. The past week, with its depression and physical weakness, faded, and I came down running.

When Johnnie arrived on Christmas leave, he was unable to believe, in the face of my enormous appetite – for food *and* climbing – that anything had happened at all. I, too, wondered if that awful afternoon in Black Rock had been a nightmare, but when we returned to the hut, there was the tin of self-heating soup, burnt out, standing on the floor.

We had a glorious leave. On Christmas Day we tramped the long ridge of Buachaille Etive Beag and watched the sun set over wastes of snow, then glissaded down to Kingshouse and Christmas dinner. We did the Aonach Eagach and I pointed out the place where Pat and I had tramped the crest that moonlit night three years ago, and watched Achtriochtan freeze. We had good sport in Easy Gully (which isn't) on Buachaille Etive Mor where I used my first piton and led my first ice pitches, cutting steps that were far too big, revelling in using the axe, with the ice chips flying until Johnnie, shivering below, exhorted me to get down to it and start climbing properly.

Then, mindful that I still had a lot to learn, we planned a solo walk for me over strange mountains. 'Better if it were bad weather,' grumbled Johnnie that lovely starlit night as we worked with protractors and map beside the fire.

He wasn't disappointed. Next morning the Grampians were clear at dawn, but little fish-shaped clouds (the *ravures* of the Alps) lay above them. Towards Glencoe the cloud was a solid ceiling at three thousand feet.

I was going to do the circuit of the Lost Glen: a long rift at right angles to the main valley. It was here (I had been told) that the sheep and cattle thieves used to hide their beasts, in a high hanging corrie above a wooded gorge – a lonely place held between two parallel ridges which culminate in Beinn Fhada and Gearr Aonach above the road: two of the Three Sisters of Glencoe. At the head of the Lost Glen stands Bidean nam Bian.

That morning I had the mountains to myself. There was a place in the corrie where the noise of water died away – all the high burns were frozen – and then there was no sound, not even a raven croaking, except, occasionally, the clatter of a falling icicle.

I struck up the mountainside soon after I entered the Lost Glen and headed for the summit ridge of Beinn Fhada.

Only a few hundred feet up it started to snow; not a blizzard, but big, soft flakes floating heavily through the still air. They gave the expedition a spice of adventure, and the clouds dropped a little lower. Now, not only the peaks, but the whole ridge, was hidden.

The hillside below Beinn Fhada was uneventful except for quantities of black ice on little outcrops, and the heavy silence. Silence in the mountains is unusual. In winter, with friends, you talk, or you breathe heavily, and there's the sound of the pick on ice, or the adze scraping out a hold; there's the little rush of cleared snow running down a gully or the malignant thud of a big fall. There's the click of nails on bare rock – and there are the burns. But when the heavy frosts come, and you're alone, there is nothing.

That day I saw no ptarmigan and no deer, but, in places, a fox had been ahead of me. Strange, how fresh these tracks seem always, running along the highest ridges, even wandering aimlessly round the summits – and yet you seldom see the fox which made them. I suppose there is a fox? Or is it some little grey fox-shape which comes and goes among the rocks and has no substance?

I came out on the summit ridge about one o'clock, but there was no view, only mist, brighter now, however, because there was no mountain behind it.

The snow was hard and easy to walk on; I trotted over the tops of Beinn Fhada in fine style, beginning to think that solo ridge walks were a little too simple, when suddenly there loomed ahead of me, vertical, monstrous and plastered with snow, a great tower. To me it was as unexpected as a Himalayan giant. I stopped and went back carefully in my mind: back over my route and the map, and our armchair theorizing the night before. I fancied the next peak should be Sgurr na Screamhach, Johnnie had said it was a tooth, but I thought the steep face was on the other side. I tried to imagine the view from the road on a clear day. I closed my eyes, and because I stood on a narrow ridge, opened them again. Very firmly I put myself in the middle of the Lost Glen and tried to remember the silhouette of the ridge. Screamhach assumed the proportions of a needle.

I brought out the map and worked it out that this *must* be Screamhach if I had been on the Beinn Fhada ridge. And I must have been on Beinn Fhada if I'd come up the Lost Glen . . . I gave it up and, with something of the old pioneer spirit which sent Whymper up the Matterhorn, I moved towards the tower. There was a little neck of snow which damped the pioneer spirit, for several people had ploughed across it already. I followed the tracks and they led me round the side of the obstacle and up easy ledges to the summit. Little snow had fallen since the tracks were made and all the holds were clear for me.

Now came the sweeping ridge rising to the summit of Bidean. There were long ribbons of snow lying on the lip of the slope, and below the drifts, the gullies dropped away into cloud. Walking up the snow-slope was like plodding up a concrete ramp. So long and easy, in fact, with nothing to focus on because the mist was only a shade darker than the snow, that there was an odd atmosphere of unreality about the mountain. I could have been in the Alps or on another planet, or dead, or recovering from an anaesthetic.

At three o'clock I sighted the summit cairn. It was none too soon, because the wind had increased as I gained height and the snow was beginning to sting. My hair hung in frozen strands and tinkled gently like clusters of glass pendants in Victorian drawing-rooms.

So far the walk had been straightforward and I had had no need of my list of bearings since all I had to do was to follow the ridge. But Bidean is the culminating point of several ridges and I thought it best to head towards the next peak – Stob Coire nan Lochan – on a bearing. So I glanced at my list and hurried over the summit.

Now, often when you are descending a ridge, you will come to a level stretch and see nothing beyond, but, secure in a preview of contour lines on a map, you are not worried, but just go a little slower, when you will find the ridge reappearing about twenty feet below, and you reach it by scrambling down a moderate chimney or a rock staircase. So, when my ridge disappeared, I didn't worry; I checked my speed – fortunately – and approached the edge.

There was nothing below.

I could look down vertically for quite a long way and there was no ridge. In a flash of intuition I knew I was on top of the Diamond Buttress.

As I went back to the summit, I became aware of another ridge coming in on the left. By this time it could have been the one I'd come up, or the one I should descend, or an illusion, but after bisecting the angle between my two sets of tracks, I found the right way and started off again, speculating on Johnnie's excuse for giving me a bearing that was twelve degrees out. Perhaps he'd forgotten to allow for the magnetic variation.

I lost height for about five hundred feet before I reached a col and started to climb again. I came to a top with two ridges running from it. This made it, indubitably, Stob Coire nan Lochan. I found this out only after I'd retreated from the wrong ridge again.

Then came some steep little snow-slopes where I had to cut steps, and suddenly, with one last glissade, I was out of the cloud, and below me was Gearr Aonach with the Lost Glen on the right, and on the far side, the black slopes of Beinn Fhada.

I came down slowly into Coire nan Lochan and ate my lunch –

at four o'clock – below a waterfall. It was thawing rapidly and everything, including my corned beef sandwiches, was damp.

Across Glencoe the slopes of the Aonach Eagach were grim under a solid ceiling of cloud. They looked like the setting for a Wagnerian opera. One felt that a few flashes of red fire wouldn't be out of place.

It was dark before I reached the main glen and, looking for the signpost that marks the bridge across the Coe, I shone my torch up the hill. I saw it almost immediately, just within range of my light, and at the same time I knew that there were lots of *things* watching me. All grouped about the post. No, I thought, it's ice glinting. But it wasn't; it was *eyes* – lots of them – and then, slowly, round the glittering eyes, grew the heavy outlines of sheep; eight of them with sixteen glittering eyes, trying to scare the daylights out of me.

Badly shaken, I slithered down the slimy track to the bridge. There I had the urge to shine my headlamp into the swirling water a hundred feet below. It may not be a hundred; it looked like a thousand. The bridge had a hand-rail only on one side and I leant over the other. Shreds of courage which had survived the sheep faded and – a shattered wreck – the Compleat Navigator crawled out of the gorge and, missing the track, through noisome peat hags to the road.

It was late by the time I'd walked the seven miles to the hut. All the way from the Meeting of Three Waters (where I emerged from the peat) I'd been worrying about Johnnie worrying over me. There was no light at Black Rock but I went on. Surely he would have left a message, saying where he had gone to look for me? Perhaps I'd missed him below the Lost Glen. I ran the last few yards to the hut. It was locked and there was no key under the stone. I shone my headlight through the window and the empty kitchen mocked me.

I turned and trudged across the moor to Kingshouse, hurrying again as I thought of him just setting out on the other road with a search party. (There are two tracks to Kingshouse from the main road.)

I burst into the bar to find him absorbed in conversation with the proprietor, sprawled on a bench with a tankard of beer, obviously settled for the evening.

He hadn't worried at all, he said. Personally, I think he had forgotten me completely. At first I was resentful that I should be so taken for granted, but then the other feeling rose singing to the surface: he hadn't *expected* anything to happen. I didn't tell him for a long time about the sudden check on top of the Diamond Buttress, and my bewilderment as the big tower of Sgurr Screamhach rose before me.

*

His leave ended, Johnnie returned to Kinloss and left me in Fort William. I was alone again, standing in the middle of a strange town where I knew no one except Mr Duff (the surgeon who had set my leg when I fell on the Aonach Eagach).

With the idea of becoming a ward maid, I went to the hospital but there were no vacancies. I wasn't sorry, I wanted an interesting job. The Labour Exchange offered me the position of housekeeper to three brothers somewhere on the western seaboard. Turning this over in my mind, I wandered to the police station and they told me that one of the grocers needed a driver for his travelling van.

I saw the van in question – and got the job. Then I rented a room in a house near the hospital, a room which was small and simple and devoid of heating but they said I could have a paraffin stove on wet weekends.

My work was to sell groceries and provisions to the remote crofts. My 'runs' radiated from Fort William following the glens: south down the shore of Loch Linnhe to Loch Leven, north and east of Ben Nevis to Spean Bridge, and up the long rift of Glen Nevis to Polldubh where the road peters out into a track crossing the desolate land in the shadow of the Mamores. And I went west to the lonely stretches of Loch Arkaig and the mountains between the Great Glen and the sea.

I was no business woman; less than half my time was spent selling, but I consumed vast quantities of tea in dim kitchens among the cats and collies and (genuine) horse brasses. I muddled the cash and forgot so many requests for the next week that I had to write them down on scraps of paper. Then I lost the paper. I took far more interest in the country and people than in my goods. You couldn't convince anyone of the cheapness of pearl barley when you were wondering if the gleam on the ridge of Carn Mor Dearg came from crusted snow or ice.

When they got to know me, my customers told me something of themselves. There were the two poachers one dark cold night who shot their stag and decided that the best way to dispose of the head was to throw it in the loch. So they carried it down to the shore and gave a mighty heave. But instead of the distant watery plop there came a long skidding sound. The loch had frozen. For days the head remained, a mute accusation – and passers-by averted their eyes . . .

There was the schoolmistress who came up from England for her holidays and married a shepherd . . .

But, as is always the case, the most fascinating people were those who didn't talk, or who talked a little and left so much unsaid. There was the old, old couple – often one of them was ill – always two ounces of Warhorse for himself and ten Woodbines for her. Did she make those Woodbines last all week? They lived in a ramshackle cottage, not over-clean, and waged passionate warfare on a ewe which was always waiting outside their gate ready to sneak in and eat the few cabbages. I, too, developed ewephobia and the sneaking hope she would be run over.

There was the thin young girl with the lovely secret face (but which, nevertheless, made me feel uneasy) in a pencil-slim skirt and good Italian shoes with fantastically high heels. She lived on a croft at the back of nowhere.

An old man lived in Glen Nevis who knew all the birds, and who would stand outside his door and sniff the air and tell me what the wind was going to do.

It was inevitable that there should be at least one ghoul living in the shadow of the Ben. She bought her few necessities as quickly as possible so that she could detain me with long and sanguinary accounts of the most unlikely accidents. But her meaning was clear – and I fidgeted unhappily, wondering with some resentment if test pilots and racing drivers had to put up with this sort of thing. Had she known I'd turned professional perhaps she wouldn't have been so hard on me. Most people were grand, and most hurt if I wouldn't – or couldn't – eat a meal in their kitchen.

There was a farm in Glen Spean which I shall never forget,

partly for the view of the Grey Corries from the kitchen window, partly for the little plump, bird-like wife, but mostly for her sandwiches: new bread and farm butter and home-cured ham, cut thick. After one night spent dancing almost until dawn (when the salvage ship *Reclaim* repaid the hospitality of Fort William with a ball in the Grand Hotel) when my course up the Great Glen was like that of a zig-zagging meteor, it was an hour in this kitchen which eventually brought me round.

The runs were not all gossip and business. I saw a lot of wild life. There was the angry buzzard who dropped his rabbit in front of the van (but I went back and moved it to the grass verge where he could return for it) and a pair of the big birds courting beside Loch Arkaig, hopping solemnly about the hillside until another – probably a second male – arrived, and the first male rose and scrapped and chased him away across the moor, while the hen followed, eager not to miss anything.

Often I saw deer. Once I cut a herd in half, coming suddenly on them through the mist. I stopped, and the stragglers eyed the van mildly, then trotted gently past the bonnet to join the others, their hooves pattering lightly on the tarmac.

The districts I moved through were lonely. For many miles I travelled over one-track roads. I became adept at reversing and squeezing through tight spaces. I was always – or nearly always – ready for the little post van, or a timber lorry, pelting round the next bend. I had no accidents, but some good near-misses. I thought I drove well, but Johnnie disagreed. I gave him a lift one day to Polldubh and, out of the corner of my eye, I saw his hands clench as we took the bends above the brawling river. He stopped breathing when we jumped the pot-holes, and by the time we reached the head of the glen he was white and speechless. He said he would walk back.

Constricted farmyards tested my skill to the utmost. I weaved my way delicately between hen houses and kennels, old mangles and cart shafts. Hens, cats, dogs, cattle and children – bent on suicide – weaved against me.

One evening I returned late to the garage which housed the van, and there was no room to park except on the hydraulic vehicle lift. I don't know if that is the correct term, but it is the thing which lifts the car so that you can work underneath in comfort. My comfort is always cancelled out by the fear of the thing collapsing and squashing me into twelve inches like a concertina.

The lift is formed by two runners with ramps at the ends. I didn't realize that these were adjustable, and, since I'd been on the lift before, I saw no reason why I shouldn't go on it again. There was no one about to tell me that a large lorry had just come off it. I approached gently with my off-side wheel in line with the off runner. The nose rose obediently – then the whole van listed and crashed. I got out and found her lying against the metal support of the lift. Then the manager of the shop arrived and, to my horror (for several men could have lifted her clear), *drove* the van off the ramp scraping my gleaming paint work from end to end. I went home in disgust.

Although I derived excitement from awkward roads and mechanical emergencies, the big thrill came from the country. I saw Nevis every day – if the clouds were up – and from a week of working in its shadow, I knew exactly what the conditions would be at the weekend. If there had been snow with a strong southwest wind the cornices would be piling up above the gullies. With the right conditions the cornices would freeze, and if a thaw set in, they would drop.

The weather, that winter, was generally mild, but there were some strong gales. As far as my work was concerned, the gales were at their worst at Ballachulish, driving straight up the loch from the sea. There were days when I couldn't stop to serve my customers on the way out, but only when I returned and the back of the van was away from the wind. Often, on bleak roads, with a wet gale blowing, my windscreen wiper would disappear, and dismounting, I would find it revolving aimlessly above the roof of the cab. There was one morning when I was coming up the shore road beside Loch Linnhe and the gusts were picking up the gravel and throwing it at the windscreen, so that I had to slow down to protect the glass.

In contrast to the gales would come the still, cold mornings, with Loch Leven black after the rain, and Bidean covered with new snow, rising very high and splendid into an intensely blue sky. I would look across the water at the long sickle ridge of Beinn a' Bheithir, gleaming like silk in the sun, and I'd long for the weekend.

But Ben Nevis was the mountain which dominated me completely. Driving up and down the road to Spean, I had one eye for the van and the other for the mountain.

Coming home in the evening I knew the exact spot where Carn Dearg would come into view, then the massive splendour of the first ridge with the Great Tower catching the light, then Observatory Ridge and the long line of Zero Gully on its left (steep and narrow and full of ice, as yet unclimbed) then the North-East Buttress, and the whole mountain was in view, with the summit cliffs snow-covered and the cornices blazing in the last of the sun.

Often the face was invisible with cloud down almost to the corrie and only a few hundred feet of the buttresses showing. There were days when even the corrie was hidden behind curtains of rain sweeping up the glen, but then there was the consolation that for every three hundred feet of height there should be a drop of one degree in the temperature. It would be snowing up there (God help the Mountain Rescue team if they had to go out tonight!) and if the thaws and frosts followed as they should, we would have all the alpine conditions we wanted.

Johnnie was often in Fort William at weekends but we seldom climbed together, as he was with the Mountain Rescue team. I had joined the civilian team, as much to meet people as to be of assistance, but the Fort William climbers preferred to ski and most of the time I walked alone.

As the winter wore on the snow hardened. Indeed, one misty Sunday morning, coming up the easy incline leading to the summit of Aonach Beag, I struck the toughest snow ice I had experienced until then (but often since, above four thousand feet). The long, swelling ridge was almost level, yet I had to cut steps – almost on all-fours, doubtless presenting an amusing spectacle to George Dwyer who had a party of novices in the corrie below. Then the mist came down and I had to proceed on a bearing. It was a strange mountain to me, but I knew there was a cliff beyond the summit cairn, which I was approaching at right angles, so I moved warily as the ground levelled off. But there was no sign of a cairn; every rock and stone was plastered with snow. I moved in a world devoid of any object on which to focus, and suddenly I stopped, uneasy and vaguely aware of emptiness ahead. As I waited I caught a movement – out of the tail of my eye, more felt than saw – the mist lifting . . . lifting out of space, and I knew that I was on the lip of the cliff. The cornice was so big I had no way of judging its size. I retreated in my own footsteps until I thought it safe to turn at right angles and head for the bealach between Aonach Beag and Aonach Mor on a compass bearing. The cloud lifted as I cut steps down to the col and when I was on the slope of Aonach Mor, and looked back, I saw the biggest cornice I had seen outside the Alps. I must have been standing right on its edge.

Before the snow became hard we did Tower Ridge. It was the first time I had climbed on the north-east face since I did the North-East Buttress with Ian in the rain. I knew all about the difficulties of Ben Nevis in winter – I had read Bill Murray's *Mountaineering in Scotland* – but I wasn't prepared for the reality of the close-up view that Sunday morning.

The great ridges running down into the corrie were plastered with snow; every ledge – even the walls and overhangs higher up – were white. It was awe-inspiring. I felt I would never have the courage – nor the experience – to lead on this face in winter.

We started on the ridge at midday – three of us; Jack Emmerson, an experienced climber also from RAF, Kinloss, Johnnie and myself. We found the snow in very poor condition and treated it gently all the way, expecting it to slide off the ledges at any moment. It was banked high and, being as soft as flour, kept us in an agony of tension.

We climbed slowly, and as the afternoon wore on and the shadows deepened in the corries, low cloud came rolling in from the sea and mist streamers played about the crest. Occasionally the wind would drive windows through it and there would be glimpses of white buttresses against a clear sky, or the dazzling summit of Carn Mor Dearg across the glen, drawing the last of the sun. And suddenly, through one of these rifts, we saw a lonely figure glissading down the long slope below the summit, skimming down the snowfields like a bird.

By six o'clock the Great Tower loomed above us, snow-covered and looking very hard. The cold began to make itself felt : a little wind insinuating itself through our windproofs. We were all feeling tired by now. For six hours we had been climbing on the crest of the ridge, for the most part on unstable snow, and the exposure on either side was sensational. I didn't feel normal physical fatigue, but a more subtle, mental exhaustion. As I paid out Johnnie's rope along the Eastern Traverse I stared, not at him, but at the slabs hundreds of feet below in Observatory Gully, and as I stared, they dilated and contracted like the eyes of a sleepy cat. I was very close to sleep myself.

When my turn came to follow along the traverse above the moving slabs I was most unhappy. The snow was banked high and loose, I could find no anchorage for my pick on the wall above, and I wished we were on the other side of the tower where the exposure was equally severe but the floor of the corrie looked softer : full of deep snow and moonlight . . .

At the end of the traverse we stood below the start of the summer route to the top of the tower – no rock showed today, only what appeared to be great blocks of snow piled vertically on top of each other.

Johnnie struck down to the left to find an easier way to approach Tower Gap (it's there, but we didn't know the Ben at all well in those days). After a while he came back and we stared at each other. Then Jack plunged down the slope, and I waited, tired and cold, and remembered tales of experienced parties turning back at the Gap. I remembered the seven hours of work behind us on snow like flour, and thought of climbing down it with horror.

Johnnie said he would try the wall above me. At first he tried unaided, then I moved closer to give him a shoulder. Johnnie is six feet tall and built in proportion. He didn't hurt as he was in vibrams, but he was very heavy. Then he lost his hold and all his weight came on me. I stood it for a moment (sinking into the snow like a pony in a bog) and then I subsided gently over my axe. Johnnie showed temperament. He rushed wildly down the snow-slope shouting, 'There *must* be a way ! I will find a way !' in true pioneer fashion. Jack and I looked at each other morosely and let him go. He couldn't go far as he was roped to me, and by the time he came back, nails had succeeded where vibrams had failed and Jack was halfway up the tower.

On top, four thousand feet above sea level, we rested, munching Kendal Mint Cake and peering suspiciously at Tower Gap below us.

It was nine o'clock now, but the moonlight was strong and the weather held. After a while Johnnie climbed down into the Gap and stayed there half an hour trying to get out again on the other side. We couldn't see him, but we heard him working, and muttering to himself.

He came back in the end and I began to gauge the depth of the snow, wondering if there was enough to build an igloo in which to pass the night. But after a while Johnnie returned to the Gap.

The way out of this cleft was a wall where all the holds were buried deep under snow – but about ten feet up was a spike of rock. After a while one of us remembered our W. H. Murray[1] and the possibility of lassoing the spike. The rope caught round the rock at the first attempt – and held – and our difficulties were over.

The party hauled itself up on the tight rope and at the top, with the summit of the Ben within easy reach, I sat on Johnnie's knee and was sick.

We reached our camp in Glen Nevis at one in the morning.

If Tower Ridge had been a great climb, it had had one drawback. I had not led. And, remembering its difficulties, I was glad. I had been too tired and too frightened. But I began to wonder if the long waits and the tension of always watching, never participating, hadn't contributed towards this fatigue. Surely I'd have been better if I could have done some of the work?

I begged Johnnie to take another day off, to climb alone with me on the Ben when we could lead through. But he had been having cartilage trouble in his knee lately, and suddenly it became so painful that he was admitted to hospital in Inverness to undergo an operation.

Monday was my free afternoon. I visited him every week, hitch-hiking the seventy miles or so up the Great Glen in the afternoon and returning the same way through the night. There was a bus back, but if I didn't catch it I could have more time with Johnnie.

Hitching home was a precarious business. There was very little

1. An authority on mountaineering in Scotland.

traffic late at night; most people were scared of picking me up, anyway.

The first time that I visited the hospital, I didn't leave Inverness until about nine o'clock, and at midnight I was still plodding down the side of Loch Ness, in a night so dark that, with no torch and no white line, I was constantly bumping into the fence at the side of the road.

I walked well over twenty miles that night. Unused to tarmac, I was blistered and unutterably bored. Had I been carrying a sleeping bag I would have bedded down anywhere, but it was freezing hard and I had to keep walking. I plodded grimly past the buildings of the hydro-electric scheme at Invergarry, and – walking down Loch Lochyside much later – had just reflected that, at this rate, I could be home at breakfast time ready to start work, when I saw the lights of a car in the sky. This was about three-thirty in the morning. It never occurred to me that the car might not stop.

It slowed down as it passed me and halted a short distance away. As I limped towards it, I could see the driver – silhouetted against his own lights – lean across the passenger seat to do something to the window.

I leaned on the glass, which had been rolled down a few inches, and talked – unnecessarily it seemed to me – aching to sit down. I could feel the waves of warmth flowing out from the car.

When the man seemed satisfied he let me in. He was the South African manager of the hydro-electric scheme and he had been working late. He was a powerful-looking man, sympathetic when he heard my story, and amusing. He told me he had had the deepest suspicions of me when I thumbed him, and had wedged the window so that I could lower it no farther while I explained myself. He thought I might be a decoy for a gang. Although he lodged several miles north of Spean Bridge, he went thirty miles out of his way to take me home. Butter was rationed at the time. On my next run to Spean, I took him a pound. After tense and muffled hammering at his window, I managed to rouse my land-lord, who seemed not unduly upset. I expect he was used to me by then.

*

With Johnnie in hospital, I languished for a time, trotting alone and fast around the 'other' peaks, the ones usually left out by the climber: Beinn a Bheithir, Gulvain, all the peaks of the Mamore Forest. I started timing myself on thousand-foot snow-slopes, and breaking my records the following weekend. And in easy gullies, secure from prying eyes, I practised glissading – of which I was inordinately afraid.

Living in Fort William was a doctor who was also a member of the Scottish Mountaineering Club – John Berkeley. He and his wife were very hospitable, giving me hot baths (there was no hot water in my digs) and lending me books. John had, at one time, been in charge of the RAF Mountain Rescue team at West Freugh, so we had much in common. He agreed to climb with me on one of his free Sundays. At our first attempt we were foiled by a member of the Alpine Climbing Group who made a sensational descent of Comb Gully very fast, and we ended the day carrying him down to Fort William with a broken neck. (He recovered and was none the worse except that he had to wear a plastic collar for some time.) Later we made another attempt, John taking the precaution of warning me that he might be off-form since he seldom had time for climbing nowadays.

The sun was blazing that lovely morning when we came up through the bogs of the lower Allt a Mhuilinn; once or twice a breeze moved in the glen and we caught the raw, exciting smell of snow. It reminded me of the Alps, and the Ben itself was a big snow mountain, with its great rock walls below the icy ridges and the sky dark and clear above the upper cliffs. Observatory Ridge, from a distance, seemed to be clear of snow for the first five hundred feet: the steepest section, then came a line of snow arêtes rising to the summit – about a thousand feet of climbing in all. It was long and it was steep, and it hadn't been climbed this winter.

I followed John up the snowfields towards the foot of the climb. It was like picking someone out in a crowd, and approaching them. Everyone else merges, superfluous, into the background, and so, as our ridge loomed to meet us, the rest of the mountain dropped back, faded, and the climb became our own immediate world.

That first five hundred feet was clear of snow but interspersed with ice. We had started happily, unroped (John said it would go anywhere), then, after a hundred feet, the angle steepened, the ice increased and the holds became, very suddenly, quite inadequate.

John was just above me, pondering, with his boots a few feet from my face, while I waited uncomfortably on two small footholds. I glanced below and realized to the full the insecurity of our position. I suggested that this was the place where we should rope. Unfortunately there were no belays and our only piton was in my pocket. One-handed, I managed to extricate it from raisins, Elastoplast, and the cable of my headlamp, and passed it to John on the point of my axe (he was too delicately balanced to stoop). He had some difficulty in extracting the hammer from his sack.

After a few false casts the peg was driven home with a high singing note that was infinitely reassuring. In the meantime I had succeeded in uncoiling the rope with one hand and my teeth. Once we were tied on, and the rope running through the carabiner on the piton, we were imbued with confidence, and John continued up the ice, casually cutting nicks for his edge nails, while – as is often the case – the second reflected that it had been a waste of time to rope.

After the black-ice pitch we led through. My first lead was a polished, holdless crack in a corner, reached by a mantelshelf move. I was pleased when John came up and found it hard.

The interest continued. At this height most of the holds were iced which made the route much more fun – and harder – than under summer conditions. Unfortunately the ridge was out of the sun and a keen breeze was blowing across the face; waiting for the leader to cut his way up the next pitch was cold work. I wondered if we would be forced to abandon the climb, but hoped that, once the first five hundred feet were behind us, we could move faster on the snow.

Once we reached the top of the rocks, and saw what lay ahead, we became light-hearted. Above us was a fine crest of snow, pointed and symmetrical, with drops below and on either side into the flanking corries. But although the exposure was sensational, the climbing was more straightforward than the rock below. However, as I chipped steps up the crest a little below its top, I cut them deep and close together; I wasn't taking any chances where the displaced snow slipped over the edge and fell hundreds of feet before it touched anything.

The snow was perfect: two or three blows of the axe and the steps were big enough to take a boot. I was disappointed that I wasn't leading all the pitches.

We were growing hungry but there was no flat space where we could stop to eat. Ahead of us rose more rock. We would eat on top of that, we said.

John led the rock pitch. It was very hard and time was getting short. Already the shadow of the Ben stretched almost to the summit of Carn Mor Dearg across the glen. When it came to my turn I tried in vain to pull myself up on one hand – the crucial hold was beyond my reach – and, in the end, came up on a tight rope. I passed John and found more snow, with a little flat space with just enough room for us both to sit down. We munched chocolate and raisins and, as our energy returned, we looked at what lay ahead. It was a series of graceful snow arêtes interspersed with rock. We decided to keep well out on the snow where we were less likely to strike ice underneath.

The best part came just after we had eaten. The crest had fined to a point but the wind had curled it over into a miniature cornice, of which the top was about a foot thick. We had to straddle it, but because of the overhang our feet touched nothing on one side, and hung, rather foolishly, in space.

'Do you actually sit on this?' I called to John, firmly belayed at the end of the cornice.

'What else can you do?' he answered, reasonably enough.

He was sitting pretty; he was across.

I lowered myself gently on to the crest of the wave, deploring every ounce of my inconsiderable weight. But John had sat on it . . . perhaps he had weakened it and my weight would be the last straw. I shuffled along, unaware and uncaring of the indignity of my position. My left foot dangled above several hundred feet of air.

The cornice held. My left foot found a purchase. I was across.

We rested for a moment, looking back down the climb. I thought, seeing our steps meandering up the arêtes, that the next people would be lucky, with the track already cut for them. And then I thought that fresh snow would come and obliterate the route and the next comers would find virgin snow again. And, thinking about other people, we realized that there were climbers far below. We could see a little group of them standing outside the hut, staring upwards. We knew from their stillness that they were watching us. We envied them their cups of tea in the hut. I had been eating a fine, salty goat's cheese, rather to excess, and was suffering from a raging thirst which ice splinters did nothing to satisfy. But our envy wasn't as strong as our satisfaction, and a smug little devil in me grinned at the thought of those below, sitting in the warm hut, eating and discussing their day while above, others were still climbing up the cold cliffs of evening.

As we went, the moon rose above the summit plateau and shone on the great bulk of Tower Ridge across the corrie. We were in shadow but there was enough reflected light by which to work, although we had to peer myopically at our steps to see if we had cut them deep enough to take a boot.

We came to a point where it was possible to traverse into Zero Gully on our left, but no sooner had we reached it when we realized that there was ice about a hundred feet above.

I led to the foot of the pitch and brought John up to me. He was feeling tired but he tackled the ice powerfully enough. Shivering and impatient, I was bombarded by chips and, once, a lump of rock. But he didn't take long. Scarcely had I had time to feel cold when I heard him shout, 'OK. Come on!'

While I led the next pitch, straight up the gully, he was able to have a rest, except for paying out my rope, but when he came up to me again, he was feeling ill. However, he insisted on leading through but he had gone only a few feet when he stopped and said he felt faint. I asked if he had put his rope round the axe. He said yes, then turned and sat down. I watched and waited, unable to do anything. After a while he brought me up to him. We ate some chocolate and I pressed on.

There were three or four hundred feet left to do. It wasn't very steep, but quite steep enough. If I came off and John didn't hold me, we would fall all of a thousand feet. I thought of this, but I didn't think I would slip. I hoped to finish the climb in four pitches. I felt rather surprised that I should be feeling so fresh. My arms were tired, of course, and I did wonder if my mind was tired without my knowing. Perhaps my apparent freshness was a psychological reaction to John's fatigue (a complete reversal of my relationship with the two men on Tower Ridge). Giving myself the benefit of the doubt, I went slowly and methodically, cleaning out the steps properly, and moving up with the pick in the snow, taking all precautions against a slip. It was a strong temptation to cut smaller steps and move quickly, but I resisted it, even then smiling at my own caution.

Although at the last halt I had estimated that a few hundred feet would see us clear of the gully, now imagination took a hand – and tricks of light – and the skyline would appear within reach of the next rope's length, and then a thousand feet away.

The moon was shining straight down the gully, dazzling me. I couldn't see if the glitter came from snow crust or ice. I hoped it wasn't the latter; even cutting up the snow was hard work.

As I cut and climbed I felt that I was being watched. There was a huge, upright boulder leaning over the gully – a monstrous thing about ten feet high, and partly snow-covered. It was horribly like a presence, inclined over the edge, watching. I would glimpse it out of the corner of my eye, and although a moment before I had identified it as a rock, I would be startled again.

I continued to cut huge steps, partly for John's boots, but mostly for my own comfort. I was needing to rest quite often now, and it was comfortable to know that, if my arms tired suddenly, my feet, and not merely my toes, would be on good holds. Besides, it was difficult to see what I was doing with the light in my eyes, and if I missed a stroke, I stood more chance of retaining my balance if my feet were firmly planted.

At the end of the hundred-foot run-outs I dug big buckets in the slope for both myself and John.

The Spinning Chorus from *The Flying Dutchman* was going through my head. There was himself sailing endlessly round the world, and here was I cutting steps into eternity – but I didn't mind. The moonlight and the snow, my glittering axe and John waiting patient and silent below were all my world, and I felt that if the gully went on for a thousand feet – with ice pitches – I could still do it.

I *must* have been tired.

The snow softened – and the gully fanned out suddenly at an easier angle. Thirty feet above me, at the edge of the fan, there was the suspicion of a cornice. We were at the top.

I belayed. John came through and I watched him tensely. It wasn't until I saw him stand erect against the sky and walk away, and disappear, that I relaxed. He shouted to me that he was ready, and in a few moments I was out of the gully and on level ground.

We lay flat on our backs in the snow and interrupted each other.

'I thought it was never going to end . . .'

'Ice would have been the last straw . . .'

'. . . lack of food and off-form . . .'

'My arms are tired . . .'

'I've strained my shoulder.'

'It's a *wonderful* climb !'

It was nine o'clock. We had taken nine and a half hours from the foot of the ridge.

The wind came sweeping up the Ben and we shivered. We picked up the rope and our axes and hurried into the lee of the old observatory to eat some more chocolate and raisins.

Southward of us all the mountains of the Mamore Forest were wreathed in mist trails, but west and north the peaks were clear. Over four thousand feet below us we could see the lights of a boat moored on Loch Linnhe, and the lights of the town. I thought of my bed and hot soup a little wistfully, and we started down.

On the bealach we saw the white hare. I had seen her after Tower Ridge, and I was to see her again, many times, but only after climbs, never before.

*

It was spring now and there were catkins in the hedgerows. The snowline was retreating and the start of my first professional season approached. As I had hoped, once I had a guide's certificate, the Mountaineering Association had agreed to employ me full time. I was booked to run courses in the Lake District and on Skye from April until October. There was no guarantee of employment; if courses were cancelled through lack of numbers, I received no fee, but in this event, I hoped to find private clients at short notice.

Four months ago, when I learnt that soon I would be financially secure, I had been wild with elation, and all through the winter I had climbed with an end in view: to improve my technique and my confidence. Reason told me that Observatory Ridge had proved one and my solo ridge walks the other. But, at the penultimate moment, reason deserted me and I was terrified!

It is difficult now to remember why I was so frightened. Johnnie had an answer for every excuse when I told him of my nightmares, but still the dread of disaster persisted. I imagined my clients demanding to be taken up Very Severes in bad weather when I would be in nails (I had difficulty *following* Very Severes in nails), I imagined myself losing the courses in rain and mist, but the picture which haunted me, sleeping and waking, was an accident: not to me – to a client. Any accident would be my fault. I saw the Coroner, the Mountaineering Association, the whole climbing world – and the Press – as a hawk-eyed enemy waiting to pounce. I knew that, already, there was hostility towards me in certain quarters, some from men who had been refused guides' certificates, some from local people who were genuinely mystified concerning my qualifications to guide in the mountains they could see from their kitchen windows.

When George Dwyer asked me to take Monica Jackson (of the first Women's Himalayan Expedition) for a day in Glencoe because he was fully booked, I leant over backwards to be cautious. Instead of taking her on a sensible climb like Crowberry Ridge (most of the snow had gone) I took her up Chasm North Wall, thinking it would be easy. I had great difficulty keeping to the route, and when I did find it neither of us thought it worth doing. But I finished the day without an accident and Monica asked me for three days in the summer. With my first professional day behind me (and I had found the way down off the Buachaille in mist without a false cast) a ray – a very small ray – of light appeared in the threatening clouds ahead.

16. First Professional Season

I left Fort William in April and spent the Easter holidays with Sheena in Sussex. I was very relieved to hear her talk about her new school with obvious enjoyment. Life became less complicated. All I had to do now was make enough money to pay school fees three times a year. These seemed exorbitant, but I had the comforting thought that if anything happened to me – such as temporary illness or unemployment – she was happy and safe. By the time I was on the road north again, heading for Langdale, I was feeling, if not exactly confident, at least a little aggressive towards the Enemy watching for that first slip.

I hitched north. I couldn't afford to go by train because my salary included expenses and I must keep these to a minimum. By nightfall that first evening I had reached Windermere. The last bus had left for Ambleside so I walked down to the shore and found a patch of grass where I could lie and listen to the ripples a few feet away. It was a clear, starlit night with no wind. After a while I became aware of something moving in the bushes.

I stared at the dark tangle of brambles until my eyes ached, wondering when this nasty man (who had, obviously, been very close when I undressed) would leap out on me. But the rustling continued and no one came. Reluctantly, I crawled out of the bag and crept across the grass to the bushes. In the light of my torch I found a hedgehog grubbing for worms.

I lay on my back and stared at the stars and remembered another night, years ago, when I came to an old straw stack on the Cornish cliffs, and thought a tramp had staked his claim before me, for the straw rustled without visible agency, and closer inspection showed that it *moved*. It was full of rats. I had been too tired to move on, so I pulled the drawstring of my sleeping bag over my head, and hoped they wouldn't eat their way through the down. They left me alone, but ate a neat hole in my rucksack and left nothing of my food but crumbs.

*

Langdale was basking in spring sunshine when I arrived the following morning. The first course was not due to start for another week, and my object in coming early was to familiarize myself with the easier climbs in the district. I pitched my tent in a field full of new lambs and celandines and went out to look for a climbing partner.

I met a girl called Maureen, six feet tall and correspondingly strong. The first day was lovely: dry, with chance sunlight and cloud shadows racing across the fells. We went to Scout Crag because I wanted to assess its qualities as a nursery cliff, and did a few routes before moving up to Pavey Ark.

We scrambled up Jack's Rake to the foot of Rake End Chimney and sat there, idly contemplating the climb. I had put on my spectacles in order to see the cliff better, and out of the tail of my eye, caught a movement on the wall of the gully below. There was a sheep on a tiny ledge about forty feet above the bed of the gully.

My heart sank. It is quite impossible for me to abandon any animal in difficulties. If I find a wounded bird I must take it home or kill it. If a sheep is stranded on a cliff it must be rescued. And here we were, just the two of us, with one rope. It meant going down to the hotel and rousing Sid Cross to action or doing it ourselves. The disadvantage of the latter course was that two ropes were necessary to be safe (and always I wanted to be *safe*): one for the sheep and one for the rescuer. We stared at the sheep gloomily, willing it to do something: to jump up the rocky rake by which it had plainly descended, or to jump off and take the decision out of our hands.

The sheep lay down, stood up, tottered, and lay down again. It was obvious it had been there a long time. Its little ledge was bare of grass.

We would do our climb, we said, and descend again. Perhaps by then – disregarding the length of time the ewe had been marooned – something would have happened.

We did the climb, hurriedly and preoccupied. Back on Jack's Rake we stared at her again. She was still there.

We decided that Maureen should tie on to the middle of the rope, belay at the top of the gully wall, and haul us both up: the sheep and me.

Rather foolishly I started climbing up the gully before she was in position and found myself perched, delicately, on a steep slab with a tiny excrescence for one foot, nothing for the other, and my hands resting lightly on the rock above. I yelled for the rope and Maureen retorted that I would just have to wait. I waited, trembling, until the two ends came down, and I could tie on.

It was something like forty feet to the ledge which was roughly triangular in shape. The easiest line – and easy only in comparison, for I was on a tight rope all the time; it was too hard to *climb* – went up to one side of the ledge, with the result, of course, that by the time I'd pulled myself level with the lip, the sheep, instead of moving to the back of the haven, was six feet away at the other end, stamping her feet and threatening to jump off if I moved another inch.

I clung to the ledge, motionless and silent, while Maureen – out of sight some distance above – asked petulantly what was keeping me. I couldn't shout for fear of startling the sheep so I told her in a gentle, reassuring monotone. I told her that if I could persuade the ewe into the back of the haven, I could leap on her. I also told her that the ledge sloped outward and was filthy with mud and sheep droppings; that the ewe looked very big, and that when I yelled she was to hold me as tight as possible, but to leave the other rope free so that I could secure the sheep.

I stopped talking to Maureen and addressed myself to the sheep. She flared her nostrils at me and twitched her ears. After five minutes of my steady monologue she retreated calmly into the back of the haven. I mantelshelfed on to the ledge and threw myself on top of her.

I was quite determined to get her on her back. She was equally determined to stay upright. We fought like a couple of jungle beasts, and in the middle of it I was horrified to realize that we were sliding towards the edge. I had yelled to Maureen as I pounced, but things had happened so quickly – and nylon is so elastic – that my rope was not yet tight. It didn't tighten until we were literally on the brink. When the pull came on my waist, I was dragged back from the edge, lost my footing, and fell. The sheep fell on top of me; I had my arms round her waist, my fingers deep in the wool, when I saw the spare rope disappearing up the wall. As I yelled for this to come back, the sheep got one hoof free, stood up, and planted it in my mouth.

This was the last straw. With a convulsive heave I turned over and got on top of her. We lay there, panting, glaring at each other.

I managed to work a sling round her head and under her front legs. There was a knot in the end of the spare rope, and I clipped her on with a carabiner, and stood up, retaining a tight hold on the rope. I shouted to Maureen that I was going to try to drive the ewe up the rocky rake at the side of the ledge and both ropes were to be kept very tight. I let the sheep stand up, showed her the rake, gave her a word of encouragement, and threw her at it.

She *did* try; she got up a few feet and then, despite the tight rope, came rolling back into my arms.

I kept her pinned on her back, and knelt beside her, studying the rock. Above the haven, and directly below Maureen, was an overhang. It wasn't a very big one, and I suggested that she should try to pull us both up at the same time.

When we were ready she started to pull. She was very strong. The sheep and I rose gently up the rock, my feet scrabbling for holds, while the sheep pretended to be dead and went completely limp. But still we rose, myself clutching the rope with one hand, pushing the sheep above my head with the other. When Maureen paused for a second the sheep sat on my head. After we'd risen about ten feet I emerged from the wool (which smelt abominably) and screamed to Maureen to relax. The sheep was in an inverted diving position with its front legs vertically above its head, and the sling just caught round its front hooves.

Maureen took her orders literally. She relaxed, and the sheep came back into my arms. We went down to the ledge again where I fastened another sling round the other end (I had tried to do this before, but the sheep had been too fat, then).

Up we went again, as far as the overhang where the sheep stuck, and started to make horrible noises. Maureen hauled me to the top and I peered down the overhang. The ewe was twirling now, and as her head came out from the rock, we heaved together. She came up like a fish, and, directly she felt the grass, she was on her feet. We threw ourselves on her (for we weren't off the cliff yet) and lay there in a tangle of limbs and wool and legs until we had recovered sufficiently to lead her off the cliff.

It was not until several sheep rescues later that I learnt the advisability of taking sheep down to the farm after they have been rescued, so that they can be confined in a small space and fed slowly, otherwise they will kill themselves after their long period of starvation.

We finished the day with an ascent of Cook's Tour, then trotted down to the Old Dungeon Ghyll, full of our rescue, to spend the night like the Ancient Mariner, pinning people in corners of the bar and telling them all about it. No one believed us, although they admitted we had been very close to sheep because of the smell.

*

At the end of the week I met my first course. They were four young men all of whom had previous experience of rock climbing. I tried to appear cool and business-like, but now that I was confronted with the situation after weeks of brooding over it, there was an element of hysteria in my welcome. Despite the fact that I had to pass or fail them at the end of a fortnight, I was the one on trial.

On that first morning I took them up Middlefell Buttress; five of us, all on one rope. It was slow, cold and boring. They climbed faster than I did, surrounded with an almost visible aura of masculine resentment. So I took them to Gwynne's Chimney on Pavey Ark, and as they struggled and sweated in that smooth cleft, with sparks flying from their nails, and me waiting at the top with a taut rope and a turn round my wrist, I knew that I had won. The atmosphere – when we were all together again – was clean and relaxed. They could look me in the eye and say,

'Have we got any more like that? I thought it was going to be easy when you went up it . . .'

And I could laugh and say, 'You'll be leading it by the end of the week.'

I was no longer a woman with a reputation, but an instructor with a technique superior to theirs, and now we could settle down to work.

I took them to Bowfell Buttress – not five on a rope this time, but in two parties. The great difficulty of these courses was that there was only one leader: myself. When Johnnie ran Mountain Rescue courses with pupils who were more experienced generally than mine, he never had more than two novices to one instructor. I might, after the first week of an Intermediate course, weed out another leader, perhaps two, who could take the strong seconds up a Difficult, even a Very Difficult, but I was always very wary of letting people lead, and the parties kept close, on parallel climbs, with myself tense and watchful and almost unaware of my own climb, all eyes for the other two leaders.

During the first few days, however, I was extremely cautious, with the result that the students received only half the rock climbing I thought they should have. When we went to Bowfell Buttress I sent two people on a walk to the summit by way of Brown Ghyll and Crinkle Crags while I took the other two straight to the cliff and climbed. We met on the top and the two who had climbed reversed the walk while I led the others up the Buttress.

By the second day of the course I had recovered my sense of proportion and was astonished when I remembered my fears of the last few weeks. Certainly the work was extremely exacting, but it was, on the whole, fun. I forgot the Enemy watching for a slip and revelled in the easier classics in Langdale. The two basic moods on a climb were, first, delight while I was actually climbing – perhaps tempered a little by the necessity to tell a dreaming second to watch me and not the view – and then the sense of confidence and responsibility as my seconds followed when I approved their style and neat movements; and I saw, with amused surprise, that they had watched me carefully. Usually I had no doubt that they were better than the day before.

It was capricious weather. The day might be spent in the hotel doing theory with the rain curtains drifting down the dale, and the night clutching the tent poles as the gales came roaring down on me, shaking and snatching at the canvas, while the guy ropes strained and slackened – and the stream rose – and finally I slept from sheer exhaustion. One night mine was the only tent left standing. Even the proper mountain tents were blown away and one of the caravans behind the farm was tossed over like a doll's house.

In contrast there were hot still days on Gimmer when, at lunch time, we sunbathed at the foot of the cliff; or (the same place) in mist when Oliverson's seemed as exposed as a climb on Scafell, and another day – so hot that we were too lazy to tramp all the way to Pavey Ark, but turned aside and, in shirt sleeves and plimsolls, ran up and down all the little routes on Tarn Crag.

Despite the pleasure I was taking in the climbing, I had been looking forward to the end of this course, for I was to go to Skye for six weeks, and Johnnie was in Kinloss. But he was posted suddenly to Topcliffe in Yorkshire, and we had only one day together in Langdale before I left for Scotland. I wasn't very miserable. My days were so full now that I had no time for anything else but climbing; after I had cooked my supper at night and written up the day's report, I was ready for bed. It was very different from being warden at the youth hostel where I had far too much time in which to wait for Johnnie and wonder why he didn't come.

My courses on Skye were not to start for three weeks; until then I was fully booked with private clients. I travelled north with the best of my students from the Langdale course. He was waiting to do his National Service, and had engaged me for a further week.

We broke our journey at Fort William, and I took him up Tower Ridge in two and a half hours. There was no snow left except in the last gully before the summit plateau. The rock was bare and nail-scratched and very easy. I told him about our great climb here back in the winter and pointed out the gap where Johnnie had worked for so long in the moonlight, trying to find a way up the other side. Even I found it unbelievable that here, where we scrambled gaily out of the gap, I had wondered if we would survive the night if we had to bivouac, and – where I had crept, terrified, along the unstable snow of the Eastern Traverse – now we walked casually, carrying coils.

From Fort William we headed west, along the Road to the Isles, crossed to Portree by steamer, and came at last, in the dusk, to Glen Brittle and the Black Cuillin.

It was a fine cold evening with the wind in the north-east. The peaks were clear as a cardboard stage set; the old, familiar outlines coming into view as we topped the rise out of Carbost. There was Waterpipe Gully cleaving the pyramid of Sgurr an Fheadain with memories of Dave Thomas and myself climbing in its rotten depths where holds came away in the hands to reveal yet more unstable rock behind, and the Inaccessible Pinnacle with memories of mist on every side: above, below, behind. And that reminded me of the traverse when we had been up there for forty hours. There was the bealach where we slept on the scree and the hail piled up round the mouth of the sleeping bag ...

The incongruous bulk of the old wooden youth hostel loomed ahead and, with a wary eye on the sky and remembering those gale-swept nights in the tent in Langdale, I was deeply thankful that, for the next six weeks, I would not be camping. The peaks were very clear, too clear, but one felt no uneasiness about the weather if one slept under a roof, with a good fire to dry clothes and cook food.

Despite the abnormal clarity of that evening the weather didn't break completely. There were showers during that first week but we climbed almost every day. We did nothing eventful and had no excitement, and my client disappointed me by saying that he thought Scottish climbing dull and the walks to the foot of the cliffs far too long. My next client was very different. He was a dentist from Shropshire, a windfall in that he had come north to climb with Jim Cameron, the Coniston guide, but Jim, on his way to Skye, had fallen in Clachaig Gully and was now in Fort William hospital. He had recommended me to the dentist.

Mr Bellamy took over so closely from my other client that they overlapped and one day I had them together on Sron na Ciche. I was elated with the trade and began to think that now, with school fees paid, a debt to my mother honoured, and money still rolling in, I could go to the Alps in August. I wrote jubilantly to Johnnie making plans for Chamonix.

My second day with Mr Bellamy was a complete fiasco. I had become quite confident in myself as a guide, and I lost my client in Coire Lagan.

I knew that the Black Cuillin were magnetic in places so I never carried a compass; it was quite useless. I thought I knew Coire Lagan, too, and this day we intended to do Collie's Route on Sgurr Alasdair. We walked into mist at about a thousand feet and continued, following the track up into the corrie. We negotiated the *roches moutonnées* below the lip of the upper corrie, and then started to traverse screes diagonally upwards to the foot of Alasdair.

Mr Bellamy was a happy little man, enjoying everything: views, company, climbs, walks – even that long walk up shifting scree to the foot of Collie's. He had great faith in his guide, too, so that when, to my astonishment, we came out on a ridge at the top of the scree (when we should have been at the foot of a cliff, hundreds of feet below any ridge) and I, after a discreet mental calculation, identified it as a point on the south-west ridge of Sgurr Sgumain, he accepted it and turned meekly to start the long, diagonal descent to Collie's.

We came to a cairn at the foot of a cliff. Below we could hear the sound of a fair-sized stream. That, I told him, was the burn running into Coire Lagan. He looked at me with admiration. We roped up.

Suddenly the mist shifted and began to disperse. I looked down the slope and saw the stream and the lochan. Everything seemed the wrong way round. The stream was running out of the lake, not into it.

We were on the Lagan Buttress of Sgurr Dearg. Collie's and Alasdair were opposite, on the other side of the corrie. Since the moment I identified Bealach Coire Lagan as the south-west ridge of Sgumain I had been a hundred and eighty degrees out in my calculations.

The only emotion Mr Bellamy showed was concern that I should feel so humiliated. Determined that he should climb, I took him up Sgumain. We went slowly, watching the mist clear from the main ridge, with Sgurr Dearg appearing occasionally above the cloud banks and looking twenty thousand feet high.

He didn't seem disappointed with his day; he was the kind of man who can be happy in the mountains in any circumstances, but I had the sneaking feeling that I was not giving him his money's worth. However, I quieted my conscience on the last day when, with a heat wave starting, we climbed on Sron na Ciche in shorts and shirt-sleeves, and the rock was like sandpaper. We reached the Cioch by way of the Cioch West, and finished the day with Archer Thomson's route on the Upper Buttress. I had never been on this climb before; we both thought it was a delightful little route. It is only a Difficult and the holds are enormous – but when you look down, you seem to be suspended in space above the plunging depths of the Cioch Gully. We came racing down the screes of the Alasdair stone shoot where the dust rose in clouds behind us and the sun beat relentlessly as in a desert, and we cooled off by the limpid water of the lochan.

The heat wave continued. My engagement ended and Mr Bellamy drove me south to Glencoe where I was due to climb with Monica Jackson. And how we climbed ! Not hard stuff, nothing more than Very Difficult, but we took full advantage of that glorious weather, out early in the morning and coming home in the dusk.

The first climb was Crowberry Ridge. Then I wanted to do something new, and what appealed to me most was that great west face of the Aonach Dubh which is such an obvious feature of Glencoe as seen from Ballachulish ferry: an elephant-grey wall supported by powerful buttresses and seamed with gullies. Monica was in favour of this face – in that good weather no day could go wrong – and I think she felt, too, that this formidable wall would repay exploration.

We set off early one morning from Achtriochtan, watched with disapproval by an elderly gentleman in a deerstalker, for nowadays I climbed in French shorts and an old and tattered lace blouse. I felt hostile eyes boring into my back as we went through the farmyard.

There was little wind that day, and none at all on the west face. On a hot June day time goes slowly, and there was no hurry; we had the whole day and evening before us. We explored at our leisure, wandering across the face towards the high amphitheatre in its centre, up a few pitches of a buttress ('B' Buttress, I think) and along a rake where the unclimbed gullies overhung us – and dropped away below – and into the amphitheatre where strange towers rose out of the sloping scree and we said how impressive it must be in mist. Then, by way of easy gullies, gradually steepening until we had to use the rope, where the sun beat into the dry and stony rifts and Monica (who had been brought up there) said it was as hot as India. I remember, on the last pitches of the last gully, looking up and seeing a tuft of dead grass shaking in the breeze on top, and pointing it out to Monica in encouragement.

It was early afternoon when we came out of the gully. There were nine hours of daylight before us and already the breeze was reviving our parched and sweating bodies.

We moved up slowly to the summit of the Aonach Dubh and then, unwilling to go down with all those grey mountains swimming in the haze around us, we tramped the circuit of the Lost Glen, reversing my walk of the winter, walking through the old snowdrifts to cool our feet, myself remembering the mist and the blizzard and cutting steps down off Stob Coire nan Lochan.

The following day we explored again; this time the steep little cliff on the east side of the Aonach Dubh. The sun still shone in a cloudless sky, and I slept shamelessly after lunch until Monica roused me to climb again. I climbed in a hazy dream until I was brought up short by a hard move, when I reflected ruefully that heat and dryness are no excuse for lack of concentration, and, with an effort, brought my mind back to the rock.

That evening we reached the road without incident and then, suddenly, fatigue overcame us, and we sat down on the bank, desperately in need of a lift to take us the last few miles to the hut. But when the first car stopped and asked if we were going to Kingshouse we said yes spontaneously, and so, an hour and two drinks later, we started the last stage across the moor, staggering a little, drunk with heat and fatigue (not with two beers) and very content.

Monica left for London the next day and I travelled, by easy stages, back to Skye. There was a haze of bluebells in the woods now, and the dream-like quality of the heat wave persisted. I stopped in Fort William to visit Jim Cameron and felt rather guilty, walking into the hospital, very brown and fit and relaxed, and there was Jim, looking rather ill and shaken, in a dressing gown and slippers, listening enviously to my tales of Skye and Glencoe. A rib had pierced his lung but his spine hadn't been damaged, as was thought when he was first admitted to the hospital. Mr Duff looked tired too; and I felt out of place in Fort William, staying just long enough to visit old friends and see the film of Everest which was showing that evening.

I hitched to Mallaig through miles of flaming rhododendrons, and then caught the bus from Armadale to Broadford where every wood and field was drenched with bluebells – and I met a man at

Broadford who had known Collie, Mallory, Irvine and Odell and talked about the old days with a nostalgia that had me almost in tears.

There was a lot of mail waiting for me at the youth hostel, among it a letter from Johnnie saying he was in hospital in Yorkshire with a broken back. He had gone to his parents' home on leave and decided to test – or stretch – an old hemp rope by abseiling on it out of a bedroom window. He put the rope round a bed and leaned out of the window horizontally with his feet on the ledge. The last thing he remembered was seeing the bed move towards him across the floor. Then he was lying on his back on the rockery. He said he would probably be fit for the Alps.

Dazed and appalled, I took the letter to a German doctor who was staying at the hostel and he assured me that a squashed vertebra was not too bad, that Johnnie wouldn't be a permanent cripple. I felt a little better and wrote fourteen pages to him before I went to bed, swearing mildly in my relief that it hadn't been worse, feeling all the time the horror of that moment when the bed started to move across the floor.

There was never any monotony in our lives.

*

The heat wave passed but the weather stayed dry for the first course. This was a Beginners' and we were to make a film for the Mountaineering Association. The cameraman was Norman Keep, the MA treasurer. I had four beginners, two of whom, a Lyons Corner House under-manager called Paul, and an Italian countess, Dorothea Gravina, were already competent on rock. The other two, George and Mary, had no experience. I approached this course with some trepidation. I had heard guides say they wouldn't take Beginners' courses on Skye for higher wages than I was getting – and others said they wouldn't take Beginners' courses in any circumstances. The Cuillin are not suitable for parties of novices with one leader. The climbs are long and difficult to escape from in an emergency : too long to have more than two novices behind you. And if I climbed with two only, I was committed to sending the others for a walk, and 'walks' on the Cuillin are scrambles of a high standard.

The first day I played safe and taught rope work on the boulders in Coire Lagan. With the hope that something had been learnt, I took two of them on the long and easy Amphitheatre Arête in the afternoon, leaving the others, under the leadership of Norman, to traverse the skyline of Coire Lagan. Two people fell off that day and one retreated from Sgurr Thearlaich with an attack of nerves. People falling off was a secondary consideration, since they were roped and with me, but nerves on the ridge was worrying. I decided to keep the party together in future.

The following day the course went into Coire na Banachdich where a fine sweep of rock ran up to the main ridge. We split into two parties, with Paul and Dorothea leading through on a route parallel to mine, following a line which I picked out as we climbed – a very moderate route, well within their limit. I had George and Mary on my rope, and Norman filmed us from an easy gully.

Roped, we went well. It was when we took the rope off that we had trouble. We were coming down the Sron Dearg ridge of Sgurr Dearg, a blunt edge, not particularly exposed, and broad enough to walk along without using our hands. I had the most competent people in front and bringing up the rear. I was in the middle with Mary in front of me and George directly behind. Suddenly aware that the footsteps behind had stopped, I turned and saw George, very white, standing motionless on the crest. He was quite unable to move. (How long had he been looking at the drop and calculating how far he would fall when he slipped?) He stared at me miserably.

The whole caravan had stopped. Quietly I told him to come on, but he couldn't move. I uncoiled the rope and gave him an end. He muttered something about its being no use.

I said confidently, 'If you come off, I shall jump over the other side.'

He said nothing, but when I moved on, carrying coils, he followed, and we had no more bad moments that day.

Such situations, although saved, were very shattering to the one who had the responsibility, and by the last morning I was getting ready to breathe a hefty sigh of relief that the course was over. But Norman wanted to film me climbing, and abseiling off, the Inaccessible Pinnacle. To reach it I gave them one last ridge walk: up Coire na Dorus and over Ghreadaidh and Banachdich. Coming down Sgurr Ghreadaidh the order was the same as it had been on Sron Dearg. I was ignoring the first three, giving all my attention to George who was coming down a steep section of the knife-edge to the level part where I was standing. Below, the cliffs dropped away on either side. Unlike Sron Dearg, this was exposed. Paul and Dorothea had continued past the level section and were about a hundred feet ahead. By a coincidence I looked away from George for a moment, and saw Dorothea leaping back towards me with her arms outstretched and a terrified look on her face. I shouted to the last men to stay where they were – and then I don't remember moving, but it must have been fast because I heard the rocks falling as I scattered the rotten crest off the ridge. When I reached Dorothea, Mary was scrambling back on to the ridge, where she sat down, trembling a little and speechless, her face completely drained of colour.

Fortunately she kept up a running commentary on all her movements and, being a parson's daughter, 'Oh dear,' in sepulchral tones, meant she was at the end of her tether. Dorothea, hearing this, coupled with the sound of a slip, had turned to see Mary clinging to her last handhold. She had raced back, wedged a shoulder and foot under the girl, and levered her back on to the ridge.

I stood there, breathing hard and staring at them. We all looked about a hundred years old. Then I went back for Norman and George.

The day ended with Dorothea and I performing for the film on the Pinnacle. The course ended with my asking Norman – as an officer of the Mountaineering Association – to recommend that, after this season, no more Beginners' courses should be held on Skye.

Looking back on that first course, it seems full of harrowing incidents. Perhaps I should have picked easier sections of the ridge for walks, but where on the Black Cuillin is there a day's walk which is perfectly safe?

Whether I was more cautious with the next course or that they were, in general, of a higher standard, is a debatable point, but the second week was less trying; the only casualty being myself, spraining an ankle scree-running, and gashing a foot abseiling – barefooted – into the sea.

It was a large course, eight in all, far more unwieldy than the first – except that, occasionally, people dropped out from fatigue. By now I looked on Coire na Banachdich as my nursery cliff and I had three parties climbing the slabs to the ridge on the first day, while I ran backwards and forwards at their head, picking out the line and the stances, encouraging, supplicating, almost barking, like an anxious sheepdog.

One day, in thick mist, I took all of them to the top of the Cioch,[1] and shivered and waited for hours on the lizard's head while slowly they crawled up beside me until the Cioch was covered with people. The Creag Dhu, coming up the gully ('Here, there's a wee blonde up here . . .'), were amazed and amused at my endless rope, but cheerfully shepherded the van across to the main cliff while I was still bringing the rear up the Cioch Slab. The Creag Dhu soon learnt my identity and watched me surreptitiously in the hostel that night. An Englishwoman guiding on Skye!

We spent an afternoon abseiling on the sea cliffs where the rollers came creaming into the gully below and, if we weren't quick enough disentangling ourselves from the abseil rope, broke over our heads.

The weather was deteriorating rapidly now. For some time I had wanted to sail round to the next loch to the east: Coruisk, and walk back across the ridge, traversing the Dubhs on the way. I kept postponing this trip as the sea was too rough for the boat and gales were sweeping the ridge, and then the last day of that course arrived, and we decided to walk round, and at least see the other loch.

The wind rose steadily, and halfway round the coastal moor, we could see the rain coming in from the west. Two turned back then, but the rest went on, the gale at our backs, until we reached Loch Scavaig and I realized, too late, that the wind had reached such a velocity that it was doubtful if we could fight our way back against it. Of course, the ridge was impossible. So we forded the outlet from Loch Coruisk in a chain. It was roaring in spate, the stepping stones were invisible and the two girls in the party – both small and weighing less than eight stone – were glad of the heavy

1. An enormous projection on the face of the cliff shaped like the head of an iguana. [Author.]

men on either side. And then we walked right round the Cuillin to Sligachan with the wind at our backs. The rain never stopped and my ankle, which I'd sprained the day before, was swollen inside my boot. I came down Glen Sligachan well in the rear, and was as glad to see the roof of the inn as I had been years ago after my forty hours on the ridge.

In the bar we steamed and dripped puddles on the floor, consuming large quantities of spirits until MacRae of Glen Brittle came to fetch us in a specially chartered bus.

*

Now the bad weather clamped down on the island. During the last of the Intermediate courses (each of which lasted two weeks) we didn't have one dry day, except perhaps the first, when we did the skyline of Coire Lagan in a mist which was like a dense, damp blanket. Otherwise it was heavy showers at the best, wet gales at the worst. But we climbed. We had to. It was my work and I was determined that my clients should have their money's worth. At least, I thought, they will have achieved something – will have climbs to look back on in retrospect, even if they don't enjoy them at the time.

No, the actual climbing wasn't enjoyable, although there were a few hours one morning when we snatched the Window Buttress while it was dry, but we weren't to return unscathed: the rain came at us horizontally on Sgurr Dearg. But memorable things happened, as the time we were nearly drowned in Cioch Gully.

Four of us had gone up to Sron na Ciche to do the Amphitheatre Arête. I never discovered the correct way to start this moderate route, but by now I had my own pet start: a scoop to the east of Cioch Gully, and where it crosses the latter, I went right and upwards across smooth slabs to a little chimney. Above this is the start of the Arête.

On this particular day we had passed the foot of Cioch Gully – dry as a bone – and then the rain started, gently at first, and the rocks became greasy, then wet, until – on the slabs below the chimney – it came down in earnest and we climbed through a sheet of water sluicing down the face. Before this started I had told my pupils (I was leading a girl and two competent men followed behind on their own rope) that we had eight hundred feet of climbing to do, and how did they feel? They deplored the wasted energy of that long drag up from Glen Brittle; optimistically they hoped it was only a shower. We went on.

It was a very long and heavy shower. At the foot of the chimney my second confessed that she preferred to retreat. My hands were cold. I guessed that she was numb. We were all very wet. So we retreated to Cioch Gully.

There was a fine waterfall coming down it now but the angle was easy to the top of the last hundred feet. Here the stream leapt over the edge and disappeared.

I belayed in the water and sent the first man over. As he lowered himself the water came up his back until, to our amazement, it broke over his head. I could see nothing then, only the wet nylon running through my hands told me he was moving. Then his head emerged, sleek and gleaming like a seal's, submerged again and the waves broke white above him.

I went down last. As the others descended it had been borne in on me that I would have to do it without a top rope : a disturbing sensation. I lowered myself over the edge, facing out, my feet probing for invisible holds in the water. Behind me the stream mounted until my head was under and I could see nothing. The incessant pounding on my head and shoulders and, above all, the noise, was alarming and muddling. I was forced to move by touch, deliberately making a great effort to go slowly, to refuse to be hurried. Somehow I found the holds, emerged, caught a glimpse of pale, upturned faces, and went under again. It was exhilarating in a way; this was the Ultimate like the thunderstorm when the Grépon rocked, or the stones singing like bullets down the east face of the Strahlhorn – but it was not so dangerous, the holds were there (under the water). One had need only of concentration.

For days at a time the lines above the hostel stove were festooned with drying clothes. It was impossible to bake in the oven; it was crammed with smelling, scorched articles. One night I found a sock in the soup.

The last Skye course ended on a Friday. On the Sunday I must be in Langdale to welcome my next clients. Time was too short to hitch and I came south as fast as possible by train and bus, arriving in Kendal about half past four on the morning of my birthday. Johnnie had said he would meet me as he was on leave, but he wasn't there.

I sat on the steps of a deserted cinema after the coach had gone, and stared at the wet and empty streets. I was tired of rain, I was hungry and cold. It was Sunday; there would be no buses until midday, and probably no traffic on the road. I felt too dispirited to move. Perhaps, if the glass porch of the cinema hadn't leaked, I would have slept on the steps, but rain, splashing down my neck, forced me to shift. I pulled myself together, hoisted the rucksack on my back, and turned towards the river.

I found a timber yard with dry planks stacked under cover. I pulled out my sleeping bag and was asleep almost immediately.

*

During the month that followed I began to feel tired. The bad weather continued and often I was soaked to the skin. I was living in my tent again. Sometimes I managed to dry my clothes at the Holiday Fellowship centre where my students stayed, but often they were damp in the morning. My sleeping bag was never dry. I had no lilo and my groundsheet was starting to tear in places. The field I had camped in previously was under hay, so I found another camp site behind Wall End farm. Unfortunately the only place that I could find which was sheltered from the south-west gales was in one corner, and close to a stream. I watched that stream as it rose a little more every day – and listened to it at night. I wasn't sleeping well, and found it hard to get up in the morning. I didn't feel like cooking when I came home at night, and I lived on a diet of bread and cheese and apples.

The weather was freakish, often clearing on the off-days, so that, taking advantage of it, I climbed with friends instead of relaxing, with the result that I never had an off-day and I became nervous and frightened.

One day, on Crescent Climb: a very easy Moderate on Pavey, I was halfway up, with a lot of rope behind me, and I paused at a place where I had never hesitated before. I pawed at the rock, tried to left and right, and came back to stare hopelessly at the next easy move. I looked down at my second – and at the screes beyond him – and knew that I was very frightened. I went up, but I was trembling when I reached the stance.

I was very, very tired, and the worse I felt, the less I ate. I was caught up in a vicious circle, and very soon I was going to the Alps.

Then one night the stream rose and water seeped through the bank, and my sleeping bag was a sodden mass of feathers. The following day, after bread and butter for breakfast, I managed one climb on Scout Crag before the rain drove us back to the Holiday Fellowship and lectures. That evening, returning late to the tent, I startled a cow who had her head under the canvas. She jumped, and one horn ripped the tent from top to bottom.

I slept very little that night in the wet bag and in the morning I gave up the struggle. There were three days left of the course, three days before I was due for the Alps. Sid Cross and his wife welcomed me at the Old Dungeon Ghyll with open arms. Everyone else had been washed out of their tents; there was no room in the hotel, but that night I slept on a camp bed in the bar.

Next day I moved into the hotel proper. It was pure bliss to eat like a civilized human being again. It was roast beef that first night (roast pork and roast chicken the following nights) and there was a Swiss waiter who came round and asked me if I wanted more. And after everyone had left the dining-room I was still helping myself to biscuits and cheese from the sideboard.

I washed all my clothes and dried everything on the hot water tanks. I bathed and slept in clean sheets in a dry bed. I had enormous packed lunches to take out with me, and, although we did no spectacular climbs, those last three days became, overnight, a holiday, and – when Johnnie arrived on the last night – I was straining at the leash at the thought of the Alps.

17. Chamonix to Borrowdale

Chamonix that year was disappointing. The weather was generally poor, and if it did clear up for a day, we were, almost invariably, caught on the wrong foot: going up to a hut or just coming down. Geoff Roberts made a third to our party: a bad number; I think we had intended originally to have two parties of two, but the fourth had been unable to come, or had gone to the Riviera out of disgust for the Alpine summer . . . Although we were stronger as a three, we were far slower and I had little or no leading, but was merely a passenger again, as on Tower Ridge.

Both the men noticed the heat. Geoff had collapsed in the street the day that Johnnie and I arrived in Chamonix, and Johnnie had not yet recovered from the weeks in hospital. He found the long grinds up to huts extremely laborious.

Chamonix itself, after six years' absence, was a great disappointment. The number of tourists had increased fantastically since 1948; there was a constant roar and bustle in the town, a stink of petrol fumes and long lines of glittering cars. But for the high prices, we thought longingly of Zermatt. Even the huts were crowded, often with parties of walkers who had come up merely for the experience of spending a night beside the glacier. If you were lucky to get a bed, it was almost impossible to sleep. Our first hut was the Albert Premier refuge. We slept, packed like sardines, on the wooden floor of the lobby. There wasn't room for me to lie straight. I had my feet propped against a door. With the earliest risers the guardian went through this door, my foot slid into the gap between it and the post (I was still asleep) and the door was slammed. I woke, screaming. There was no apology. We were all of us, but myself most of all, unfit for anything that day; we loitered resentfully across the glaring glacier, raging against tourists – and wardens who should give priority to climbers. We took pictures and glared at the Aiguille du Chardonnet, hotly disputing the comparative dangers of the routes on its north face.

The following day, at the tail of a great bevy of guided parties, we traversed the mountain, an expedition mainly memorable for our sleepy meander among the great crevasses having lost the way on the glacier, and our new variation to the foot of the Forbes Arête. This by-passed a dull hanging glacier and went up a sub-sidiary ridge for about a thousand feet. Johnnie led in vibrams, Geoff and I coming up the delicate slabs in crampons with a tight rope. Above, I led the ice bosse, not very excited about it as the passage of many people had enlarged the steps to the size of buckets.

Later we did the north-north-east ridge of the Aiguille de l'M – in rain: a route very similar to the long rock climbs at home, except for the boulders chasing us down the Nantillons Glacier on the descent.

There was an abortive attempt on the Aiguille de Peigne (on the Chamonix side) where, reacting painfully to too many bilberry tartlets and cream the night before, I trudged across the Plan de l'Aiguille in misery, through a mild, dark morning, and when the sun came up there were ravures streaked across the brassy sky. The climb proper was reached by way of a long easy couloir: a couloir rendered unbelievably dangerous as a party ahead sent down a cascade of stones. I was very angry and frightened, but all my yelling was to no avail; the bombardment continued.

We lost the way – and a lot of time – which was a good thing since we were foolishly pushing on despite that ominous dawn. But when our difficulties became insurmountable and we had been forced to abseil a hundred feet and everyone was in a bad mood, we retreated – and the rain started while we were still on the little snowslope at the foot of the face.

We glissaded down the hard snow without unroping. I was coming down last, diagonally above Johnnie with about a hundred feet of rope between us. Geoff and he had stopped some distance above the foot of the slope. With nothing below but scree I came down fast, braking hard as I drew level with Johnnie (but still a hundred feet to the side of him). The snow was too hard for me to stop so suddenly, but the rope tightened and round I went in a gigantic pendulum, still on my feet but my legs going so fast the onlookers vowed they were blurred. As I leaned outwards against the rope, brandishing the axe above my head in case I fell, I saw Johnnie goggling, with fascinated eyes, straining on the tight rope, and Geoff, beside him, doubled up in agony.

From the Peigne we went to the Couvercle hut to climb the Moine and the Evêque. There was far more ice about than usual; holds had to be cut in normally easy cracks, and, on the Evêque, a moderate chimney was a ribbon of green ice and the hardest pitch of the climb.

We had intended to spend three weeks in Chamonix, but the weather deteriorated, money was being wasted and enthusiasm ebbing as we ate and wrangled in the town. After a fortnight we cut our losses and came home. We had done four climbs, but something – was it the air of commercialism surrounding Mont Blanc? – had taken the spirit out of the holiday. I didn't keep a journal and produced only one article, and this I shelved on completion since it conveyed no enjoyment to the listener or the reader. No nostalgic memories remain; the one vivid picture is of me galloping round Johnnie on the snowslope like a circus pony.

*

With the autumn the professional season was drawing to a close. I realized that I must find work during the winter to make up for the lack of clients. I wanted a home, too. Mother couldn't continue to have Sheena indefinitely during the holidays, and I wanted to see more of my daughter than those few brief periods during the year. I needed a place which we could look upon as home, and of necessity in the mountains and close to my work.

Since Johnnie was stationed in Yorkshire and my last two courses were in Borrowdale, I started looking for winter work and a cottage in that area. I found temporary lodging in a barn at Rosthwaite (I was still waiting for my tent to be repaired from the ravages of the Wall End cow). The barn belongs to the Weirs of Chapel Farm. All my landlords had been extremely hospitable this season: the Myers at Wall End, Sutherland at Glen Brittle youth hostel – and now the Weirs. Mrs Weir was worried about my sleeping in the barn, but it was far superior to camping, particularly as the weather was typical Lakeland: rain and mist and gales for the most part. There was hay in the barn – and an assortment of animals for company. There was a turkey hen and her chicks, several beautiful white cats and about six kittens. In the byre below was an aggressive bull who spent the night dreaming and sharpening his horns on the side of his stall. The cats welcomed me with open arms, for the nights were getting chilly and my sleeping bag was a boon to them. Every time I turned over in the night kittens flew off in all directions, to come scuttering back immediately with shrill little curses. Sometimes I woke up with the whole mob of them *inside* the bag.

Borrowdale was strange and delightful country to me. I had visited Shepherd's Crag once from Langdale, wandering (with the students) lost and helpless along the foot of the crag – for the trees obscure the first pitches in summer – until an Outward Bound course from Eskdale came to our rescue and pointed out the routes. It was on this occasion that I met John Tyson again. He was the man who had been on the edge of the little group that spent the night on the Zinal Rothorn – the one with the snowdrifts on his shoulders. Now he was one of Eric Shipton's instructors.

I met Shipton himself once or twice. He made no impression directly, probably because we were both shy of each other. What did impress me was the way in which he seemed to sift through the climbing world for the best potential instructors and when he had found them, kept them – and their affection.

The instructors at Outward Bound, Eskdale, were not great tigers; on their off-days they preferred to enjoy Very Severes rather than to compete on Extremes. They were remarkable for their toughness. One might, putting one's tongue slightly to the side for fear of ridicule, call them clean-living. They hardly smoked or drank, and their occasional cider orgies were innocent and almost asexual. And after their innocuous evenings in the Scafell or the Borrowdale, when I was going thankfully to bed having spent the day on streaming cliffs, they – with a similar day behind them – would be moving up the fellsides to bed down under a boulder in the rain.

My own courses struggled through that September, coping with greasy rock, high winds and insufficient leaders. (The only advantage that the Outward Bound instructors seemed to have over me was that they never took more than two novices at a time.)

Sometimes Johnnie came over from Topcliffe and helped out for the day. We took no account of weekends but climbed on Saturday and Sunday if the weather allowed, for often there were days during the week when the gales were so strong we could do nothing but theory. Sometimes I thought about next year and tried to forget the nights when the tent poles bent and quivered before the wind, and the stream rose beside my head. For the moment I was very comfortable. Mrs Weir dried my clothes and gave me hot baths; she would have given me an evening meal had I not dug in my heels and supped among the cats.

September came to an end and the last of the '54 courses. The summer visitors moved out of Mrs Weir's furnished cottage beside the farmhouse and I moved in – at a nominal rent 'to keep the place aired'. I went after work.

I rejected the pencil factory at Keswick and was advised to refuse a job as cowman at a remote farm. For some inexplicable reason the proprietor of the Lodore Hotel thought I was unsuitable to be his dairymaid – but the manageress of the Borrowdale agreed to employ me as gardener at half a crown an hour. Optimistically I calculated that this would be a pound a day: six days a week (one for climbing): six pounds.

I had reckoned without the weather. Had I been an experienced gardener I suppose I could have found something to do under glass when it rained; as it was, my two jobs, making a strawberry bed and digging, were often interrupted so that my earnings seldom came to more than three pounds a week.

I learnt to bed out strawberries from a book in the library.

Then the manageress had a difference of opinion with her barman. The rest of the staff (they were all related) packed their bags and left. I arrived one morning to find my employer frantically coping with breakfast on her own. She pleaded with me to come indoors during the emergency. She even offered me a guest room: not the staff quarters but the right side of the baize door. It was pouring with rain when she asked me. It looked like pouring with rain for eternity. I agreed at once.

I established myself in the hotel that evening. Unfortunately I had come to Borrowdale ill-equipped for anything but climbing. My domestic uniform was climbing trousers, a naval jersey (which, owing to good food, I was forced to wear outside my slacks) and espadrilles. Old Isaac Postlethwaite, a kind of privileged retainer who resembled a grumpy gnome in a trilby, loathed me: for my accent, my clothes, but mainly on principle. He would sit on 'his' chair by the Aga, ostensibly reading the paper, but shooting hate-ridden glances at me occasionally and mumbling curses. Mrs Mettam, the manageress, cursed too, but with cheerfulness and ingenuity.

My duties began early in the morning when the alarm clock rang and I started as boots. I had many duties (four of the staff had left) but I began the day with the boots. My first mistake was not to chalk the numbers of the rooms on the soles of the shoes (I had wondered what the chalk was doing in the boot-box). The result was that having cleaned them superlatively, I was faced with twenty pairs of shoes and the absolute impossibility of returning them to their owners. Guests breakfasted in puzzled silence and slippers, and I had to leave the washing-up to shepherd the long queue through the baize door to the boot-room.

After the boots came the early morning teas. Some people (notably honeymoon couples) were shy and only after repeated and furious knocking (my arms aching and my eye on my watch) would consent to open the door. By this time I was usually too annoyed to make a polite pause before my entrance, and swept in aggressively, glaring at the husband leaping shyly into bed, and sweeping everything off the bedside table to make room for the tray. But with the personages I was on my best and most winning behaviour, astonishing an Archbishop one morning by drawing aside the curtains, telling him what the weather was going to do and what it was doing now. I thought this was how one woke the upper classes. My appearance would be strange at dawn, and I was often unaware of the odour of cow which hung about me due to helping the Weirs at milking time. I embarrassed many people by forgetting the milk, or the sugar, or making the tea without any tea (of course, I seldom knew about the latter) and embarrassed them further by running back with the milk or the sugar . . . but I *did* knock. There was a lot of running up and down stairs, because after the first time that I tried to carry two trays and fell down the stairs on to the tiled hall, I carried only one at a time. Mrs Mettam had a Siamese cat who watched me from dark corners, sniggering.

At breakfast I was given the toast to look after, where, perhaps, it was felt that I could come to no harm. Then there were the fires to be lit, the bars re-stocked from the cellar, breakfast dishes to be washed and lunch prepared. During the morning the fires must be kept stoked and coffee served. On occasions I forgot myself and sat down with climbers for a coffee, to be recalled by Isaac who would come and stoke the fire with such abandon that he couldn't have been more obvious had he stood in the middle of the lounge and thrown lumps of coal at the grate.

The afternoon was a repetition of the morning, except that instead of coffee I served teas, and instead of lunch I prepared dinner.

The emergency lasted a week, when all the renegade staff returned and I retreated to the garden. All this time I was looking for a cottage, but with no success. There was none to rent, except furnished holiday cottages which would cost as much as five guineas in the summer. I had no capital, in fact, during the winter, I kept out of debt only by the skin of my teeth. I had grown very fond of the Lakes and it was with reluctance that I started corresponding with friends in North Wales, looking for a house there. In the meantime I rented a cottage in Matterdale, above Ullswater, for Christmas.

I relinquished my job at the Borrowdale (for after the Christmas holidays I would be going to Fort William) and Johnnie combined a visit to the Air Ministry with one to Sheena's school in Essex and brought her back with him.

The cottage in Matterdale was delightful : tiny, dark and warm. It had Calor gas, piped water and – the supreme luxury – a bath and water closet ! The weather was intensely cold and the hours of daylight short, but there were pleasant low fells all around the house and, to Sheena's joy, a Lakeland terrier to walk from the pub.

Then, at Christmas, the Mountain Rescue camped near by and the whole team came for Christmas dinner, squeezing into our tiny living-room until food had to be passed from hand to hand through the kitchen doorway because I couldn't get in. There was one great advantage to giving Mountain Rescue teams this dinner (I had done it at the youth hostel too) – I didn't have to wash up, and there was always someone who had celebrated too well on Christmas Eve – while I had been preparing the stuffing – who would baby-sit on Christmas night.

Johnnie took leave after Christmas, but the team came back to the district for New Year and Bill Kelsey, who was then in charge, called in one evening to ask if I would like to watch a stretcher being lowered down Gillercombe Buttress the following day. I had seen a lot of stretchers being lowered by now, seriously and in practice, but I was glad of the outing so on the Sunday morning I left Johnnie and Sheena sailing boats in the icy river (it was hopeless telling them not to; I knew they would, and I was the only one who seemed to notice the cold on these occasions) and trotted round to Borrowdale.

When we reached the top of the buttress it appeared that I was the lightest person present and it was suggested that I should guide the stretcher down. Reflecting that I might have to do it in earnest one day, I agreed.

It was a sensational experience. Not so much being on the front of the stretcher but being at the centre of an extremely well-organized exercise. Gillercombe Buttress is nearly five hundred feet high; taken direct it is a Severe, but we weren't following the route: the stretcher went over the top and down like a plumb-line, with myself wrestling with it all the way down like a frantic spider. I had to keep it from catching on the rock and to ease it into a level position on the ledges. There was no one on it, merely a sack of rocks weighing about ten stone. It was lowered on two ropes with a third coming to me. I was also clipped to the forward cross-bar with a sling and carabiner. I went down backwards in the abseiling position, holding the two projecting handles and thinking occasionally of Johnnie falling out of the bedroom window. My back felt naked. There was no question of climbing. I was lowered, and if I jibbed at an overhang the stretcher would give me a sly dig and push me off. If my rope wasn't synchronizing at that moment with the others I dropped and dangled from the cross-bar. But even in extremity I was aware of the slick manoeuvres on either side of me as pairs of men abseiled fast to the ledge below, ready to take the stretcher from me and pull down the ropes for the next lower. While they were doing this the men above who had been lowering were abseiling in their turn. It was a very well-integrated performance. Lying injured on a cliff one would feel reassured if these men were coming up.

*

The Christmas holidays came to an end. There came the dismal business of packing – I was used to it by now but oh, so tired of it – and the journey south to London and school.

Then came the tooth episode. It seems that I can do nothing conventionally, even sprouting a wisdom tooth.

It started in the ordinary painful way of a normal toothache. The first day coincided with Sheena's return to school, and another of Johnnie's stag parties at the Air Ministry (he was going to the Himalayas in a few months' time with an RAF expedition). Another coincidence was an interview with the producer of 'In Town Tonight'. Doped with Codeine and nicotine I tearfully said good-bye to Sheena at Liverpool Street, waited the inevitable fog-delayed hours at Euston for Johnnie and then rushed to the studio for my interview. This time it was for television, not radio, and it is scarcely surprising that, since I acted drunk and looked like a corpse, I was turned down.

Friends and Johnnie took pity on me but dentists didn't. For two days I tramped the streets of suburbia trying to find a dentist who would just *look* at my mouth and tell me what was wrong. But I penetrated no farther than the receptionists, and it was the same story everywhere: I could make an appointment for a week or a fortnight from now ...

Relief came at Jackson and Warr's, the mountaineering specialists. I had wandered into the shop to meet Johnnie, gaily buying equipment for his expedition, and John Jackson and Ted Warr stared at me in horror and started telephoning. Then they sent me to Guy's in a taxi where it was found I had an impacted wisdom tooth and a large abscess.

After daily treatment for a week two surgeons managed to relieve me of the tooth, not without some trouble. After the gum had been stitched I retired to a friend's flat for a few hours. I was catching the night coach to Scotland. My friend was still at the office when I reached the flat and, although I talked to her landlady, when she did arrive, shortly afterwards, we were astonished to find that I couldn't speak. My jaw was clamped shut and when

I tried to talk, strange sounds came from the back of my throat. We trusted that this would go off in time and we concentrated on feeding me for the journey. Having had toothache for about ten days I hadn't been eating very well. I dribbled soup carefully through the quarter-inch gap between my jaws – and more Codeine. The anaesthetic was wearing off now.

The journey north would have been horrifying for me as a backseat driver but for the fact that I was almost comatose. The roads were iced; it shone dully on the tarmac like verglas, and we passed countless lorries at unaccustomed angles on the grass verge. At intervals we were held up by powerful lights and, dimly through the steamed windows, I glimpsed police and cranes round great bulks across the road.

But the coach went on and we reached Glasgow – I now unaware of my physical self and in no pain thanks to the Codeine, unaware of the weight of the pack on my back or the travel bag and the typewriter wrenching my arms. But I did notice the strange looks people gave me as I tried to ask the way to the railway station. My jaws were still clamped shut.

Johnnie – now running the usual winter Mountain Rescue course on Ben Nevis – met me in Fort William, and stared in astonishment. My jaw obscured my ear. I had looked in a mirror on the train.

We went to John Berkeley's where I was pumped full of penicillin and put to bed. After two days of bed, and sherry and port and raw eggs, I was removed to hospital with an abscess in the throat.

Mr Duff received me with glee – he is always happy to have climbers about him, as long as they're not seriously injured – but he lost me next morning for, awakened by the inevitable wash in the small hours, I realized that I could talk. The abscess had broken and I was ravenous with hunger.

Outside the window snow was falling thickly. The Ben was hidden, not in mist, but behind that shifting curtain.

Trapped in his office, Mr Duff struck a bargain. He would remove my stitches and let me go if I promised to do only training walks for the next few days. I promised.

Next morning Johnnie and I were tramping up Glen Nevis with axes and ropes en route for a training walk over the Mamores.

John Berkeley overtook us in his Zephyr and we had some difficulty in persuading him of our intentions. Only Stob Ban, I assured him, just a little walk up Stob Ban and down again.

We did Mullach nan Coirean too, and, misjudging time and terrain, floundered down to the glen in the dark, wading through forestry plantations where the snow was a foot deep on the ground and a foot deep on the branches – and all the latter came down our necks as we swung from one resiny trunk to the next. Johnnie was exhausted when we arrived back at the hostel and I had to cook supper.

I was camping in the glen above the hostel. It was bitterly cold but I was bringing camping to a fine art. I used a hot-water bottle. There were raised eyebrows in the hostel when I filled it at night, but I slept warm although the river was frozen hard and temperatures were abnormally low in the small hours. I have heard that this habit has spread now to members of the Alpine Climbing Group.

At the end of Johnnie's course, the members of the RAF expedition held a pre-Himalayan meet in Glen Nevis and wives and fiancées were invited to attend. I attended too. But the good snow lasted only a few days, just long enough for me to climb Castle Ridge and South Castle Gully and to have a day walking alone along the arête of Carn Mor Dearg. The cold spell had been disastrous for the deer and smaller animals. On this last day I came down Coire Giubhsachan and the frost was clamped down hard on that lonely place. Tracks of hare and fox led to the banks of burns where there was no water, or where there had been waterholes now fast frozen. I hacked at the ice with my axe and hoped the animals would come quickly before it froze solid again. Farther down, round the ruins of upper Steall, deer were feeding, moving away sluggishly as I approached. There were pathetic patches in the snow, cleared by tired hooves, exposing only a few dry brown stalks of last year's grass.

Coming through the gorge at the head of Glen Nevis, I saw a large animal ahead of me which turned out to be a young deer: about a year old, I thought, one of last year's fawns. As I came round a corner I saw it sink to the ground and stay there. I expected to find that it had a broken leg. It didn't move as I came up, but its legs were uninjured; it allowed me to run my hands over its body. It was quite unmarked and obviously starving. I knelt there rubbing its ears and staring down the path, calculating the distance to the first house: Polldubh. It was probably three miles. If I could get it on my back, as a shepherd carries a ewe draped round his neck, I might be able to get it there. But would they shoot it? Perhaps I could get it to the hostel and telephone a keeper. I tried to lift the deer to its feet so that I could heave it on to my shoulder. It struggled gamely but seemed to have no strength.

I stood up and stared at it hopelessly. Then it got to its feet and started trotting down the path. I followed slowly and saw it sink again, but this time on the edge of the drop. I quickened my pace, trying to move smoothly in an effort not to alarm it, but I was unsuccessful. It moved and started to slide, crashing down through rocks and undergrowth into the gorge.

It was dusk now but I started to climb down after it. I had no rope and after a few yards I realized I was being rather silly. Suppose I slipped and lay in the gorge, unconscious? Who would think of me being here, and what would I do if the deer were still alive and I reached it safely? I came home heavily, debating with myself all the way whether I had done the right thing, and rebelling against Fate which sends me more than my share of responsibilities. It is always to me that the mangy old cats and the stray dogs come. No one else sees the ewes with broken legs, lambs with great abscesses in the cleft of their hooves, cows with ingrowing horns. When I was in the Land Army life would be unbearable for days because I had seen a horse thrashed or a puppy dragging paralysed hindquarters across the floor.

Fortunately for the animals the thaw came very soon after I had seen the deer in Coire Giubhsachan. The climbing was over for a while. Johnnie went back to Topcliffe but I stayed in Fort William. An invalid friend had just lost her daily help so I did her housework during the week and walked on Sundays. The weather was poor and the local climbers preferred to ski anyway. However, I had some lovely walks: the Mamores, the Aonachs again, Gulvain – and then one glorious frosty day on Beinn a' Bheithir in Glen Coe, when I stayed on top until late, watching the sun go down behind Ardgour, and coming down through the forests by torchlight.

18. Guiding in Snowdonia

During the winter friends had written to tell me about numerous vacant cottages in Wales, but they were all for sale; I wanted to rent a place. Oddly enough, I had known of an empty cottage for several years. Like the youth hostel it stood on the mountain above Ro Wen; in the old days Sheena and I used to walk across and peer through its grimy windows. I never took it seriously. I would stand on its weed-grown terrace that looked out across the sea and moors and mountains, reflecting idly that it was a perfect situation but, of course, quite impossible. It was on no road and was accessible only by Land Rover or tractor. It was over a mile from the bus stop and six hundred feet above the village. The occupier would have to carry everything: food, fuel and furniture, up the mountain on his back. Being twenty miles from the climbing centre it would be impracticable for any guide, even one in possession of transport. But now I was desperate: I wanted a settled home for Sheena – and a base for myself, somewhere to go when courses were cancelled, somewhere to live and write during the winter.

With this house in mind I came to Ro Wen after leaving Fort William. I had arranged to meet the owner in the village. It was a bright fresh day in April when we trudged up the cart track to the farm and I, always easily affected by the weather, was ready to fall in love at the rustle of a leaf.

It stood among its sheltering sycamores, the purple roof slates shining in the sun, the grey stone of its walls rough and warm to the touch. Grouped about it were the crumbling byres and stables, the pig sties and the great barn – unused now, the landlord told me, except when they were shepherding.

There were sheep in the garden that day, browsing among the nettles, and sheep had sheltered in the dairy for years to judge by the floor of trampled droppings. The sink was here, for the house had a piped water supply – a very old rusty pipe leading from a spring.

This was an unlooked-for luxury, for there were many houses in the village where people had to carry every drop of water from a pump. Plumbing, electricity and gas were, of course, non-existent.

There was a kitchen with a tiled floor, and an ancient range with a kind of gibbet and chain for the kettle. The range was at the back of an enormous ingle nook. Then there was a small parlour, rather genteel, with a wooden floor, a lined ceiling (the beams were exposed elsewhere) and a hideous tiled fireplace. Upstairs there were two good-sized bedrooms and a boxroom.

I was charmed by everything, already looking at the place with a possessive eye. In imagination I was redecorating the rooms and scrubbing out the appalling dairy and clearing the garden. So it was a blow when the owner told me that another woman was interested and that he must contact her as she had first choice. I was horrified. I had fallen in love, but even from a practical point of view, if this – the last resort – failed, where else could I look for a home?

A day or two later, by an astonishing coincidence, Johnnie was posted to Anglesey – to his old camp and the Valley Mountain Rescue team. I *had* to get the house. And, of course, I got it. No one else wanted to live there. I paid a year's rent in advance and now, with my own home a few miles away, I continued placidly with my work in the Llanberis Pass, living in a hovel with a few hens and many rats.

I was running an Intermediate course. The first week (while I waited for word of the cottage) was wet and miserable; the second, when word had come, was warm and dry. One wondered if, at last, we were going to have a good summer.

One Saturday evening in the middle of the course I sprained my ankle by falling down some steps. We spent the rest of the fortnight on the more accessible cliffs, myself hobbling up to the Milestone, to the Idwal Slabs and to Craig Aderyn, and trying, when climbing, not to put too much weight on that right foot. This was difficult on Tennis Shoe when, near the end of the week, lulled into a mood of false security by the hot sun and rock as dry as a bone, I decided that my best students should do something delicate.

The first pitch of Tennis Shoe went well for the holds are adequate if a trifle sloping and polished, but the second pitch – where you traverse on to the main face of the slabs, and the hard move comes shortly after you've abruptly become aware of the exposure – here I felt a little insecure. I reasoned (standing on the last good hold and staring at the crack above that is merely a line across the rock) that it wasn't really exposed, it was my nerves . . . But reason told me that a slip here would mean an uncontrolled slide down the slabs until the rope tightened, then a spectacular *pendule* over the first pitch and down the east wall, and there the shock of the last vertical drop would come on your second, pulling him off those two little belays which were quite adequate for bringing him up the first pitch but – as my leg started to shake on that last good hold – now quite useless.

With a mental shrug (not bravado; I'd done it many times before and knew the flesh was quite confident even if the spirit gibbered in fear), I hooked the top joint of my index finger into the only place where the crack is wide enough to accommodate the top joint of an index finger and moved up carefully. The bad ankle gave a twinge and I winced, my foot slipped the fraction of an inch on the polished crack, slipped and held, and then I had the good finishing hold and I was up – and already wondering how the students would cope.

In the evenings I returned to my hovel and, at the end of the course and with Johnnie going to the Himalayas, I threw a party. Someone, going outside in the dark, tripped over my landlord who had come, he said, to ask us to curtain the window. We thought of asking him in for a drink but decided, kindly, not to disillusion him. Probably he got quite a kick out of imagining the nameless orgies in his hovel. So he kept his illusions – and charged me double the rent on which we had agreed originally 'because I had had so many men in the place'. Well, to one man, at least, I was dangerous.

The course ended with a heat wave. I thought I was climbing well, and on my first free day I was inveigled by John Turner, a chemist from Cambridge, to follow him up Unicorn. This after he had helped me with my students the previous day on Crackstone

Rib, the Wrinkle and Spiral Stairs. Possibly my performance on these had given him an exaggerated idea of my capabilities, for, having followed him up Unicorn, he suggested Spectre.

Johnnie and I had long had designs on Spectre. It was something to work for when we had become very fit. When we did climbs like Rowan Tree Slabs or the Blade Finish to Javelin Buttress, we talked about Spectre in the evenings. Several times we had done the first pitch and then stopped, staring, rather awed, at the crack leading to the overhang above. He had even gone some distance up the crack but had retreated. We were saving Spectre. Now John was adamant that I should second him. I pleaded fatigue, staleness, laziness – and all the time we were drawing nearer to the foot of the climb.

Perhaps the climb was hard, perhaps I was tired; I made a shocking exhibition of myself. Dave Thomas, watching through a glass from the door of Cwm Glas cottage, saw every movement and avoided my eye in the evening.

John went up so fast and smoothly that I lost all sense of proportion. I started well and casually, but I became tense and anxious as the crack progressed, and I went more and more slowly until I came to the overhang and stopped. To the right was a stride which was long for a tall man, to the left it was harder; straight up – taking the overhang direct – it looked impossible. But it was a poor resting place; there was no time to choose my route. After one or two half-hearted attempts to make the stride to the right I had little strength left. I must move before it went completely. I shouted to John to keep my rope tight and then realized that I no longer had a choice of routes. John was a weight lifter. I took the overhang direct like a sack of coal, grabbing – for form's sake – at the holds as they passed. Above the overhang came the top crack. John wrestled a little here and my heart sank. I was so demoralized that when my turn came I couldn't even get into the crack. I went round the side. The last few pitches (of Nea – parallel and only Severe) were easy and, normally, delightful, but I was deeply resentful. Why had I allowed myself to be persuaded to do this route? I had been happy and confident leading Severes, and now I suffered a dramatic reversion of feeling. I was no good. Not for the first time I realized the great gap between a Very Severe and an Exceptionally Severe.

Later I recovered some confidence on Javelin Buttress and Holly Tree Wall but still I wasn't happy, and telling myself that I was getting stale, I went round to Ro Wen, to lick my wounds at Maen y Bardd.

*

The house, untenanted for years, was damp and mouldy. There were patches of mildew on the back wall where it was built into the mountain, and the chimney-piece sweated when the fire was lit. Johnnie took leave and we heated water and swept and scrubbed, throwing open all the windows and doors so that air circulated through the musty rooms. We ate off packing cases and slept on the floor. I wanted to make the place habitable in time for the summer holidays. I had no idea what we were to do for furniture; there was no money to spare after school fees had been paid. But we had four walls and a roof which was a great advance on last season when my home was a tent.

Suddenly, thinking of tents, I was reminded of my next course – in Langdale – and I had a recurrence of stage-fright. Strange, that I should have been quite confident at the beginning of the season, and now, with the first course over, I should be frightened of the second.

As I left Maen y Bardd to travel to Langdale, I picked up a book to read on the train: Winthrop Young's *Mountaincraft*. On the way north I read the chapter on Management and Leadership. I had read it before but now it held a deeper significance for me. I was reminded that I was not only a climber but a leader, yet this point, made with understanding, instead of frightening me with its threat of great responsibility, filled me with exhilaration. As the Pikes came into sight on the way up Great Langdale I watched them eagerly – as eagerly as an amateur on holiday, not as a guide who must climb in all weathers with poor people, with reckless people, with people who refused to watch the leader, who tangled the rope when one was on the hard move . . . I had recovered my sense of proportion.

Perhaps something of this feeling of insecurity had been due to the fact that Johnnie was now on his way to India. Despite the fact that I had sympathetic friends in Langdale, in particular the Crosses at the Old Dungeon Ghyll, I felt very much alone. He would be away for two months. He was an extremely experienced mountaineer, inclined at times to be over-cautious, but the Himalayas were big – very big – and the objective dangers were far greater even than the Alps. I thought of tents pitched below a slope that no one dreamt would avalanche, of unexpected storms at great altitudes, and of those terribly Heath Robinson bridges across glacier torrents . . . It is a moot point who suffers most when men climb: the women who know little of mountains except the view of them from the kitchen window, or those who are climbers themselves. I had my knowledge *and* my imagination. I had been on snow bridges which collapsed without warning into crevasses and had spent the night shivering under an overhang, and knowing that if the weather broke, it would be luck that saved the party, not experience or technique.

I forgot about him during the daytime, and in some inexplicable way, if I did remember, I felt more confidence in him if I were on a cliff myself. It was at night, just before getting into my sleeping bag, that I remembered. I wrote him long letters, my old typewriter tapping away in the candle-lit tent while the owls called about Wall End and lambs came to stare at me, their eyes shining like coins in the dark.

The weather was mixed that May but June and Whitsun arrived in a blaze of sunshine. Vibrams replaced nails and again I knew the pure delight of Gimmer on a still hot day: Oliverson's, 'B' Route and Gimmer Chimney during the week, and harder routes on Sundays: Bilberry Buttress and the Severes on Raven Crag, Diphthong and 'D' Route (with the Severe layback at the top of the Forked Lightning Crack).

There seemed no chance of my going stale now. I was well away, climbing almost every day, with one morning a week for shopping in Ambleside, and the occasional very wet day when we ran over the usual theory. This came pat now with a season of impromptu lectures behind me, although I was still flummoxed by some questions ('Why are there 360 degrees in a circle?').

Warned by last year's experience I was eating well and sensibly; I had bought a lilo and found that I slept far better with something between me and the ground.

Evenings were spent happily in the Old Dungeon Ghyll. Sutton was up for a time, and other friends. Mr and Mrs Winthrop

Young were on their annual visit and, almost literally, we sat at his feet and listened to his reminiscences – and his opinions. It was entertaining to hear the incidents you had read in his books told again, and in greater detail, to elicit the answer to your query, 'What happened *then*?' I would have liked to tell him how his book had encouraged me recently, but I was too shy. I dreaded the thought of being the palest shadow of those gushing females who haunted me.

An odd thing happened one night. It was after a weekend and all the campers had gone, leaving me alone in my field. It was raining gently and some time in the small hours I woke, aware that there was something heavy across my legs. I stretched out a hand and felt what I concluded was wool. My immediate reaction was to think that a sick sheep had come to me for company but, exploring further, I found a shoulder – not a shoulder of sheep. I was fascinated. My hand travelled below the shoulder, down an arm – and was clutched by another.

In a flash I had reviewed the current residents in the dale – and dismissed them.

'Who are you?' I hissed.

'Let me stay! Do let me stay!' It was tremulous, but it was unmistakably a man's voice. It was unnatural. He wasn't violent and this made the situation quite incomprehensible. There was no smell of drink.

'But who *are* you? What's the matter?'

He mumbled something about friends and having nowhere to sleep.

'But you can't sleep here,' I exclaimed. 'Go away. Go and sleep in the barn!'

Still he pleaded, and since there seemed to be nothing wrong except this peculiar desire for company, I found myself losing my patience.

In the end, still mumbling, he went. Against the paling sky I saw that he wore a raincoat and carried no pack.

Later that morning I told Sid Cross. No one could offer an explanation, and the whole incident remains a mystery.

*

On 2 July I returned to Wales and spent that night in the Climbers' Club hut at Cwm Glas. It was a night of torrential rain. In the morning, instead of waterfalls coming down Clogwyn y Grochan, water flowed over the top of the cliff in a sheet. The river was like a glacier torrent; no one would have survived had they fallen in. About midday the sun came out and the ground steamed. We were not to have another drop of rain for six weeks.

I was due to start an Intermediate course in Nantgwynant on the Monday. This was Sunday. When I hitched round from Llanberis to find a camp site, the road to Nantmoor was flooded, so I abandoned the idea of a site there, and settled for a high, grassy dell in an oak wood above Llyn Dinas. I pitched the tent beside a stream and went to meet my students who were quartered at the Holiday Fellowship centre near by.

We had a glorious week. There was no gradual clearing up of the weather. The heat wave came with the sudden violence of a thunderstorm. Already, on the Monday, we were climbing in shirt sleeves and plimsolls. The stream beside my tent dried up and I had to go some distance for water. By the Thursday we were looking for climbs in the shade, and, for some, the scree slopes below the cliffs were purgatory.

On this Thursday, having worked our way lazily upward from the Gribin to Glyder Fach, having sweltered and struggled in the Chasm, one man collapsed on the summit and another was missing.

That day a climber from West Africa, called Peter Lord, was helping me. He had a party on the Direct while I took the less competent people up Chasm Route. It was one of the latter who collapsed from the heat on the summit blocks. It was while I was pondering whether to descend with him to Pen y Gwryd or to go with the rest of the course down Bristly Ridge to Ogwen and the cars, that my notice was drawn to the fact that one of Peter's party was no longer with us. He was last seen scrambling up the easy rocks between the Direct and the summit. Reflecting, with some bewilderment, that no one could have had an accident there, I went down a little way and shouted. We all shouted. There was no reply.

I scrambled down a hundred feet or so and thought I could hear scree shifting far below. Still there was no answer to my shouts. I had the feeling that the man was descending the cliff. I shouted to a French nurse that we had in the party to take the tired man to Pen y Gwryd, to the others to descend Bristly with Peter, then I started to run.

The scree of Main Gully is abominable stuff : more loose rock than scree, but I kept moving fast for I had glimpsed, far below, a figure moving downwards in East Gully. In the latter, and from above, the scree seems to descend unbroken to the foot of the cliff. Actually there is a sixty-foot pitch in the gully : not a moderate route where a falling climber might bounce down, but a great overhang above a cave. The scree runs down right to the lip of the capstone.

The boy below looked back at me once, but instead of stopping, continued downwards. I hurtled after him, shouting.

He was only a hundred feet above the cave when I reached him. I was very angry. He had been tired, he said, and hadn't felt like going to the summit. We climbed carefully down East Gully Ridge, myself watching the silhouettes on Bristly anxiously, thinking that, with one nasty accident averted, and the party split into three, it would be just my luck to have someone come off there. I dismissed the two going down to Pen y Gwryd; they were in no danger, at the worst the invalid would collapse in the heather and we could collect him later.

We all met without incident in the Gwryd and there was nothing to warn me that it was to be the guide on that course who would come to grief.

That night Johnnie arrived back from the Himalayas, very brown, very happy, and with several hitherto unclimbed peaks to his credit. We spent the weekend carrying paint up to the cottage and working so hard that it was not until late on the Sunday evening that he suggested doing some routes on the boulders above the house.

These rocks, where Sheena, Mais non ! and I used to practise, looked bland and innocent that July evening. We had no rope – why take a rope on boulder problems ?

Johnnie went first – up a steep crack with a delicate move at the top.

'You'll find that hard,' he called down, 'I doubt if you'll do it.'

I moved up the crack slowly and stopped to look at the hard

move. After a careful appraisal I did it more neatly than himself, and went padding in smug silence up the easy slab above. There was no need of holds and my hands rested lightly on the rock. It was with some surprise that I realized I was no longer moving up but down. I couldn't believe it and continued to paddle frantically with my hands, but definitely, the rock was going up and I was going down. When the moment of truth came and I knew I was falling, I turned on my back (much to the admiration of Johnnie who was watching every move with intense interest) and continued to paddle. I suppose I was trying to slow my descent. Then I was in the air, saw a large rock below, tried to twist away – and hit the ground. I fell about thirty feet and the jar was considerable but my shame and guilt were such that, almost before I landed, I was shouting to Johnnie that I was all right.

When I stood up, one ankle seemed rather weak but there was very little pain. I managed to hobble home and in the morning it was scarcely swollen. But with a rucksack on my back the walk down to the bus stop was agonizing, and by the time I reached Llanrwst I had to consult a doctor. I was sent to Bangor and X-rayed. The bone was cracked and I was put in plaster to the knee.

This was a setback to the course, but fortunately help was at hand. Johnnie, frantically telephoned on Anglesey, agreed to take a few days' leave, and he and Peter would take the students for their last week.

I lay sulkily outside my tent, wearing nothing but the plaster and my only company a red squirrel. It was far too painful to hobble to the stream to wash my breakfast dishes, so I left them outside the tent and every morning the squirrel came undulating through the wood and, a yard from my recumbent body, cleaned them meticulously.

On the last day of the course I had to make out my reports, passing or failing the students. I had never made my reports on the basis of the quantity – or quality – of the climbs done, but on the safety of the students' technique. If a man led Very Difficults it was no guarantee that he would pass the course unless he led them with safety. Conversely I might not get Intermediates up to leading, but if they were competent, safe seconds I passed them. Both during their first and second weeks the present people had done a lot of climbs, some were following Severes, yet I felt that I couldn't make out a report unless I saw them myself on the last day.

So we went round to the Idwal Slabs and, feeling very conspicuous – almost an exhibitionist – I limped slowly up the path to the foot of the slabs.

The plaster came to my toes, but by breaking away the end of it I found I had these free and could get them on a hold, although, of course, I couldn't flex my foot. Not daring to try Tennis Shoe with that delicate second pitch I took them up Hope and then Lazarus. I found the plaster made the climbs considerably harder, and my foot, vainly trying to bend on the holds, was raw by the time we reached the top, but I had found out what the students were like and could write my report with a clear conscience.

Throwing caution and clean living to the winds that evening, I stayed at the Pen y Gwryd until closing time, and had to walk most of the four miles back to the tent – until, in fact, I realized my great asset, rolled my trousers up to the knee and continued with a limp so exaggerated that the next motorist stopped for me.

*

There followed a fortnight of decorating at Maen y Bardd when I found that standing on chairs and painting ceilings, or going up ladders to the roof was just as hazardous as climbing in my present condition. But even without the plaster I never overcame my feeling of exposure at the top of a ladder.

The house was beginning to look homely and fresh. I had whitewashed most of the interior, and painted the oak beams black, and the rest of the woodwork in pastel shades. Some friends who had bought a large old house in the district had given us all the furniture that people didn't want at the auction. We had a brass bed with proper knobs on the corners, a wardrobe, and a great looking-glass that had to stand on the floor because the wall would never support it. I had bought mattresses cheaply from the Youth Hostels Association, camp beds from Millett's, and Johnnie had made tables, chairs and cupboards from packing cases. We had cleared the garden and started digging.

After a fortnight of intensive work during which I did no climbing although the plaster had been removed, Johnnie came one evening to ask me to go to Craig yr Ysfa the following day.

We had had the drought for a month now. Every night there was heavy dew and glow-worms shone in the bog. Mornings dawned hazy, and the haze increased throughout the day until none but the nearest mountains was clear. The sun blazed through this haze and tanned us the colour of old gold.

That day on Craig yr Ysfa, drenched with heat and light, is un-forgettable. With another member of the Valley team we came to the foot of Pinnacle Wall and Johnnie asked me to lead. I hadn't led it before, but now, remembering that superb wall above the quartz ledge (we were too close under the cliff to see it), the tra-verse out to the pinnacle, the delightful upper pitch, so exposed above the amphitheatre, I was filled with excitement.

The first pitches aren't particularly impressive, except that you know, as you traverse rightwards and up from the gully, that un-derneath the drop is growing rapidly. Then comes the walk – the light cat-pad – along the quartz ledge, the delicate step at the end and the comforting assurance of the piton in the corner. Above is the wall.

I brought up the men and Johnnie belayed me.

Above us a groove ran up the wall. This is followed for about twenty-five feet when, with sensational abruptness, the route breaks out to the right, following a rough crack to the pinnacle. But the crack – which is sensational – isn't hard. The crux comes near the top of those first twenty-five feet. There are runners in the crack: tiny things to take a loop of nylon line. With your toes balanced on excrescences and your right hand on the rock, with infinite delicacy you take the sling off your head and place it round a knob. Everything is in slow motion, and perhaps, this day, every movement in this moment of time is perfection. You bring up the rope, clip it one-handed into the carabiner, the nylon drops again with the faintest jerk on your waist – and the second breathes a little easier as he stares upwards in the deep silence. And so on, stepping slowly, aware more than ever now of that silence, through which comes, perhaps, the cry of a peregrine.

Near the top of the groove there seem to be no more holds, but you know there must be, so you look for wrinkles, and you find them; you choose the biggest and you step up and, amazingly, they are adequate. They bring you to the crack, the big, rough friendly crack which leads you over all that exposure to the flake and the belay. From there you look down at the route with the eyes of a lover, and across the gully you catch a movement. You hear a cry again and there is the peregrine slipping through the sun shafts in the amphitheatre.

It was the hottest day of that hot summer. On the way down we sent the others ahead to swim (some had been photographing us from Amphitheatre Buttress). After waiting an hour – while I lay half-asleep on the parched grass and even a fox pattering idly among the boulders scarcely roused me – we followed slowly down the cwm, seeing, far ahead, pale shrimps dancing on the bank beside the pool.

When we came to the bridge they were gone and we had the water to ourselves. It was deep and clear and it had had four weeks to grow warm. There was no cringing and no shock as you plunged. It closed over your head like a caress.

There was a Pinnacle Club meet that weekend and on the Sunday we went to Lliwedd – a Lliwedd so dry that there was dust on the ledges, and Mallory's Slab, like Pinnacle Wall, was delicate and smooth and delightful: reminiscent of Lot's Groove without the crux. On the Monday we went to Carreg Wastad where I, contented and willing to let others have their day, placidly followed a former student up her first Severe, Crackstone Rib. Or did I lead Crackstone Rib and she led the Wrinkle? It was hot and we were lazy; I remember only that the climbing was easy. It is pleasant to speculate on the heights to which we could rise if autumn and winter did not separate summer from summer.

In the middle of August Johnnie took three days' leave and we returned to Craig yr Ysfa. We walked there in the cool of dusk, carrying only sleeping bags and food. No tent was needed. We walked through the darkness while curlews bubbled across the moor and owls hooted in the tiny ravines. But the stars glittered too brightly; in the morning there were clouds above the mountains. Unbelievably, it was cold on the cliff. We did Shean Treuse, a dirty, unfrequented climb, and hard.

That night we slept in the ruined quarry buildings at the head of the cwm, where gaunt pillars rose against the near-black sky, and the tips shifted restlessly.

The next day, after a delightful little route, Gomorrah, we came to the top of the crag and it rained !

It cleared after the shower, but the drought was over – and the fantastic summer. Those six weeks have become a yardstick by which we measure all summers.

'Hot,' we say, 'but not as hot as in 1955.' Or, 'I've never known water so warm as that day we swam in the pool after Pinnacle Wall.'

*

There were no more courses for the Mountaineering Association. Sheena and Mother came up for the second half of the school holidays and both were very impressed with the house. I became domesticated. I continued the redecorating and I made pounds and pounds of jam. In the autumn I wrote a great deal and had many rejection slips. For social relaxation I played darts in the local pub and travelled round with the darts team, marking for them in matches.

There were a few private clients but not as many as I would have wished. I seemed to be entering on a period of professional inactivity, but it didn't last. In the middle of October, and without any warning, came a letter asking me to lead a women's expedition to the Himalayas. It was a fantastic offer. I talked it over with Johnnie and then accepted provisionally, pointing out the fact that I had no money. As yet the expedition seemed very nebulous. Neither the composition of the party nor its destination had been decided upon. I suggested Kulu: the area where the RAF had been, where there were lots of small mountains of moderate height and difficulty, and vast tracts of unexplored country. This suggestion was accepted and we turned to the RAF for help. I borrowed their equipment lists and after amending them slightly, circulated them among the members of the women's expedition. In December I was asked to help with the task of begging for support from the newspapers. I went to London and was demoralized and frustrated as we went from newspaper to newspaper, from shoe shop to mountaineering specialist – and all with no success. Private people were more sympathetic. I spent an evening with A. E. Gunther on whose information concerning Kulu the RAF had based their expedition. He was extremely helpful, as were the

RAF themselves, who invited us to the Air Ministry to see their film. But as the organization progressed I began to have doubts. Originally I had tried to persuade Nancy Smith to come on the expedition as a fourth. At first she was enthusiastic, but then she, too, had second thoughts. Neither of us relished the responsibilities. As the climbing leader and a professional I had everything to lose. I had refused to go to the Alps as a climbing instructor for the Mountaineering Association; it was ludicrous to contemplate going to mountains half as high again and where, in the event of an accident, any rescue would have to be effected by ourselves. Early in 1956, reluctantly, but certain that I was right, I decided to withdraw.

It was ironical that soon afterwards one newspaper, thinking that I had withdrawn through lack of money, should offer me five hundred pounds to return. When I refused they suggested I should form my own expedition, but I was tired of organizing – and I had my doubts about the five hundred pounds. I stuck tight at Maen y Bardd and wrote furiously, trying to recoup the losses of the two weeks in London.

I had a lot of publicity over the affair and this had an amusing sequel. One morning I had my first anonymous letter. It didn't tell me nasty things about myself, or anyone close to me; the writer said – and reiterated several times – that he was coming up to cut my throat with a razor. He didn't say why. The postmark was Bristol; the writing illiterate.

I took it to the police who waxed avuncular, appropriated my letter, patted my shoulder and told me not to worry. The people in the local pub were more concerned and advised a large, fierce Alsatian.

At five o'clock that evening I was sitting by the fire with my back to the window when I felt an itchy feeling between my shoulder blades. I got up and pulled the curtains. On my way back to the fire, I picked up the carving knife (a fine piece of Sheffield steel) and laid it on a corner of the table, between me and the door.

At six o'clock someone knocked. I never had visitors who knocked and waited. I froze, staring at the fire. The knock came again. I picked up the knife and, standing just inside the front door without opening it, asked firmly (more firm than I felt):

'Who is it?'

A little voice answered:

'I've got a telegram for you.'

I'd heard that one before, dozens of times: at the cinema, on the radio, in thrillers.

'Who is it?'

'The postman.' The voice sounded scared – as well it might.

I debated telling him to put it under the door. But if it *were* the postman, it was criminal to send him away like that, after he'd walked all the way up the mountain in the dark.

I opened the door carefully, standing aside – partly to avoid the rush, but mainly to let the light fall on the wicked blade of the knife.

It *was* the postman. He drew back, appalled.

'Oh, come in,' I cried in relief, brandishing the knife, 'come in and have a cup of tea.' I'd forgotten the telegram completely.

He wouldn't come in until I'd put the knife down, and when I explained my behaviour he wouldn't wait for tea. He kept glancing at the window as if any moment a homicidal maniac was about to leap in, with a naked razor. He wasn't a young man, and he was so worried I said I'd go down with him to the place where he had most inconveniently (tonight of all nights) bogged his van.

We went down the mountain carrying sacks and the Tilley lamp, but we couldn't get the van out of the ditch. I said I would run down to the village and telephone for the breakdown waggon. I felt so sorry for him. I ran down fast, but by the time I'd put down the receiver he was in the bar behind me. Nothing was going to keep him up there alone – nothing!

*

Now I acquired a car. It was a 1932 Morris Minor, which was immediately christened the Daimler. Despite the fact that the steering was so bad I got cramp in both hands on long runs, I was jubilant at this new acquisition. It was a long and tiring hitch-hike to Ogwen – and I had to hitch for the buses didn't connect. Now I could be there in an hour, could even ferry my clients quickly from one centre to the next, and take them for a drink in the evenings. But first I must do something about the steering.

It was found, on inspection, that a ball joint on the drop arm had worn so badly that it was no longer a ball but a hemisphere. A lump was welded on and the next day I started south to lecture at Oxford. I had gone only ten miles when the lump dropped off the ball joint and the steering reverted to normal. But not having driven since the days of the travelling shop in Fort William, I wasn't unduly disconcerted and chugged southward happily, overtaking only bicycles and electric milk trollies and leading long lines of traffic up the hills. I felt like Boadicea.

In the Vale of Evesham the coil dropped off, but worked just as efficiently jammed inside a bracket that might once have contained an oil can. A few miles farther on, when I had stopped in a lay-by for personal reasons, an A A man could not resist raising the bonnet (few people can) and found that I was firing on three cylinders because the leads were lying on the block. I wasn't surprised; I had been having difficulty in overtaking the electric milk trollies in the last few miles. We fastened the leads to the dynamo with string from the A A man's sandwich packet. Intimidated, I gave him an enormous tip because he said he was supposed to take the string home.

On the return journey I lost several bolts out of the springs at Rugeley, and spent the afternoon lying on my back in a garage under the erroneous impression that by helping the fitter, I could lighten the bill. Instead of returning to Wales from Oxford, I was driving to Manchester to record a talk for Woman's Hour. The BBC had booked a room for me at the Queen's.

It was one of the few times I saw sables – coming out of the revolving doors as I went in. I was in motoring dress: cords, submarine jersey (with a large white 48 painted on the back) and espadrilles. I flamed with sunburn, having driven with the hood down for two days, and I hadn't washed since we'd greased the springs at Rugeley. I directed the porter to bring in my bags from the convertible and gave him the keys, forgetting to tell him that a 1932 Morris Minor has the accelerator *between* the clutch and the brake. Dave Thomas, who was waiting to dine with me, was losing his habitual *sang froid*.

'I must bath,' I told him. He agreed pointedly.

On the way home – after a bad moment on the Chester by-pass when I shot like a rabbit under the nose of an enormous lorry at a roundabout – and the driver was rude – the radiator sprang a leak on the coast road. I came home spasmodically, jerking from pub to pub from Saint Asaph to Llandudno Junction, begging kettles of water from the landlords and courteously drinking with each one.

The Daimler's finest performance was Skye: over a thousand miles without so much as a puncture. Having obtained my divorce in May, Johnnie and I were married in June. We had to wait for leave and the honeymoon for two weeks. We planned to do all the 'new' routes on Skye: things like Doom Flake, the Crack of Double Doom – and Shining Cleft, a climb whose name alone is pure temptation.

We left Wales one afternoon in a heat wave. We carried an enormous amount of gear, for now that we had a car we lost all sense of proportion. The hood was down and the boot filled inside and covered outside. A big double sleeping bag was spread across the seat giving some insulation from the springing, and there were large packages on the wings. The tent and all the ironmongery were strapped on the front bumper to keep our nose down on the hills, so she boiled readily and had long rests at the tops of passes.

Never doing more than 28 mph we pushed steadily northward, and midnight found us crawling down the Patterdale side of Kirkstone Pass. Some belated cyclists, plodding uphill, asked if they could help. Hurt, we bade them goodnight. The brakes screamed on a high, uninterrupted monotone. I had been warned about them several times by the police. My garage taught me a little speech to be delivered in a cultured, pleasant tone with a now-you're-an-intelligent-man air. It began: 'But *all* the models of that year made a slight noise with the brakes; in 1933 the makers . . .' I forget what they did in 1933. The brakes were quite efficient; it was merely that they had to be so noisy about it.

We slept that night on the shore of Ullswater, and the following evening we were in Glencoe. It is remarkable that when I'm alone in the car I arouse a feeling of amused and tolerant interest in other motorists, but when accompanied by a man everyone glares. You know they're telling their passengers that you shouldn't be on the road. Coming along the shores of Loch Leven, with a long drop to the water on our near side and the mountain above, a horn hooted imperiously from behind. It was quite light and I saw a big black saloon bearing down on us. Johnnie was driving, which was fortunate, as he had stronger arms. Instead of waiting for a wide piece of road, the saloon swept past when we were as close to the grass as possible without hanging over the edge, gave the Daimler a passing blow, and went weaving fast towards Kinlochleven. It was pub-turning-out time. When we stopped, we found the metal strip on the running board had been ripped off. We reflected happily that we'd marked our aggressor anyway.

That night Johnnie had his first encounter of the season with the midges. They didn't bother me much, and after one hasty glance at the Aonach Eagach, still and high against the stars, I was able to sleep.

While in Fort William we did Slav Route on Ben Nevis. The north face was as dry as we'd ever known it; there was no water anywhere, only the drift of old snow at the foot of Zero Gully. It was a lovely route: delicate, with long run-outs (I wonder if there is one route on the Ben which is uninteresting?). To climb anywhere on the face is a delight – to my mind – incomparable with Scafell or Clogwyn du'r Arddu. It is so big, so high, so isolated. It is, of all cliffs, the most intimidating and yet, for that solitude and mystery possessed only by the great, and perhaps for something of its implacability, it has captured me completely.

And so to Skye – to cliffs more friendly, less serious – and to rain. We pitched the tent well down Loch Brittle to escape the crowds – a mistake, for we would have welcomed company in the wet days that followed. We had to content ourselves with the normal routes which were still fun: Cioch Direct, Mallory's, the White Slab, but they weren't what we'd come for. In the evenings we sat in the kitchen at the House, gossiping with the Mac-Raes until late at night, when we stumbled back along the sea cliffs through rain and wind, and wondered dismally if the sun were shining farther south.

We endured the weather for a fortnight – and Johnnie fought the midges. One night, in uncontrollable anger, he tore his ear. Then his bites turned septic and we left Glen Brittle. In Fort William John Berkeley prescribed gentian violet. I applied this on the shore of Loch Leven when we'd found a sheltered spot away from the tourists. John had told me to paint all the spots. Johnnie looked absolutely appalling when I'd finished. Not only was his face bright purple but even his head. He was taking penicillin and already, with the rain having stopped and Glencoe basking under a hot sun, he felt better. So much so that when we stopped at Clachaig (and I'd carried a beer to him – he couldn't go into the bar with a head like that) we stared up at Clachaig Gully and reminded each other how much we'd always wanted to do it.

Although it had stopped raining, the gully was full of water. We were soaked to the skin after the introductory pitches. We were in nails and we revelled in the climbing. The holds were big and rough, not water-worn as one might expect, for the route kept more to the side of the waterfalls as it can do in big gullies.

Everywhere there were flowers, and, framed in golden rod and foxgloves – as he peered over the top of a pitch at me – Johnnie's monstrous face took on the aspect of a horror film in Technicolor.

We returned to Wales with the holiday saved by two good climbs: the last one and Slav Route – and Johnnie went back to camp cured of his bites but still with a faint flush of purple behind the ears.

*

For a long time we had been agitating for a Scottish certificate for guiding. At the moment we were allowed to practise anywhere, any time, in England and Wales, but in Scotland only during the summer months. After many delays the Association of Scottish Climbing Clubs, in early 1957, asked us to go to Glencoe and 'sit' for this new winter certificate. There were two grades: one for all-round winter mountaineering, the other for winter hill walking.

I was a little hurt when I found I'd been put down for the latter, but I was assured that it included the easier snow and ice climbs – routes where steps must be cut and ropes worn. When I realized that the higher grade meant the ability to lead clients competently up things like SC Gully and the North-East Buttress, I agreed wholeheartedly on the second grade.

Another guide present was Bob Downes, but his appendix was giving trouble on the morning of the examination and he was unable to come out with us.

Johnnie didn't have to undergo an official test. Instead he followed me up my route. I had been given North-West Gully on

Stob Coire nam Beith. I had indignantly rejected Broad Gully when it had been suggested, and instead, in mist and with a poor guide book illustration, took my two examiners up the wrong gully. Johnnie had to come up and lead the crux. It was a complete fiasco. We were late on the summit, no one had torches except Johnnie and me, one of the examiners lost her axe (and control) glissading, and I, coming down last, tripped over it and gashed my thigh. I was reprimanded sharply by Tom Weir, which was turning the screw. I felt terrible about that gully. But we found out later that both Bill Murray and Betty Starke had, on different occasions, made the same mistake. Indeed, a few days later, when Johnny and I had grimly and indubitably climbed North-West Gully with me stubbornly refusing to relinquish one foot of the lead (nine hundred feet of step-kicking with about a yard of ice in the middle) and we emerged on the summit, we met another party who had just done my examination gully but assured us they had done North-West. We explained, argued and expostulated. We quoted Murray and Betty Starke. We failed to convince them.

It was as we were coming down the glen after an unsuccessful attempt on SC Gully (I'd taken too long on the first pitch, and we had to be at the Clachaig for dinner) with the crust scrunching under our nails that, suddenly caught up in this world of snow and ice knowing and regretting this would be our last expedition of the winter, I said, 'How about Zermatt this year?'

Johnnie had never been there. I'd told him what the Matterhorn looked like from Zermatt, and Monte Rosa from Macugnaga, and he'd been forced to listen many times when I described the Marinelli and the east face of the Strahlhorn. Now, suddenly, in a frost-clamped Glencoe, I remembered it all again and said breathlessly, 'What about Zermatt?'

And Johnnie, catching fire, agreed.

19. Mainly the Breithorn

I had never been in an aeroplane before and I found even the most mundane preparations novel and exciting. The flight left Blackbushe at eight in the morning, so we had to catch the last coach from London and spend the night in the airport lounge. We passed a few absorbing and hysterical hours repacking our kit. By the time we'd fined our rucksacks down to the specified thirty-five pounds, we were faced with about seventy pounds overweight. Much of this we divided between our two small rucksacks and called it hand luggage. Trying to heft it lightly with one hand was singularly difficult. The remainder of the overweight, like smugglers, we distributed about our persons. Despite the heat of the morning, I wore an anorak full of pitons and, clasped round my lower torso like a chastity belt, a dozen carabiners and slings.

I was occupied with the thought of accidents. I had insured myself and was worried that, in the event of a crash, when all this ironmongery was found on my body, the claim might be invalidated. Instead of sleeping in the lounge armchair, I brooded. In the small hours I had reached the conclusion that the crash would be my fault. At breakfast time when the large and jolly Northumbrian party – who had chartered our aircraft – erupted mysteriously through the doors (we wondered if they'd spent the night under a hedge) Johnnie pointed out that some were children. This we accepted as justification for my excessive overweight.

As things turned out we missed all our calls, and the aircraft was waiting on the tarmac when we were bustled through the clearing house, so no one seemed to notice that I was carrying my hand luggage in both arms, and that I clinked.

We had a front seat, just forward of the starboard wing. The interior seemed very cramped and to me, who had seen plane interiors only on the cinema screen or in glossy advertisements, rather Heath Robinson. But the engines were reassuring. All the children and myself watched the propellers with fascination. Johnnie was quite blasé.

Then we were moving and I was wondering about the sensation as we left the ground. But nothing happened. We stayed down, running very fast, slowed, turned like a two-wheeled cart, and lined up at the end of a runway. I could just see the empty tarmac stretching away into the distance. The plane was stationary for a moment, throbbing like a greyhound in a trap. Then we were moving again, gathering speed, and suddenly, unbelievably, the ground was drawing away. We looked down on the tops of trees and sheds, and as we rose one lost the sensation of speed until, at a few thousand feet, the ground was floating very slowly below – and I knew that I'd seen it all before. It wasn't strange at all. It was the same view that you have from the top of a cliff, but a very steep one, for the ground was vertically below.

The sea was strange, glimpsed occasionally through windows in the cloud; tiny cat's-paws wrinkling the surface, and then a ship – like a model on grey frosted glass. Sometimes there were other planes speeding away very purposefully on lines of their own. Then we were in thick cloud, at least, there was cloud all about us, but sometimes there were gaps which the pilot seemed to make for, so that we flew along below towering masses like great ice walls, and the shadows looked like crevasses on a wet glacier. There were vast snowfields, and when the cloud sea sank and levelled off, it looked like the Yorkshire Moors or the Cairngorms on a winter's day.

We landed at Basle, and went quickly through the Customs and out again to a waiting coach. There were flowers in tiny metal holders, and a very loud radio playing a kind of Swiss edition of Music While You Work. The Northumbrians effused *joie de vivre*. They sang to the music, and people, walking along the bright wide streets, turned to stare as we passed. I hadn't seen a mountain nor smelt the scent of pines but I was choking with nostalgia and anticipation.

After leaving our baggage at the railway station, we found a workmen's café where we lunched cheaply and well, and the coffee was superb. Our train left in the afternoon. It was a long journey through the Oberland; we shared our compartment with a priest and a German family on holiday who, like the train passengers on Snowdon, rushed from side to side as each new prospect appeared. We followed more staidly. The waterfalls were, indeed, very lovely, dropping like lace down their black cliffs, but the cloud was down to eight thousand feet so we saw no peaks until we came twisting down the side of the Rhône valley, and the Weisshorn shone clear and bright above the murky depths of the Vispthal.

I had pictured it so many times in the last six years, this return to Zermatt. We were on the same train – the eight o'clock one – that I had taken with Vicki. I remembered the hair-raising road hundreds of feet above the glacier torrent, the avalanche sheds, the glimpses of the Breithorn at the head of the valley, and the lights of Zermatt beyond the flat pastures. But there was cloud on the Matterhorn; I felt that Zermatt was letting me down. I had wanted everything to be perfect for Johnnie.

We stayed at the Bahnhof which was run by the guide Bernard Biner and his sister Paula. It was this hotel where I had first heard the word *concubinage* but, ostensibly, I went unrecognized. If I was remembered it was with a tolerant air that said we were young once but now were responsible and respectable.

There was a sliding scale of prices at the hotel. You could sleep in great comfort in a bed with sheets (with a view of the Matterhorn) and have baths for some phenomenal sum outside our means, or you could share a room with another couple (four beds) for a more moderate amount. The plutocrats ate in the town, but those who had to husband their francs bought their own food and cooked it in the cellar.

However, for the first few days the weather was deplorable and, with money melting away on cafés, maps and all the superfluous trivialities one buys on off-days, we moved from the room which we shared with a Spanish couple, and climbed many flights of stairs to the attic and the cheaper communal dormitory.

On the third evening the weather cleared so that at last Johnnie had his view of the Matterhorn, plastered with new snow. He shuddered. He admitted during the holiday that the mountains here were big. Plainly he was impressed with Zermatt.

Bernard had suggested the Leiterspitzen for our first day. This is the rock ridge which cuts across the faces of the Dom and Täschhorn as seen from Zermatt. Its west ridge is bare of snow, a

rocky crest of gendarmes and brèches rising to a summit which is
a little over ten thousand feet high. We were told it was no more
than Difficult (not by Bernard but by an amateur who had just
done it). Bernard advised us to wait until the morning before we
went up. It could be done in a day from Zermatt. We believed
him. He said that we would have no difficulty. We believed that,
too.

Next morning we had our first taste for a long time of an early
start. We were up at four and away by five-thirty. It was a lovely
dawn with all the peaks clear, but later the ominous little cloud
appeared on the Furggen Ridge and there were signs of ravures
making as we went up through the pinewoods towards Täschalp.
There were crested tits in the trees and I saw a nutcracker. I was
anxious to go slowly and look at the birds and flowers (the path
was fringed with the biggest grass of parnassus I'd seen) for I was
carrying Johnnie's spare rucksack, which hung well down my
back like a second bottom; it was cutting my shoulders to the
bone.

It was chilly at Täschalp, chilly enough to drink our coffee
wearing duvets. My divine padded jacket I had bought at Jackson
and Warr's a few days ago. It seemed an enormous outlay at the
time, but I knew only too well how useful it would be in an
emergency. It was incredibly light and I insisted on taking it with
me on the climb. We left most of our gear at the café, taking, in
addition to a little food, only the duvet and one torch, and even
the latter was included only on my insistence. Johnnie's argument
was that it was an easy ('Difficult') rock ridge, and it would all be
extra weight. My answer was that we were in the Alps.

To one who had known only the well-trodden paths of Chamonix and the popular Zermatt tracks, that ascent to the Leiterspitzen was a revelation. At first the path, little more than a sheep
track, rose slowly, running under the south face of the mountain.
There were flowers everywhere: scabious, harebells, sheepbit
and a dwarf forget-me-not, pale blue and perfect. Higher there
were gentians of an intense and vivid blue. There was a sedum
with a cactus-like rosette, a red stalk and pink and red petals. I
thought this was house-leek. There were alpine pinks and cushions
of moss campion, and a big yellow daisy like coreopsis. Everywhere
there were edelweiss and starry saxifrage, and a lovely violet aster

with a yellow centre. And as the ground steepened and I trod close on Johnnie's heels, the scent of crushed thyme was almost overpowering.

After the first thousand feet we struck up towards the ridge. There was a col far above, but to reach it we had to traverse steep, smooth slabs interspersed with slopes of unstable scree. We lost an hour here, taking three hours to the col instead of the guide book time of two. But when we reached the ridge about twelve-thirty, still with the thought that there was only an easy rock climb between us and the summit, we were unconcerned and took our time over lunch. A rock thrush watched us curiously from a boulder. We might have taken his interest as a sign that few people came this way . . .

We started on the ridge at one-fifteen p.m. I had the first lead and went wrong immediately. The guide book warns the climber not to leave the crest because the rock is loose. Goodness knows, the crest itself was loose enough, but the stuff at the side was rotten to the core. I tried to move out to the left because straight ahead looked far too hard, but I was forced to retreat and then Johnnie led straight up the ridge. Now we knew that our in-formation was wrong. This first gendarme was Severe but there were two pitons in place for protection and, at the top, an enor-mous iron spike for a belay. Wondering silently how much I was committing myself, I led through with a mantelshelf behind Johnnie, and so over the top of the gendarme and down into the brèche on the other side.

The rock was as rotten as anything we had met on any climb. There was a gendarme split by a crack which looked as if it would part when you wedged a fist in the fissure, and there were loose blocks perched lightly on the crest of the ridge itself. The expo-sure on the north side was alarming and later, when we saw this wall from the floor of the Vispthal at Randa, we were speechless with astonishment to think that we used rotten holds above that drop. Only Difficult![1] There was a steep wall with four great bolts cemented into the rock: strenuous work pulling from one to the other, particularly as a sling had wedged round the second

1. Of course we had confused the British Difficult which is merely difficult with the Continental Difficult which is severe. See also glossary. [Author.]

and I had to retrieve it while hanging off-balance on one hand.

When we topped each gendarme we could see the ridge stretching ahead – and still no sign of the summit; it was like the Cuillin on a colossal scale. And now the sun went in, and snatching a glance southwards, I saw the rain curtains creeping down the Vispthal.

By the time we came to a huge overhanging fang where it was obvious we would have to abseil, it was snowing heavily, and anxiety about weather was added to that of daylight.

I could find no bollard for the abseil rope so I passed it right round the top of the fang, running it through a nick and over a sharp flake. I stared at those razor edges dubiously, then tied my best lace handkerchief round the nylon, and, with Johnnie shouting for speed, climbed down gingerly to a ledge. Looking below to find my point of arrival, I realized with a shock that the abseil was free – and free over that great north wall. I shivered in the blizzard, thinking of those sharp flakes with only my lace handkerchief protecting the rope; then I swung off the ledge, lost one rope, retrieved it, slid down the overhang, touched the rock again with my feet, and continued more happily now that I was no longer surrounded by air.

I was interested in Johnnie's comments as he came to the top of the fang and stared, fascinated, at the glacier below.

As we pulled the rope down, my handkerchief detached itself, opened to a square – the delicate border showing pathetically for a moment against the cloud – and then it floated gently away and was lost to sight. I was heart-broken.

We continued along the ridge thinking each new gendarme was the last, but always the crest rose higher ahead. We passed a little cairn but pressed on, ignorant of its significance (we are still), knowing we couldn't escape before the summit. At six-thirty we stopped. We had no way of knowing how far we were from the top, and our one desire now was to get off the ridge before we were caught in a worse storm and darkness. Johnnie thought we might be able to traverse the face below the summit and link up with the easy descent.

We retraced our steps to the little cairn, wondering now if it marked an escape route. There was a gully running down the face here, and we descended it for about six hundred feet. Occasionally we left it and traversed across smooth slabs in the dark, meeting scree which shifted alarmingly above the bottomless drops, and sometimes the scree lay on the slabs themselves. Eventually, and again in a gully, we came to a place where the angle steepened abruptly and to continue we must abseil. There was no place to belay, and I waited anxiously while Johnnie crawled about the slabs with our one light, like a gigantic goblin, vainly trying to find a crack that would take a piton. He found one in the end but the peg didn't sing as it was hammered home, and it wobbled when he tested it.

I refused to abseil. I said that there was a strong doubt that the peg would hold; that we were guides – he should know that a bivouac was the wisest course. Besides, how did he know the length of the abseil? We were tired after fourteen hours out: neither of us would have the strength to climb the rope again if the bottom hung free above an overhang. When the argument grew really hot I reminded him of Sheena. I won. He couldn't force me to abseil.

With the situation decided and a bivouac inevitable, we were calmer, and climbed slowly and in silence up the scree again to a kind of earthy ledge below a great wall. It was Johnnie's first bivouac, my third, and with the experience of an old campaigner, I started spinning out the time. We took an hour arranging ourselves, putting in the piton, tying ourselves to it, reckoning our food supplies, our cigarettes, the matches, carefully choosing our seats after levelling the ground, and dressing against the long cold night. At length I settled down on the rope and my head-scarf. I was quite warm in the duvet, and it was this comfort that kept me silent for a time after I had settled down; I was wondering whether I should give Johnnie my pullover. He had only one and no duvet. After some time during which my conscience wrestled with my comfort, I gave up the struggle and stripped. After that I shivered all night. Johnnie said he was quite warm.

We had enough cigarettes left for one every hour; there were some boiled sweets and some grubby Kendal Mint Cake; these we would have between the cigarettes. We agreed that we would smoke on the hour and eat at the half hour.

Johnnie insisted on my taking off my gloves and holding his hands. He had only fingerless mitts. We talked.

The storm had passed. There was a cloud sea now in the valley (and heavy rain, we were told later) but all the peaks were radiant in the moonlight. Across the ridge opposite, we saw Monte Rosa, the Lyskamm and the Breithorn, remote and dream-like and very still. There was no wind. I was conscious, as the night wore on, that the streams which had run down the rocks after the storm, were now silent, frozen hard. Our clothes didn't freeze and the wet elastic in my cuffs was unpleasant. It became an agonizing effort to move, to push up my sleeve and look at my watch.

Time went quickly. We were amazed how soon the hour and the half hour came round and it was time to smoke or eat.

With my captive audience I talked relentlessly. I told Johnnie the complete story of *The Well of Loneliness*. When I had talked that out we played word games, but in the last few hours before the dawn we were both very tired, and sunk in a half-stupor, I found I could drop asleep in the pause between question and answer.

In the long silences at the end of each game, I looked out across the valley at the opposite ridge, and the snowfields, high in their hanging corries, assumed strange and perfect shapes. There was a flying swan and a rhinoceros, and the head of a lioness. Once an avalanche fell and we could hear the séracs bumping down the cliffs.

Above us the moonlight moved across the great towers. Everything was in slow motion, conducive to sleep. Occasionally I lurched forward and the rope at my waist brought me up short. I looked at the watch and shook Johnnie's hands.

'Time for a cigarette. You've been asleep!'

'No, I haven't. I was thinking.'

'Give me a mountain beginning with "A" and a route up it.'

At three-thirty the sky began to pale, and after another hour we started to get ready. I wondered how long it would take to get warm. I wondered what warmth felt like. Was I too tired to hurry? But, climbing back to the ridge in duvet and gloves, I soon stopped shivering. As we had known all through the night, we had been within easy reach of the top, for when we struck the crest again we were on the summit in no time.

There was a lot of ice and verglas on the rock and we had to

climb carefully, but now we had no worries; we weren't unduly
fatigued by the bivouac, and the sun shone brilliantly. I was still
wearing my duvet, which was fortunate, for, as I was abseiling on
the descent, a large rock, loosened by the rope, came down and hit
me on the shoulder, but the padding dulled the shock and I stayed
on the rope.

After the abseil we came down a long, long stony couloir for
about two thousand feet. We coiled the rope at the top and,
glancing idly down the gully, I saw a figure working slowly up the
screes, picking things off the ground. Beyond were more figures:
about three altogether.

'What *are* those women doing, right up here?' I asked. 'Do you
think they're gathering amethysts?'

But Johnnie was impatient and refused to look.

'Listen!' I said, 'there's a peg hammer!'

Up on the rocks I caught a movement.

'I know,' I said, 'it's a geologist, and he's recruited the local
women to collect specimens.'

The people in the couloir weren't geologists themselves; the
leading one wore a long peasant skirt.

Johnnie started down and I followed more slowly, peering up at
the women as I passed below, but, unaccountably, they had
moved out of sight, although I still caught a flicker of movement
here and there.

Johnnie never saw them and he had better eyesight than I. I
wasn't so tired that I was seeing things, nor was it like the strange
shapes I saw at night. I *let* myself see those; I could pull myself
deliberately out of that mood, focus on the shapes, and they became snowfields again. I was perfectly normal that morning at
the head of the couloir – and there were women in it gathering
something among the rocks.

Johnnie, eager for coffee, had no time for my curiosity, no
time for a slow plod down the mountainside under the sun, revelling in the comfortable security of grass after the blizzard on the
rotten ridge. He galloped ahead and I became resentful, trying to
catch him up, then angry because he was leaving me no time to
enjoy myself. When I did come up with him and he sneered at my
slow progress I came right back with the nastiest jibe at my command – his acceptance of my pullover last night. Speechless with

fury, we glared at each other, and then I sent him ahead, reflecting wickedly that they would give him hell at the café for leaving me alone on the mountain.

When I reached the Weingarten torrent at the foot of the couloir I found that the way led down the banks of the stream where loose boulders perched on slopes of wet earth. I kept tripping and sliding, cursing the absence of a track.

At the Täschalp I found to my amusement that Johnnie *had* been lectured for leaving me behind. We both felt better now and settled happily at a little tin table in the sun, eating soup at a phenomenal price. The café people told us they hadn't been worried the night before. They had thought we were at the Täsch hut. I felt a little resentful.

We came slowly down through the pinewoods to Zermatt. Over an enormous meal we told Bernard about our adventure, then, at six o'clock, I went to bed. I learnt afterwards that Johnnie, unpacking the large rucksack which had been left at Täschalp, found that a tube of tomato purée had burst, and he had to wash all the spare clothing. He set the alarm for eight since we had intended to have two hours' sleep and go out to eat again, but neither of us heard it, and we slept for fourteen hours. My eyelids were swollen like table tennis balls in the morning.

Two days later saw us slowly plodding up to the Rothorn hut with heavy packs. This time I was determined to reach the summit of the mountain by way of the Rothorngat. Six years before we had retreated from the Gabel which is several hundred feet below the top.

The cloud was down. We could see only the Unter Gabelhorn and the lower slopes of the Wellenkuppe when we reached the Trift Hotel. Then it started to rain so we decided to have coffee and give the shower time to stop. But the weather deteriorated further and we spent the night at the hotel. Everything but the beds was primitive. There were candles in the bedrooms which I passed, but I couldn't inquire too deeply into the mechanics – not plumbing – of the lavatory. I was locked in it, too, as there was a handle only on the outside, and was released by a member of the Alpine Club. When we went to bed it was snowing hard.

We continued to the hut the following morning, plodding dismally up the moraines through intermittent snow showers. We spent the rest of the day playing Battleships in the hut – a game which fascinated the Swiss and French who shared our involuntary inactivity. After a few hours the whole hut was playing Battleships. This is a paper game. The warden was astonished at the great demand for lavatory paper.

The following day was glorious, but not having expected it, we got up late and were, therefore, among the last to leave the hut.

We followed the ordinary way to the place where the route to the Rothorngrat branched off to the left. We stared across the glaciers and saw that the ridge was well plastered with new snow. We agreed that it might go tomorrow; for today we must be content with the ordinary route. So we turned and trudged up the gentle slope to the snow ridge, and stopped there to stare up at the Gabel. The couloir – that 'easy' gully which we had descended so slowly six years ago – was now in even harder condition. Guided parties moved up it in slow motion. There was ice everywhere. We were far too late for the mountain under these conditions, besides we would have to pass all the other parties as they descended. We turned back.

The following morning I awoke with an aching head and a churning stomach. I forced myself to eat breakfast and pack and we left the hut at five forty-five a.m. The clouds were low on the glacier, but the steep glassy ice among the moraine was frozen hard and we made good progress. We stopped in the same place as yesterday to consider the Rothorngrat and the weather. Ravures were forming above the breaks in the low cloud, and there seemed to be a strong wind higher up. Things didn't look very hopeful. Once again we relinquished the harder ridge and turned to the ordinary route.

I was becoming familiar with this now: the long slope to the snow ridge (it was somewhere here that we went wrong six years ago and struck off to the right instead of traversing left) then the ridge itself with a great green crevasse gaping in the Upper Trift glacier on the left, and, on the right, a cornice above the Hohlicht ice, and then – seeming to overhang – the east face of the Rothorn, dropping like a plumb-line to the glacier.

This time we didn't stop long when the snow ridge ran into the rocks, merely paused a moment to leave the crampons and my pack. The couloir looked much easier than yesterday: fairly clear of snow and – we found later – the verglas melted. Our late start won us this slight advantage.

The couloir was pleasant climbing with traverses across the snow ice and good scrambling up the rocks, but already we were meeting the first parties descending. However, the ground was fairly easy and we reached the Gabel without incident. We had been curious to know if the Rothorngrat would have 'gone' that day. Now, standing on the ridge and looking at it a few feet away, we were astonished to see that it was still plastered with snow on the Zinal side; there was no rock visible where the sun hadn't reached. Then we looked up the ordinary route – and the mountain was alive with people! On every pitch parties were coming or going, and the air rang with their shouts. Like the Rothorngrat the route had lost none of its ice, for it was on a western face. I had not yet found my alpine sense of proportion and all the time I was aware of the exposure. There was one place where you traverse along an overhanging ledge above the east face. There are good holds, but the drop is so steep that stonefalls on the glacier two thousand feet below seem to be under your heels.

'Look down,' chuckled Johnnie, as I edged round the corner. I swore at him.

After this move the rest of the exposure assumed more normal proportions.

Passing other parties held us up considerably. Below the exposed ledge we had met Gottfried Perren driving his three clients down the Binerplatte like three race horses. At least, we assumed it was the Binerplatte. This may be easy in normal times; today it was an ice slope. There were steps cut in it, but we relinquished these to Perren's team and Johnnie struck out on to virgin ice, chipping little nicks for our feet. Neither of us was belayed and neither wore crampons.

On the summit we found nine people, apparently all together and all big, blond Germans speaking no English. There was a wind here and shifting mist. We had one terrifying glimpse of the ridge towards the Schallihorn with the inevitable exposure on either side, then I looked towards more familiar ground and saw, away on the snow ridge, my little rucksack looking very forlorn and very far below.

The Germans gave me an inferiority complex.

'Let them go first,' I whispered to Johnnie.

I didn't want them treading on our heels all the way to the Gabel. I shall always be a sucker for good looks and muscle and tough talk – particularly in another language. The Germans started off: *six* of them roped together, then a party of three. I tried to avoid Johnnie's eye.

It took us two hours to reach the Gabel; we could have done it in a quarter of the time with a clear run. There was no question of my inching my way round the exposed corner; I had to wait there, my boot heels hanging above eternity, while the people in front made room for me on the stance. It took me ages to sort out their rope for them afterwards. Here they offered us cold tea with lemon and rum which was nasty, but the thought was kind, and we were patient, talking careful German to the last blond giant, asking if we could pass, please, at the Gabel.

So the word was sent down the long column and we padded silently and self-consciously down beside them, accepted glucose at the Gabel and were waved politely ahead. We were at the foot of the rock ridge when their first man was only halfway down the couloir. We were moving singly too, with belays, while they moved together.

It started to snow on the rock ridge, and we paused only long enough to pick up our crampons and the rucksack and then we were rattling down the mountain, warming up with the speed. The snow fell softly, pleasant and exhilarating if you knew you were on the right track back to the hut; terrifying if you were lost.

We had picked up our gear at the refuge and were starting down to Zermatt when we met Gottfried Perren for the second time that day, coming up the moraine. He told us he had taken his clients down to the Trift Hotel, nearly three thousand feet below, and there picked up another party. Tomorrow he would do the Rothorn again. He was then sixty-seven.

Darkness fell as we came down the steep path below the Edelweiss and I slowed down with blisters on my heels. Johnnie went on and after a while I stopped and sat on the bank. Below me the town was brilliantly lit. I could hear faint sounds of music from a hotel. I was aware of the great contrast between the comfort and security of the mountain village and the remoteness of that other world above the snowline. I thought of all the people who had sat on ledges – perhaps with an injured companion – and stared through the night at the lights in the valley, and I thought of the people down there, who had waited, wondering what had happened, for a guide who was overdue. I shivered a little; bad weather and the crop of accidents since our arrival were demoralizing me. Johnnie wanted to do a hard climb. Should we – in these conditions? Would we return to Wales unhappy with only ordinary routes behind us? I thought about the Z'mutt ridge of the Matterhorn – but the Tiefenmatten face would be covered with snow now. The Ober Gabelhorn traverse would be good – but not great – and two parties had fallen off it recently. All the big ridges were out: the Schalligrat, the Viereselsgrat, the Younggrat ... Was the Younggrat out? It was from just above this point that I had first looked at the Breithorn seriously, idly thinking what a grand route that ridge would make, unaware that it was a climb.

I limped down to Zermatt, thinking, resolving that Johnnie should have the next choice.

*

We waited for two days for a good weather forecast: days of eating and writing the journal and talking to the younger members of the Alpine Club, which was celebrating its centenary that year. John Tyson was staying at the Bahnhof with his wife. He had just done the Younggrat. Ice climbs, we said, they were the things to do: the north face of the Dent d'Hérens, or the Younggrat itself, for the crux was ice and there were the steps of John's party already cut. Actually the Alpine Club had followed a guided party and it was this guide, Elias Julen, who had cut the steps. Julen, who was reputed to have done the Younggrat over thirty times, said that this year the conditions were the hardest he had known. But, said John pleasantly, we would have no difficulty.

For us everything had to be perfect for a great climb, so we waited for a good weather report. It came three days after we had done the Rothorn – but the visible weather signs didn't tally. With that slight doubt in our minds we dropped the Younggrat in favour of an attempt on the traverse of the Rimpfischhorn.

We went up to Fluhalp in the chair lift: a procedure which terrified Johnnie as the chairs dipped and swayed through the tree tops. Cloud was down to the Hörnli so we hadn't that wonderful view of the Matterhorn rising above the valley. Floppy, furry marmots stared curiously as we floated above them.

It was Saturday evening, and when we reached the hotel on the Fluhalp the adults had gone down to Zermatt for Sunday, leaving only a small boy in charge. Unable to make him understand our requirements, we forced our way into the kitchen – together with some Alpine Club people and three Irishmen – and cooked our own supper. Then the boy called us at five instead of four the next morning.

It was a lovely day and, trying to recover that lost hour, we went too fast to the snowline. My heart was hammering and blood throbbing in my ears; I kept stopping, bent over my axe. Johnnie was in little better shape. We were both relieved when the long snow plod ended and we emerged on a great white dome below the final steep step to the summit. To the south we could see the three Irishmen going up to the Adlerhorn, and the two AC members on the Strahlhorn slope. To judge by their speed, they, too, were finding the going hard.

We had the Rimpfischhorn completely to ourselves. There is a lot to be said for climbing on Sundays when the guides are all at church.

To reach the last rocks we had a snow-slope and then a hundred-foot traverse left across ice where steps had to be cut. Then came rocks and another, shorter, traverse, then a delightful scramble to the top on easy rock. It was very cold and we climbed in duvets. From the summit we looked along our intended route. There was a lot of snow on it, and we had the feeling that the great gendarme would be iced. The weather seemed to be deteriorating, too, and regretfully, we decided to abandon the ridge, retreat to the saddle below the summit, and cross the great glacier basin below the north face of the mountain. This would bring us to the Täsch hut.

On the descent, when we were nearly down, I was glissading below the last traverse when I lost control, and the ice axe belay failed (Johnnie was using an odd method he had just evolved – of passing my rope through a carabiner hanging on the head of the axe, and this slipped off), but since I was trying to stop myself and setting up some friction he was able to hold me from his stance. Mutual recriminations followed and we came down sulkily to the saddle.

As we ate our lunch a family of choughs arrived and settled in the snow watching us like vultures. But it was our crumbs they wanted, not our bones. They couldn't keep still, and shuffled about the saddle, frantic that they would miss something if they stayed in one place. When I threw a crust they came running and lurching with a kind of hop, step and jump. Some birds hop, some run, others walk; those choughs did everything from a polka to a soft shoe dance. And where most were resplendent with their black plumage, yellow beaks and red legs one was moulting round the neck; he looked like an old clown in a tatty boa.

That descent from the Rimpfischchorn must be one of the easiest in the Alps. Below the saddle a gentle snow-slope, not steep enough to glissade, ran down to the Mellich glacier, and it was with some surprise that I received Johnnie's warning of crevasses. We moved down carefully to a kind of rock rib running out from the mountain towards the west. As we approached we realized that stones were falling from it, landing with a dull plop on the glacier. There was a bergschrund which we crossed by way of a snow bridge, and then we hurried round the end of the rib and out on to the open glacier again. Here speed was unimportant for there were no more missiles from above, and we loitered across that great white expanse, completely untracked, enjoying to the full the vast solitude. The clouds had gone again and the sun blazed down on us: the sky was purple through our goggles.

We kept the rope on, of course, for there were hidden crevasses everywhere. We skirted several of the largest, going well out to the end round the last thin shadowed line in the snow, and then we came to a little slope and – a short distance out from its base – another gaping rift. By this time I had relinquished all responsibility to Johnnie, merely taking care to tread in his tracks and keep the rope above the snow. I was lost in a soft and pleasant dream so that when he told me to belay at the top of the slope, I didn't question it, although I wondered why he was fidgeting about, beating at the snow with his axe.

'Right,' he shouted suddenly, 'watch it!' And jumped into the air.

The urgency of this command awakened me, and I watched the rope like a hawk, trying to feed it quickly round the shaft and making sure it didn't snag. At forty feet (we were using only that length) the nylon ran out and I was aware of a pregnant silence. I peered over the edge and there he was, flat on his back, forty feet below and on the lip of the big crevasse, surrounded by wind-slab. Another crevasse ran along the top of the slope. I had been meant to hold him on the other side of this, but I hadn't known – and his impact on the slope had made it avalanche.

At the next crevasse he crossed on a bridge and then belayed me, but as I started to move, he discovered he was on top of another rift . . . Even when we reached the dry part of the glacier (but where snow still filled the ends of the crevasses) we weren't safe. I fell in a narrow one and wedged like a cork.

It was dark in the valleys when we reached the narrow track above the Täsch hut, but the sun was still on the tops. Above the black and lesser mountains, the Nordend rose, bright pink and clear: the only colour in that eastern view. But in the other direction there was cloud just above the Rothorn and the east face – red at any time – smouldered duskily like the reflection of great fires burning on the Hohlicht glacier.

We had hoped to do the Rotgrat on the Alphubel the following day, but Johnnie was now obsessed by the Younggrat. I, too, with the weather holding, preferred to do something big. We had done three climbs, but none of them what we had wanted to do, all second choices because the weather had been too poor for the great routes. But now that we were at the Täsch hut it was a pity not to do another climb here; we had carried all our food over the Rimpfischhorn, it seemed an awful waste of energy.

We wasted the energy after all. In the morning we had no enthusiasm for the Alphubel (perhaps because of the long grind to the foot of the climb?). We went to sleep again and woke at nine to a magnificent day. We had no regrets for the Rotgrat, suddenly we were both caught up in wild enthusiasm for the Breithorn. We couldn't wait to reach Zermatt, and trotted gaily down through the woods with the heat bringing out the scent of resin and cicadas shrilling in the grass.

*

Our enthusiasm didn't last. The following day was bad again: threatening, cool and windy. The holiday seemed to have been one long chart of ups and downs: a good weather report, then watching the Föhn build up over Italy and high cirrus forming – and the spate of accidents. Seeing our time drawing out (we had four days left) we became bad-tempered and miserable. By day Zermatt was quite gay with its throngs of tourists, among them many English or American climbers who would join us for coffee or wine in the dim cafés, but in the evenings our bad temper deepened. We tried to find some life, touring the hotel bars in our best clothes, but we found only tiny orchestras and bored singers playing to empty rooms.

We decided that we would go up on the second day whatever the weather – only to be greeted by the news in the morning that a party was overdue from the Rotgrat. Rescue operations were already in progress (they had been out all night) and Geiger, the Alpine Rescue pilot, was flying round the Alphubel, trying to pierce the cloud. We waited all day at the Bahnhof, sitting in the sun and staring at the Matterhorn, in that peculiar state of listlessness which descends on superfluous climbers when a rescue operation is in progress. In the circumstances we couldn't leave and go up to the Breithorn; Johnnie had offered his services, but Bernard (who organized the operation from Zermatt) said he should wait to see if more men were needed.

In the afternoon the news came that the party had been found uninjured and were being brought down to the valley. We relaxed – but it was too late to go up to the Breithorn.

On the Thursday, with three days left, and the weather just managing to look settled, we packed our rucksacks and left for the Gandegg hut. There was no longer any need to be careful of money; this was our last expedition and nothing was to be spared to make it a success. Not only did we travel light – as light as one can travel with ironmongery and ropes, duvets and spare clothes – but we took the new cable car to the Schwarzsee Hotel to save time and energy.

We were very cramped in the little metal boxes that were the cable cars, and earned black looks from passengers and conductor because of crampons strapped on the backs of our rucksacks. But it was pleasant, rising three thousand feet or so without doing any work – although it cost us sixteen francs. We sat on the terrace outside the hotel sparing only a glance for the Matterhorn towering beside us, but staring long and silently (even paying for the use of the telescope) at the Breithorn across the glaciers. We could see the whole length of the Younggrat, even the great gendarme near the top which was glistening as it caught the sun.

We came to the Gandegg hut by a way that was seldom used. It skirted the Oberer Théodule glacier, passing through a no-man's land of tumbled moraines where silty lakes gleamed in the hollows, and the ground was too arid for anything but a few stunted alpines. When we reached the hut we had taken almost as long as the walk up from Zermatt.

There were several parties in the refuge, bound for the ordinary route up the Breithorn the following day. They were all German or Austrian. At first we were accepted as another party for the same route, but when we had asked the guardian – a plump, bespectacled young woman – for an early call, and she had said that that was ridiculous for the ordinary route, and we'd said no, the Younggrat – then the atmosphere changed.

Elias Julen had climbed it recently for the thirty-second time and it was the hardest . . . yes, we had heard. He had had thirty metres of step cutting in the couloir and had returned to the hut at six in the evening, having left at four. We hadn't known *that*. And now, regretting my inconvenient memory, I recalled the second ascent of the ridge when a party had fallen at the crux and all had been killed.

Later I heard the others discussing us and learnt that tomorrow we were to do the North Wall of the Breithorn. It sounded a little like the Eigerwand.

We arranged a call for two-fifteen a.m. with Mademoiselle who was still heavy with disapproval. I slept little and was up early, distrusting her, but she turned up trumps; I met her on the stairs in a chic nightgown.

Outside on the terrace I stood and looked at the weather. It was very mild; the stars glittered. I was uneasy.

I went back to the common room and started making sandwiches. Johnnie came down and I responded listlessly when he asked for a weather report. He went outside and returned almost immediately. There were no stars, he said, and flakes of snow starting to fall.

A little later I went out. It was snowing heavily.

We ate our breakfast in silence. Afterwards half an inch of snow was lying on the terrace.

At five o'clock we went back to bed, dozing sulkily through the bustle of other climbers getting up to do the ordinary route.

We spent the day scrambling along the top of the cliff on which the hut was perched, making out our route for the following day: the descent to the glacier, the line through the crevasses above the ice fall, the traverse of the two snow bays, and beyond those, another glacier, invisible from the hut.

In the afternoon a member of the Alpine Club arrived with his wife and their guide. They, too, disapproved of our proposed expedition, but they gave us a lot of ham and chicken for breakfast next morning.

I heard hail on the roof before I went to sleep, and in the lull that followed, I thought I heard the snow sweeping past. I felt utterly miserable. I thought I would never come to the Alps again, that the holiday was a complete failure; that never again would I have any confidence in myself or Johnnie, and – thinking like this – I fell asleep.

*

The night before, standing on the terrace with the Swiss guide, he had said, 'Either the cloud will come up . . . or it will go back into the valleys . . .'

I said, 'Either the cloud will come up and we'll have two or three days of bad weather' (for it had deteriorated slowly and steadily over the last eight hours) 'or there will be a miracle.'

When I went outside that morning it was the miracle; the cloud had retreated to the valleys and all the tops were clear in the starlight. It was even a little chilly. I was tremendously excited.

We breakfasted on the chicken and ham and I cut sandwiches, but that breakfast was the last food I was to eat – except for Kendal Mint Cake – for thirty-two hours.

We left the hut at three-forty a.m. and Mademoiselle stood in the door and wished us good luck. A wraith of cloud crept across the terrace, but as we dropped below the hut it was clear again. We came quickly down the rubbishy cliff, following the path by torchlight, and in half an hour we were on the glacier.

During the last two days, while we stared at the Younggrat, it had seemed a vast distance from the Gandegg to the ridge, and I had thought of that distance as the first great obstacle. The guide book time is three hours, but never for one moment did I think we could approach it. But we made good progress across the dry ice of the Unterer Théodule glacier, skirting the ice-fall without incident, but it seemed a long, long time before we were stumbling through the medial moraine. Then the rognon – the little island of rock that was the next landmark – loomed ahead, and here we had to climb a neck of rock at the foot of the main cliff. I had expected, pessimistically, that this would be likely to provide a hard pitch, but when we reached it we found easy rocks that were only a walk. Then came the two glacier bays strewn with old avalanche debris. Dawn came while we were crossing these: a clear cold dawn promising a lovely day. But there was no time to look at it; we were aware of the daylight only as an aid to speed.

We came out above the last glacier on a little col called the Triftjijoch, and stared down the steep, dirty couloir at the jumbled ice-fall below. John Tyson had warned us not to reach this point before dawn, for between the ice-fall and the Younggrat there were several large crevasses and our route through these had to be planned from the col.

The couloir was less formidable than it looked and the muddy scree went quite well in crampons. Johnnie proved his worth as a route finder on the glacier, where we weaved back and forth between the crevasses without one check. As we walked I shot occasional glances at our ridge, clear in the morning light. I reflected that it must, indeed, be very hard to take the guide book time of four to eight hours. (It is about two thousand feet in length and looked a good deal less.)

We toiled grimly up the last snow-slope, going ever more slowly for our quick dash across the glaciers was taking its toll. Johnnie was swearing that he had frostbite but my feet were quite warm.

We came out on the ridge and into the sun at six fifty-five a.m., only fifteen minutes past guide book time. Our speed, the warmth and good weather, raised our spirits, and, looking up the lovely snow arêtes which seemed to go on for a thousand feet, we laughed and promised ourselves second breakfast on the summit. We stayed there nearly an hour, Johnnie removing his crampons and warming his feet, taking photographs, and myself – just lolling in the sun and thinking what a pleasant climb we were going to have: a larger edition of Observatory Ridge . . .

We started at eight, and moved together at first. The guide book says that this first section is *parfois cornichée*. That day it was completely corniced, and soon we were moving singly – and the drop on the right was growing, although, as yet, it was an ordinary snowslope and one could disregard the bergschrund as the slope was convex and it was invisible. The exposure on the left was a different matter: a rocky cliff dropping to the ice-fall of the Schwärze glacier, again not particularly noticeable when we were low on the ridge, but growing insidiously, sneaking up when one's back was turned, as it were. The guide book mentioned small gendarmes which could be turned on the left, but we took them direct – in crampons. There were good holds, and the front points gripped like tricounis although the noise and the sense of insecurity were disconcerting at first. One gendarme had to be descended *à cheval*. I felt top-heavy with the rucksack on my back, like the hunchback of Notre Dame, and not nearly so agile.

Between gendarmes there was powder snow on ice, or pure ice, or rotten snow, with all their different variations of durability, and my waits were long. The steps of the previous parties were too close to the cornices for our comfort (some of the snow would have melted since their ascent) so we had to make our own route below their tracks.

In one place it took Johnnie an hour to climb fifty feet, while I waited and shivered on the stance, and wished devoutly that I could do some of the work. But I couldn't cut nearly as fast as a man, my job was the second's: to stand on the stance watching every movement intently, always ready for a slip, my hands tense on the rope as he plunged in the pick and moved up on the holds. He led superbly, never faltering, working often one-handed, clearing, cutting, climbing, and the ice chips flew in the sunlight and rattled off the ridge in a constant stream.

I shivered and felt tired and miserable. I was dying to put on my duvet, but Johnnie, warm with his work, suggested scornfully that halfway up a climb (where there were no natural stances) was no place to start dressing. I knew that my fatigue was derived from the cold and became resentful – then angry with myself for feeling this way on a hard climb. I tried to occupy my mind with statistics. If we were halfway up now – at two o'clock in the afternoon – we had taken six hours on what was reputed to be the easiest section; another six hours and we would still be below the crux. Yesterday I had said we could retreat from the Grand Gendarme. Yesterday I hadn't suspected the condition of the snow. The route was *descended* in 1936. They must have had superb conditions. Indeed, conditions must have been better when John Tyson did it, when the Pinnacle Club did it, Geoff Roberts, Mike Harris, John Mawe, Old Uncle Tom Cobbleigh and all . . . Were they watching us through binoculars from the Gandegg? They would be worried by now, noting our speed and realizing it must be due to bad snow and ice. (They weren't watching from the Gandegg but from the Gornergrat, until four or five o'clock, when they left us at the critical time – they might have watched until sunset.)

I came up to Johnnie and I was shaking with the cold. At last he looked at me instead of glancing only at my belay before he moved off. I was allowed to put on my duvet. Immediately the mercury in my mental and physical barometer shot up; the eiderdown closed round me, enfolding, protecting, and I stopped shivering and started to enjoy myself – almost.

The prospect of benightment intruded itself. I dreaded the thought of a night on that ridge. The wind was very cold – even now, in the afternoon – and I had to keep wriggling my toes to bring them back to life. But I wriggled carefully, for the stances were only steps in the ice (there was no time to cut buckets), in fact, we'd been hard put to it to find a place where I could put on my duvet. In the end Johnnie held my pack and anorak as I passed them to him; and both held our axes with one hand throughout the operation.

I had a bad moment on the penultimate gendarme. There was a long stride to the left into a corner, too far to step, too delicate to climb across in crampons. I leant forward and fell into the corner, but the crampon on the back foot had wedged in a crack and my knee was badly wrenched before the weight of my body freed the crampon. For one terrible, painful moment I thought I'd put the patella out, and that would be the end of us. But I kept moving, the pain went, and I forgot the incident as we reached the Grand Gendarme.

Above us were steep rocks interspersed with ice, and covering the lot was a thick layer of flour-like snow. Then Johnnie found a piton in a crack, and, threading the rope through a carabiner, continued more happily – until the rocks steepened abruptly. Here he hammered home an ice peg, traversed delicately round a corner on the left and was lost to sight. It was a long run-out, perhaps eighty feet, and had taken some time. After he'd gone, I had spent it contemplating the ice fall below. When it was my turn, I followed quickly to the second peg, the hammer was passed down the rope, and I got to work. I always feel that it is unfair that the weakest member of the party should have the hardest job on such occasions. So much more strength is needed to take out a piton than to put it in. I could just reach the peg and I hammered away, while the other hand which held me on, weakened fast. I pictured myself slipping, swinging under Johnnie (he was away to the side) dangling under an overhang, oscillating gently above the Schwärze glacier. The piton, I shouted, cost only three and six – and it was mine. Let's leave it. Johnnie said that was all right, as long as we didn't need it later on. (We had a snow peg, homemade and tubular; it had collapsed the first time it was used. We had some rock pegs but no more for ice.) Thinking of the ice traverse which was the crux, I redoubled my efforts, but, although it wobbled, it must have bent as it went in (what on earth possessed him to put a long ice peg in a rock crack?). I couldn't retrieve it, and, putting our trust in rock pegs, we went on.

At five o'clock we stood on top of the Grand Gendarme. This top, and the descent to the brèche between it and the main cliff, was a knife-edged arête of rotten snow.

We took two or three pitches – and a lot of time – to reach the brèche, kicking through the snow into the tough ice underneath. I led here. There were no belays. Johnnie balanced on the crest ready to jump down the other side if I fell. Occasionally I put an arm over the top of the arête to steady myself. It felt sickening, like taking armfuls of cotton wool. Every time I took my axe out of the snow, light showed through the bottom of the hole. In one place a large lump of snow (I measured it carefully: I spent a long time looking at it: twelve by three by one inch thick) was balanced on top of the arête by a tiny neck about the width and thickness of an inch and the light showed through *that*. The only thing that held it there was the dropping temperature. I used it as a handrail. Despite the fact that I'd eaten breakfast fifteen hours before, I felt sick. The exposure then would have been about two thousand feet.

But we could see the top: a little icy chimney above the traverse. It seemed very close. The summit cliffs loomed above us. Snow arêtes led to the traverse but, after our experience of the morning, we distrusted them. I pictured a bivouac here and found the prospect infinitely distasteful but likely.

We reached the brèche and started up the snow. Immediately our fears vanished – for the snow was good! Not perfect by any means but good compared with the first part of the climb. We could actually *kick* up it. I don't think we'd kicked a step since we started; every hold had been cut. Johnnie was very tired and had to keep stopping. I felt guilty at doing no work but he was determined to finish it off himself. I felt – a little empty. The struggle was over. The crux was still to come, but what was ninety feet of ice across a couloir? Ice was firm. Hard, perhaps, but not dangerous.

I looked at the other mountains for the first time that day. Monte Rosa was still in the sun, but the shadows on the west face were no longer dark as in the daytime, but soft and tinged with violet. They deepened and the sunlit slopes held a touch of gold. As we climbed and the sun sank, the snow flushed and we saw the whole of Monte Rosa pink – as pink as the Nordend when we came down off the Rimpfischhorn. The sky was a glory of colour: primrose and gold with flaming orange bands in the west.

Then we came to the ice traverse, much shorter than I had imagined and looking – as John Tyson had said – like an anticlimax. Here we could see Julen's steps below a thin covering of powder, and Johnnie was quickly across, up the little chimney beyond, and calling to me to move. As I took off the belay, my movements were deliberate. The words of the guide book ran through my head, *lieu d'accident*. I was at the place now and I stared down that grim ice sheet, and, for a moment, I was *them* and I felt the jerk on the waist as the rope tightened, and then the hard fast ice under my back as we fell, all limbs . . . I shut my eyes tight. I wouldn't move until Johnnie shouted that he had a belay.

It was only a walk after all: in good steps, on good ice. I didn't glance down the couloir as I went across; the ferrule of my axe pressed lightly on the slope, the only sound the gentle scratch of steel on ice. At the top of the chimney, beside Johnnie, I stared at the last obstacle : the cornice.

He found a place where it was vertical, not overhanging, cut some steps, mantelshelfed on the top, and disappeared.

I shouted foolishly,

'Is it the top?'

There was silence for a while and then I heard him shouting to me to come on.

Of course the rope had to saw through the snow and jam as I was working my way along below the lip of the cornice, and while he was trying to flick it free and growing more violent every moment, I was hanging to the axe with one hand (with the pick *just* in the ice) and trying to flick the rope out with the other, and shouting that he would have me off. Then he calmed down, and lowered some slack so that, by hanging to the axe, I was able to free the rope. Apologies floated down to me.

It was eight o'clock when I mantelshelfed on the top of the cornice and stood up in the moonlight. Eight o'clock and the valleys dark, and the lights of villages gleaming in Italy. We had spent twelve hours on the ridge.

We came straight down the Verra glacier to turn the southern spur of the Breithorn. Below, in the dimness, we could see vague troughs and domes softened by moonlight. It was very cold and we were tired. It needed a lot of willpower to concentrate on the snow as we walked, watching for the thin lines of hidden crevasses.

We came under the spur and started the long uphill climb to the Breithorn Pass. As we gained height the wind increased – a north wind, bitterly cold.

We came to the level ridge and there were no more crevasses and we walked side by side. Occasionally we stopped to examine each other's faces by torchlight, looking for signs of frostbite.

My senses were a little dulled and life held no problems. Life was the sound of crampons scrunching the snow, the lights of the refuge coming up, and Life was the power and the glory of all the mountains I had ever climbed – as I walked along the frontier in the moonlight.

Glossary

abseil. descent (where it is impossible or inconvenient to climb down) by means of a doubled rope round belay or through a loop of cord attached to piton.

arête. a narrow ridge.

bealach. a pass.

belay. securing the party by means of a projection: bollard of rock, piton, etc. The projection itself.

bergschrund. large crevasse between glacier and steeper slopes above.

bivouac. voluntary or involuntary encampment without tents.

bosse. dome of ice or snow. Miniature replica of same.

brèche. a gap in a ridge.

capstone. wedged boulder roofing a cave.

carabiner. metal snap-link for attaching rope to pitons, running belays, etc.

cheval, à. astride.

chimney. fissure wide enough to admit climber's body.

chockstone. stone wedged in gully, crack, chimney, etc.

col. a pass.

cornice. overhanging wave of wind-formed snow on a ridge.

corrie, coire. normally a high, bowl-shaped valley.

couloir. gully.

crampon. metal frame with spikes to fit on boot for use on hard snow or ice. To move wearing crampons.

Creag Dhu. a select group of hard Scottish climbers.

cwm. hanging valley.

Difficile. Très Difficile, etc.: grades used to assess the general standard of a route on the Continent. The harder pitches on the climb are then numerically graded, e.g.: Four Inferior, Four, Four Superior, etc. Five might conform to a British Very Severe.

Difficult. British climbs are graded Easy, Moderate, Difficult, Very Difficult, Severe, Very Severe, Extremely Severe, with confusing shades between. Difficult is not the same standard as the French *Difficile* but much easier.

dry. of glacier; one on which there is no snow so the crevasses are unabridged, open and visible.

duvet. padded jacket, trousers, etc., filled with eiderdown.

étriers. miniature rope ladders with three or four metal rungs used in artificial climbing.

Föhn. bad-weather southerly wind in Alps.

gabbro. very rough rock of Black Cuillin on Skye.

gendarme. rock tower.

girdle. traversing line across wall or face of mountain. To traverse wall or face.

glissade. controlled slide down snow using ice axe as brake.

ice fall. very broken and crevassed area of glacier where the angle or direction of ground beneath changes.

jug. jug handle: a very good hand hold.

lead through. lead alternately. ...

mantelshelf. levering oneself on to ledge by hands and shoulder strength without, usually, being able to use the feet. The ledge in question.

Mer de Glace. long glacier in Mont Blanc massif.

moraine. accumulation of stones and debris brought down by glacier.

munro. in Scotland, a mountain over three thousand feet.

pitch. section of climb between belays.

piton, peg. metal spike with ring or hole in head which, used in conjunction with carabiner, can be used to safeguard the rope between climbers.

powder. powder snow: new, dry, non-adherent snow.

ravures. cigar- or fish-shaped clouds. Bad-weather signs.

roches moutonnées. rounded rocks, glacier-smoothed.

runner. running belay: intermediate belays on pitches where a sling and carabiner are slipped over a projection and a climbing rope run through the carabiner.

run-out, the amount of rope used on a pitch.

scarpetti. felt-soled shoes.

sling. short loop of rope or line.

solo. alone, unroped.

stance. standing or sitting space by belay.

top rope. rope from above.

tricouni. boot nail.

verglas. veneer of black ice on rock.

vibrams. moulded rubber boot soles. The boots themselves.

wet. of glacier: snow-covered glacier, with crevasses mainly filled or bridged.

windslab. wind-blown snow which peels off in slabs when disturbed.